As I Lay M

For Craig and Georgina

As I Lay me Down to Sleep

A devastating true story of neglect and abuse

Eileen Munro
with Carol McKay

MAINSTREAM
PUBLISHING

EDINBURGH AND LONDON

First published in Great Britain in 2008 by
MAINSTREAM PUBLISHING COMPANY
(EDINBURGH) LTD
7 Albany Street
Edinburgh EH1 3UG

ISBN 9781845963842

This book is a work of non-fiction based on the life, experiences and
recollections of the author. In some cases, names of people and places,
dates, sequences or the detail of events have been changed to protect
the privacy of others. The author has stated to the publishers that,
except in such respects, not affecting the substantial accuracy
of the work, the contents of this book are true.

A catalogue record for this book is available
from the British Library.

Typeset in Garamond and Lizzie Longstocking

Printed in Great Britain by
CPI Cox and Wyman, Reading, Berkshire RG1 8EX

Acknowledgements

Eternal thanks to Paul Lockley, Marcello Mega, Sara Trevelyan, who were always there and never gave up on me, particularly on the darkest days. Invaluable. Sandra Brown, who inspired me. Adam Ardrey encouraged and advised me. Lesley Martin kept my house in order. Without them, there would be no book. Also the staff at Mainstream; Ailsa Bathgate, editor at Mainstream; Bill Campbell, my publisher, who was crazy enough to take me on. Carol McKay, who took up the journey with me. My family, past and present.

www.eileenmunro.com

Great spirits have always encountered violent
opposition from mediocre minds.

Albert Einstein

Contents

Foreword

In this memoir, Eileen Munro revisits what should have been the warm, familiar cradle of a Glaswegian childhood; instead, she takes a journey to the not-so-swinging '60s and '70s of the East End, where survival was crucial in a family pushing every self-destruct button imaginable. Dysfunctional doesn't start to describe it. Only the streetwise skills she learnt, her own intelligence, sheer persistence – which some might view as a bloody-minded, devious determination – and a feisty attitude to the Establishment, gave her not only the will to survive but also the emotional glue to thrive as an adult despite having odds any Glasgow bookie would have rated as 'nae chance'.

Eileen's resilience, coupled with an unshakeable sense of humour, ensures an authentic East End voice is heard, and she breezily portrays the era, the city of her birth and the bleak industrial landscape of the west of Scotland in evocative style. For the first time, a significant voice is given to those survivors of Scotland's care system – those who have emerged from shameful treatment that Government ministers now agree is a running sore in our history of looking after children who could not live at home. This book, however, is far from being a 'misery memoir' – gut-churning glimpses of poverty and abuse are mixed with a story that in true Glaswegian style makes you laugh and cry, and occasionally renders you speechless with the power of its testimony.

The publication of Eileen's story coincides with an independent review by Tom Shaw into how residential schools and children's homes were run in Scotland between 1950 and 1995. In 2008, dedicated funding has been put in place to support survivors whose childhoods were lost to brutal, often soul-destroying regimes. It has been acknowledged that more than an apology is needed to help those affected throughout their lives by suffering experienced in care settings where vulnerable children should have been safe but were not. As a member of the Advisory Group taking forward a national strategy on childhood sexual abuse, I welcome the response of the new Government to our work and specifically to those tasked with raising awareness of the existence and impact of abuse on in-care survivors. There is a wind of change blowing through Holyrood at our Parliament, and traumatised victims of a terrible system are *finally* being listened to. It is clearly not before time.

I pray that this fresh approach, and a willingness to set up a truth and reconciliation forum in Edinburgh, will continue. A major tragedy exposed by Shaw's report is the low value that was placed on record keeping. Some survivors, like Eileen, have found their histories were imposed on them by manipulative individuals who held all the power, while others – in an eerie parallel with Holocaust victims – can find no trace of themselves in the system, never mind their family's details. Other former survivors have discovered siblings unknown to them for decades, and often now too late to contact – so many voices unheard, so many childhoods destroyed and far too many life-long consequences of the most devastating kind.

Eileen is someone who lights up a room through sheer personality and her story ensures that here is one who has not lost her unique identity. They did not manage to grind down her spirit. Her indomitable strength of character inspires, as does her underlying message: *to safeguard future generations, we need to keep listening to those with lost childhoods.*

This book ends as she reaches young womanhood. I look forward to reading a sequel and in the words of one of the '70s songs that kept her going: 'Come on, Eileen!'

Sandra Brown OBE
Scotswoman of the Year 2005–06
www.moiraanderson.org

Prologue

WINTER, 1968

The fire crackles. My mother is sitting, one thick ankle crossed over the other, in her fireside chair with her knitting needles clacking and her mint imperials tucked down beside her. Her hearing aid whistles intermittently, the square, beige battery box breathing up and down on her chest. Occasionally, she puts down her needles and twists the earpiece.

In the far-side corner by the window, the metered television flickers, black and white. I'm on the floor by her feet, shoulder leaning on the side of her chair, dreaming about school or the story I've just finished reading in the *Dandy*. I'm trying to ignore the cold draught at my back and not taking much notice of the television programme.

'Do you see that?' she says.

It's something about children without families, about boys and girls in homes. I look blankly at my mother, then at the screen, confused, not knowing why she wants me to be aware of that. I understand from her tone that it must be significant but its relevance is lost on me. I'm only five.

'That was you,' she says.

I look at her familiar face, her eyes tiny behind her clumsy glasses, her brown hair with its curls loose. She jiggles her needles while I wait for an explanation.

11

'When you were born,' she says, letting her needles rest, 'you had another mother.'

I look back at the screen. Another mother? The pictures flick through faces of women gathered in a room, talking. Have I another mother on the television? I watch a rabble of kids running about the grounds of a big old house and hear the word 'orphanage'.

The woman I call Mum seems breathless. 'She loved you and gave you away so you'd have a better life – with a good family.'

I'm sitting quite erect now, fully focused. All my dreaming's gone. 'How did I get here?' I ask her.

'Your dad and I went to the hospital and picked you out from all the babies.'

The coal fire spits and takes her attention while I think about what she's said. She picks up her knitting again, pulling at the wool.

A thought occurs to me, one that still does.

'Was I bad?' I ask.

'No,' she says abruptly, then recovers. 'You were special; that's why we picked you.' It's her rehearsed reply.

I smile. The room's still cold. It still smells of damp. Am I lucky? I'm thinking.

Later, she sings to me: 'Nobody's Child'. I hate it. She's always drunk when she sings it to me, her arm thrown round my neck, clinging to me, trapping locks of my hair. Her breath smells too minty as she breathes out where I'm breathing in. No other mum's breath smells the way hers does. She squashes me against her and I can't move away.

She must have felt relieved to have told me. Now when I started school, no one in the playground could surprise me by repeating anything they had heard by their own fireside.

Naive and pragmatic, I told my friend Beth, in front of our pals. 'See me? I'm adopted.'

Everyone stopped playing ball to have a good look at me. Being adopted was special. I had never heard of *illegitimate bastards* before. If I had, I'd probably have thought I was a special bastard.

1

Cuckoo in the Nest

At six weeks old, I was legally on loan. By 8 November 1963, and with the consent of Glasgow Sheriff Court, I was legally bound. I was nine months old.

My 'good family' life began at 74 Budhill Avenue, Springboig, in the East End of Glasgow. My adoptive parents were James and Dora Cooke. We lived in a tenement building, one storey up, with three doors on the landing. My aunt Helen – my mother's older sister – and her family lived next door to us on the same landing. She later told me they would often hear my father's drunken homecomings, signalled by the echoing as he urinated in the stone entrance close and usually accompanied by singing that was Orange Order and Irish in its nature.

When I was six months old, we moved to a new home, one with our own back and front door, in the so-called steel houses, which were set out four in a block, with two flats downstairs and two upstairs. Our flat was the bottom right, which meant we had a front and back garden, and this is where my memories begin. What came before this, I don't remember. My family history comes to me through paper documents and childhood images.

Grey paint on grey steel. The house at 40 Hermiston Road, Springboig, was ten minutes' walk from the tenement my parents had escaped from. Perhaps my arrival had earned them the right to escape it. Until then, they'd been childless for nine years. Cooped up in dour, overcrowded tenement flats, it was the dream of half the population of Glasgow to have a house with its own back and front door and a garden. All that space and privacy.

Our back garden was sectioned into three parts. The middle part was the lawn, where my mother would hang out her washing and where most of my playing took place. For a short time, my father grew flowers and vegetables on either side of the lawn. I spent long days wandering about in that garden, blocking out the noises from the house behind me. I loved to search for caterpillars in the cabbages and was amazed at the white butterflies they would become.

There were caterpillars within the leaves of the privet hedges that enclosed our back garden, too: eggs and tiny green caterpillars, which I would find by searching for leaves with an uneven arc that had turned a papery beige colour. Splitting the leaves open, I would watch these tiny creatures wriggle around, helpless, their lives dependent on my whim. My other pets entranced me, too: my 'wee tortoises', which I later found out were actually 'slaters', though the English dictionary listed them as woodlice. I played with them for hours. I spent much time watching spiders in webs, never afraid of them, just watching and letting them run about my hands, sometimes up my arms. Looking back, I wonder if I was a contented child or an isolated one. Wherever I've lived, I've loved gardens.

My father used old railway sleepers to box and set apart the three sections of the garden, and spare wood lay around in great ridges. When he worked in the garden, the weatherbeaten tan on his swarthy body made him seem somehow larger than he was. He taught me how to create a whistle by placing a blade of grass between my lips and blowing. Many times, the grass split my lip and I'd be blowing away with a mouth full of blood. Time in the garden was good.

See-Saw Marjory Daw
Johnny shall have a new master,
He shall have but a penny a day
Because he can't work any faster.

See-Saw Margery Daw,
Sold up her bed and lay upon straw,
Wasn't she a dirty slut,
tae sell her bed and lie in the dirt?

When my friend Beth came round to play, we'd drag the sleepers together to make a see-saw. We'd pile shorter pieces of wood higher and higher, reserving the longest piece for the seat. I never tired of trying to work it higher or bumping down harder so either I or my friend on the other side would fly up fast and high – the faster and higher the better. Sometimes, with the sheer exuberance of our game, the wood on which the seat balanced would topple. We'd start again. Nothing mattered other than the thrill of near-flying.

I also spent hours in the back garden playing with a red plastic tea set. I would mix water with dirt till I got the right consistency to fill the cups, then I'd turn them upside down and pat them to reveal my perfect cakes. I can see myself: the elasticated slip-on penny blacks making my bare feet sweat, my knees brown from the sun and dimpled from crawling in the dirt, wearing my mother's favourite outfit of mine, one she'd had crocheted for me. It was a pink, grey and white flecked waistcoat and skirt.

The best muck was at the side of the house under a hedge, where it was slightly grey in colour. When mixed, it was smooth and creamy; it felt silky, without any grit, and it left chalky off-white trails up my hand when I squeezed it between my fingers. It was the crème de la crème of muck. It was perfection, or at least felt like the creation of it. Looking back, I suppose it must have contained cement.

The section to the left of the garden was completely filled with tall green stalks of white flowers. Potatoes. My father would sit and eat a plate of potatoes on their own – something I still do. I never made an Irish connection there till much later. It was normal.

In so many ways, it appeared to be an ordinary East End childhood, especially when I was very young. What can I remember of my earliest years? Sitting in the kitchen playing in a large soup pot. Skipping on the path then freezing when I felt the tickle of an eariewig crawling up my white sock. For the most part, I slept, woke and accepted the drinking and violence and the wide, empty days.

My first and sharpest memory of being a new girl in primary one at Budhill School is of being put in the paint cupboard as a punishment. I have no idea why. I just remember that my knuckles stung from being rapped with a ruler and that I longed to steal the paint and brushes: all those different colours of paint in little circles set in a white plastic rectangle. Each palette contained six colours: rows and rows of lovely colours to wet and mix. Maybe it reminded me of my creativity in my garden.

Home again from school, I'd hear my mother's voice coming from the house and know that she'd been drinking. I escaped to the garden to avoid her. I didn't hear those peals of unreserved and uninhibited laughter from any of the other women in the streets and shops around me. Yet soon she'd come looking for me. I'd hear the catch of the back door open, then her voice shouting, 'Eileen!'

My stomach would turn and I'd keep my back to her, curling small, close in to the hedge at the side of the house, hoping she wouldn't see me.

'Eileen. Where are you?'

She would want me to run to the shop for her. When I was young, it was for cigarettes or a pint of milk. As time passed and I grew a bit older, she would call me in and send me to fetch 'a message' for her: a heavy bottle wrapped in a brown paper bag. I knew it was alcohol, though I never saw her drink from it – just smelt the masking mint imperials on her breath. To me, it's the way it always was. I don't remember a time when my parents didn't drink.

Behind the scenes and unknown to me, people were talking. Of course they were talking. People had been talking since before I arrived. Talking about how my mother and father shouldn't have been allowed the responsibility of children.

Did my mother care for me in her own way? She always let me have a pet, as we shared a love of animals. I was the one who named them. I had a budgie called Joey. How original! Found dead at the bottom of his cage. A tortoise called Horace, buried because he had supposedly died but who was most likely hibernating. A white rabbit named Snowy, that I later found dead down at the burn and brought home. Next door's dog, a boxer named Bruce, got the blame for that. There was a cat called Tiger, who had to be put to sleep after Bruce attacked her and left her with one eye hanging out and lockjaw. I watched as my poor wee cat meowed almost soundlessly and constantly, her eye wobbling. I begged my mother to save her. She took her to the PDSA vet to get free treatment but came back without her. I knew in my heart she would. There were several dogs, one of which went missing; another a collie whose name was Lassie, of course. She was always chasing cars. I remember the screech of a lorry's wheels outside the front door and she was under it. I watched from the living-room window as the lorry ran right over the top of her. She was on her back with her legs and paws flailing away at the undercarriage. Incredibly, all the wheels missed her. She appeared in the kitchen through the back door, untouched but shaken, and I ran to comfort her. Not long after that, I was told she'd gone to a farm to live. Various dead fish and a missing frog should be on my pets list, too. My family was made up of waifs and strays.

My last pet was a cross terrier named Queenie, so called because she was white with a brown spot on her crown. My mother and I found her wandering about the streets near the shop by the burn and brought her home. We contacted the local police; no one reported the dog missing, so we kept her. I was relieved at this, as we had previously found a dog and had had to give it back. I wandered by the owner's house several times, sad and angry they had taken *my* dog.

I think it was in the late '60s that a new type of gas came out that was safer and cleaner – 'natural gas'. We got rid of the coal fire and had a gas fire installed then. For some unknown reason, however, it didn't last long in our house and soon the coal fire came back. But I do remember the gas fire stayed there long enough for my hamster, Hammy, to go missing behind it.

Maybe it was at this time that I remember our house having renovations done. My mother, sleepy, told me to play in the garden while she stayed indoors to keep an eye on things but through the windows

I could hear her laughing. 'Come away, hen,' the workmen would tell me, seeing me standing at the doorstep. They kept me amused and out of the way. One, called Pat, would run me around the garden and the street in a wheelbarrow. It was years later that the proverbial penny dropped and I understood the probable reason why some of the men took turns in keeping me out of the way.

I had a swing in my back garden, too; it was red and blue metal, with four hooked stakes in the two bottom rods to keep it from toppling. Like the supports that were put in place to protect me, this swing's metal restraining rods weren't foolproof. Through a combination of an excess of vigour and Glasgow's wet weather, the swing sometimes toppled over with someone in the seat. Perhaps that's where I developed my attitude towards life: whenever the swing topples, you pick yourself up, dust off the dirt and get back on again.

As I got a bit older, my friend Beth and I would attempt daring and palpitation-inducing feats on this swing, like the 'runny under', which was executed by pushing the person in the swing so high that on the final push you could run under the swing before it came back down again. The pinnacle in daring was the 'bronco'. Here, one person would be seated on the swing while another would stand up facing them, with one foot between the sitter's legs and the other foot free to push and start up the swing. Then, between the two of us, we would lunge in unison to gain height and speed. The crucial point of this feat came just when the right height was gained and the stander would use their foot on the swing to abruptly push it away from them, jump off to run underneath and hope to get out of the way in time. Meanwhile, the sitter would be flying high. Heady stuff and action packed. I guess I was an adventurous child but no more so than any others growing up in the area. Not at that stage, anyway.

Summer was the time for sheets to come out and be hung over the washing line. Not for laundry but for tent making. Once they were pegged over the rope, my friends and I would fetch our drinks and pieces and thought we could live in there for ever.

One summer, there was a large crate on our back grass. It had a section that opened like a door and, seeing it, my imagination set to work. I called it my summerhouse. This was the late '60s, when I was six. What did I know about summerhouses? I must have read about them in a posh book. I set about covering it in light-coloured sheets and filling it with jars of flowers and cuttings from hedges. At the same time, I kept a so-called winter house made from a darker sheet hung over the washing rope.

My mother didn't have many female friends but one woman was more constant than others. She drank with my mother. This woman, May, was visiting one day and her son Allen, who was the same age as me, was playing outside with me in the garden. We sat together in the winter tent, close, the smell from the crushed grass under our legs tickling my nose. I felt strange, awkward, yet a weird excitement was beating inside me. We'd played together many times before, I had even been allowed to play football with him, but never before had I experienced this new sensation. I had no words to tell me what I was feeling. His sticky boy's hands and knees were close to mine. Beyond the fluttering wall of the sheet tent, sparrows were arguing and I could hear my mother and May laughing. He asked me if I had heard about 'shagging'.

'No,' I said, but my heartbeats were telling me something different.

'Do you want to try it?'

I wanted to say yes but I was scared. How could I reconcile feeling so scared with the excitement? It was just like on the swings. Did I enjoy the risk factor here, too?

I went into the house, recognising the familiar sweet scent as I tiptoed past the partially opened living-room door. On the other side of it, May and my mother were rowdy with laughter. When I reached the toilet, I stared into and beyond my eyes in the mirror, going over what Allen had said to me. Curiously, I remember thinking at the time: will it make me all grown up?

Back in the tent, we kissed, lips and eyes closed, and he lay on top of me. Where did he learn that? What door or window had he been peeking through? Embarrassed and awkward at not knowing what to do next, in true children's fashion we ignored what had just happened and returned to our play.

19

2

Lavender and Lace

Dirt doesn't appear overnight. It gradually builds up, like neglect. It takes time to show itself. Little by little, our house became shabbier and so did I. No kids except Beth and Allen came to my house to play, the rest pre-warned by their parents to steer clear. I was glad other kids didn't come, because then my shame wasn't on show.

Often when someone knocked at our front door, I'd stop what I was doing and hold myself stiff so as not to make any noise, in case they had come to collect money for something my parents hadn't paid for. Creeping to the window, I'd check to see who it was. If it was safe – Beth or May or a salesman – I'd relax and go and open the door.

I liked it when a certain travelling salesman came. 'Mum,' I'd shout. 'It's the Betterware man.' The Betterware man roamed the streets of Shettleston, Budhill and Springboig, going door to door and selling all his household wares from a suitcase. As I opened the door, there he stood in a smart trenchcoat and with his case already open and ready to put down so it would wedge the door open, his foot-in-the-door sample of lavender polish in hand ready to ingratiate himself with children. He always gave me a free sample and I took it, returning his fixed grin with one of my own. It was a ritual. I did it because I loved the smell of the lavender polish and I liked dipping the home-made duster in the waxy polish and shining up the teak wood of our radiogram. Once it was emptied, I'd use the tin in games of 'beds', otherwise known as hopscotch.

The debts must have been mounting up. Even as a young child I knew most of our money went on drink. Although I don't remember a time when my parents didn't drink, I know it was a gradual thing with my mother, becoming less secret as time progressed. Slowly, furniture and ornaments disappeared from our house. The radiogram I so loved to polish was the first piece of furniture to go to the pawnshop, followed eventually by the beautiful three-piece bedroom suite with the tallboy my mother was proud of. Everything of any value went.

Despite the drinking, my mother and father must still have been considered a 'good family' by the adoption agency. I vividly remember being in a neighbour's car when I was six, my mother and I in the back seat. I remember looking at the little baby in my mother's arms and listening as she told me this was my wee sister.

I was fascinated by the strawberry birthmark on her neck. Her name, my mother said, was to be Cathleen, after the daughter of the neighbour whose car we were in. This was my first introduction to my wee sister, whom I was to grow to love fiercely. I remember sneaking into the bedroom with my mother and laughing at the way Cathleen had fallen asleep sitting up in her cot. We laughed, too, on the occasions that my wee sister would throw yet another glass bottle of baby milk out of her pram.

Both my parents enjoyed teaching me to blow massive bubbles with the soap bar when it was bath time on Sundays. Mostly, though, my father was difficult; he was still the drunk my aunt recalled from the time I was adopted and I soon learnt that I had to be careful around him.

It was my father who taught me the words to 'The Sash' and other tunes that were never to be sung except on the occasions when he would take me to the Orange Walk. I felt slightly frightened yet thrilled by the emotions aroused in me when the Orange bands played their music and I could see all those arms swinging in marching unison, the banners and bright colours; I felt I would be consumed by it all.

I had similar feelings when my dad, an ardent Rangers fan, took me to football matches. It was my mother who made him take me. Presumably she thought he might drink less and return home straight from the match if his daughter was with him.

All his football friends would give me money and he encouraged me to swear and shout when I was on his shoulders. He would roar with laughter when I was shouting. Maybe I shouted to please him: to hear him laughing. Maybe I enjoyed his attention. Part of me found his unleashed energy and that of the other men on the football terraces exhilarating but another part of me knew I had to be wary.

Back home again, his sense of humour would be cruel. His favourite game to play with me was to curl his fist up in a ball and place it onto the open palm of his other hand. 'Smell the cheese,' he'd say, then punch me on the nose as soon as I lowered my head to pretend to smell. Time and time again I fell into the trap for him and refused to cry.

I ended up having to go to hospital once after he hurt my wrist badly while teasing me over which hand he had a chocolate bar in. Too much rough and tumble. Another time, laughing raucously, he turned from stirring up the coal fire to jab me with the poker. It was red hot and I still have a faint scar on my face and leg from that time. He and my mother argued about that incident. Cathleen started crying and the dog jumped up and down, barking. I ran into the bedroom to keep out of the way but his big Irish voice rumbled through to me: 'Get those adopted bastards out of here.' To hide, I climbed into the big Narnia wardrobe. It was there I found his Orange Order sash and pulled all the silver threads out of it. I don't think he ever forgave me.

About a year after my new sister arrived on the scene, not long before Easter of 1970 when I had just turned seven, my parents split up. I remember listening in my bedroom to my mother shouting before my father left. Crouched at my bookcase, I raised my head and tuned in my ear.

'You've been with Wilma Cairns,' she was yelling. 'That fucking conductress!'

In my bedroom, I sat with my books, arranging them in my newly learnt alphabetical order.

'Fucking shut up,' he swore. 'You know nothing, woman.'

Doors began to bang. His work boots would now be thrown in this all-too-familiar scene. I sat with my back to the sounds coming from my parents. As they grew louder, my books went more slowly into position on the shelves. The books weren't heavy but my heart was. My father's violence would be followed by my mother's increasing violence, probably as an eruption of her frustration. I knew it would filter down to me at some point. A punch from my dad to my mum had my name on it by proxy.

After the shouting had died out, I went into the living room. My mother's glasses hung by one leg on her ear and her hair was as distressed as she was. From the other side of the room, our eyes spoke to each other. I knew that if I went near her, she'd slap me.

'Where's Dad?' I asked her, my voice deliberately restrained.

She was reaching for her cigarettes. 'Pub,' she said, lighting one with shaky hands and taking a long draw. The Dalriada and The Pipe Rack were the second homes my dad's wages supported.

I watched the red glow of the cigarette become brighter and the white paper disappear. There was nothing else to say. I went back to my bookshelf. My comfort came from dusting my books: at least something could be kept in order. My mother's comfort came from a bottle.

Shortly after this incident, we had a visit from Social Work. I don't know who alerted them or why, though perhaps they had been told that my father had left home. I do remember my mother telling me I wasn't to say anything bad or the social workers would take me away from her and put me in a home.

As we waited for them, I sat close to the hearth, on the floor by her side, quiet. That was my usual position, where she would sing another of her favourites to me when she was drunk, 'Have I told you lately that I love you?'

She wasn't drunk when the social workers came to visit us. She even tidied up the house and cleaned the dust out of the hearth. Baby Cathleen was given an extra bath and I had my face and hands scrubbed at the kitchen sink. I think I wore a stripy nylon jumper and skirt. Anyway, I was clean, if shabby, waiting anxiously for the car to draw up outside and the letter box to be rattled. As if they needed to do that to get our attention. I could tell from my mother's sober shakes that this was a caller we couldn't hide from behind the couch.

My mother opened the door and showed two strangers into the living room. Throughout their visit, I smiled and spoke politely whenever they asked me any questions, never leaving the floor by my mother's side. When the woman asked my mother about the bruises on my legs, she told her I was always climbing. Soon they were gone and I no longer had to smile. My mum and I stood at the door to nod to them as they got into their car. When she closed the door, my mother put her hand on my back and said, 'You did well, hen. You did well.' I could sense her relief. Then she told me to go away into my room to play and I knew she'd be going into the pantry for a drink.

After the terrifying visit from Social Work, we went on a day trip to Hamilton, to a place called the WRVS. For me, it was a lovely day out in the country. We went on the train and I remember all the baskets of colourful flowers when we arrived at Hamilton Central Station. A short walk from the station found us at the Women's Royal Voluntary Service offices. The woman there was very kind to me. I was allowed to choose clothes from a cupboard and in particular I remember choosing a lacy party dress. I don't think I'd ever had a party dress before. It was blue taffeta with a chiffon top layer and it had a lovely silk ribbon round the waist with a blue rose sewn on the band. The attention made me feel special.

I wore this dress to the only birthday party I ever had. Prior to the party, my mother had painted the living room. It was the current interior fashion to paint one wall a different colour from the rest and my mother had painted the main wall purple. Despite her efforts, I cried at the party. We played a game of statues in which we had to stay still when the music stopped. Anybody who moved was out. I stood frozen but then Allen, May's son, pulled at my new dress and I was deemed to have moved. I was put out of the game. That was the source of my unhappiness. Years later, I came to realise how my mother must have felt about the visit to the WRVS – the unhappiness she must have felt and maybe even the shame. I hope today that in some way my innocence and excitement might have cheered her up.

3

Heat Spots and Other Irritations

My mother was old fashioned in her ways and carried in her head lots of trusted homegrown remedies that her mother had passed down to her. I remember once watching her administer the treatment for baby Cathleen's constipation, which involved self-styled soap pellets. This was macabre and curious to see; I found it embarrassing.

A chesty child, I was always wheezing and seemed constantly to have a kaolin poultice on my chest under my pyjamas. The hot menthol clay smelt medicinal: a smell I still think of as a kind of doing-you-good smell. A Vosene shampoo memory.

For skelfs and boils, the treatment was a mix of hot bread boiled in milk with sugar added. Wrapped around a skelf or boil, its heat would draw the poison. It hurt but that meant it was working. You could actually feel the boil burst and the pus being drawn. Your hand felt cleansed: the pain was worth it. In this way, my mother took care of me. Then I'd be made to sit by my bed and say:

As I lay me down to sleep,
I pray the lord my soul to keep.
If I should die before I wake,
I pray the lord my soul to take.

Then I would list all the usual suspects for God to bless, including the latest dog or cat. I might even have blessed the frog I brought home from the burn and kept in a goldfish bowl, which eventually disappeared. It must have been of some comfort to my mother to hear her daughter at innocent prayer.

'What about "God bless Dad"?' I asked her one night during the time they were separated.

'Bed!' was her reply.

Tucking the covers under my chin, I looked at her with her thin lips pressed together tightly as she waited for me to settle.

'Where is Dad?' I asked her. 'Is he coming home?'

'Mind your own business,' she said and turned the light out.

As a child, I spent a lot of time off school, ill. I enjoyed curling up in a blanket on the couch while my mother chatted away to me. One morning, I awoke on the couch after feeling poorly and my mother brought me a mirror. I was covered in spots and she said I had the measles. I looked in amazement at my reflection in the mirror. It seemed like there were hundreds of spots. We laughed and she said she'd buy me some calamine lotion to cool the itch.

Calamine lotion came in a brown glass bottle. It was applied on wads of cotton wool, which my mother hated the feel of. Over the years, I was caked with it many a time to combat the heat spots that I suffered from. I'd have to scratch at them, as they were horrendously itchy, and sometimes they'd wake me up at night with the pain from the itch. I scratched till they bled. My legs were covered in large hard lumps with a broken top brought about by the scratching. They often became infected.

Like a Dulux paint chart, I'd walk around looking as if I'd been dipped in white emulsion: white with a hint of pink. I had these spots again while my dad was living away.

'Stop scratching,' my mother said, seeing me sitting in front of the fire at her feet, digging my claws into my legs.

'I can't help it,' I moaned, rubbing at a spot on my shin with the bunched-up cloth of my skirt. 'They're itchy.'

She reached down and pushed her face closer to examine them. Then, 'Heat spots,' she said, seeing I'd an eruption of them. She shook her head. 'Leave them alone.'

'Beth doesn't get them,' I complained. 'How come I get them?'

'Away an bile yer heid,' she said, or maybe it was 'Away an raffle.' It was expressions like that she'd throw at me when I annoyed her with questions.

'No, but how come?'

A skelp to my head. 'Give me peace!' she said.

I rubbed my head where she'd slapped me.

A nudge to my shoulder. 'I'll put calamine lotion on them at bedtime.'

Why did adults have no neat answers for you, about why you had heat spots, why other people didn't and what made the heat spots appear? Or about why your dad had left home and your mum was sleeping in her chair when you came back from school, with her legs apart, skirt ridden up – my dad had never let her wear trousers – and her mouth gaping. And why there was that ever-present stink in the house instead of the smell of stews or ribs cooking for you and your wee sister's dinner? Dampness, dirt and disorder were what awaited me.

Perhaps that's one of the reasons I spent so much time in the library, looking for answers to so many things, trying to find information. In the absence of explanations from her, I had to develop my own theories, either invented in my head or as a result of reading something in a book.

My mother's other regular war cry to me was, 'Yer bum's beef an ye'll never eat it.' This one always shut me up, sending my mind into a spin. I took it literally and for years kept trying to visualise the meaning. 'Head to bum. Head to bum.' My mind would picture it but still the meaning eluded me. Eventually, I realised it wasn't anything to do with being fit or supple enough to reach round and bite my own bum. She meant I was 'havering': talking nonsense. It felt as if I had discovered something important when the penny dropped, when really it was just another example of me working things out for myself.

When I got back from school, Cathleen would be ready to wake up from her afternoon nap and I'd pick her up and give her a cuddle; then, while my mum carried on sleeping, I'd take her into the kitchen to see if there was any sugar in the house so we could have a piece. Two slices of bread with a thick layer of butter coated in sugar was a meal on many occasions.

'You'll get worms, eating that sugar,' my mother would say.

She had me convinced that the pieces 'n sugar – not poor hygiene – were to blame for my years of suffering from intestinal threadworms.

Sugar and worms also got the blame for me being hyper. 'You got worms?' she'd ask me as I jiggled and fidgeted about. 'Ye cannae sit on yer arse.'

Despite this, in the absence of anything better, my pieces 'n sugar continued.

4

Emeralds, Rubies and Pearls

My father was still living away from home and, increasingly, men I didn't know would visit our house with drink; I was usually told they were friends of my father. On these occasions, I would take Cathleen to bed, closing the bedroom door tight so as not to be too aware of my mother's 'entertaining'.

Often, however, we were on our own and my mother's drinking meant an early night for her. Sometimes I had to help her to bed and then put Cathleen to bed by myself, too. I was left to watch television into the wee hours if I wanted. Sometimes we would have a telly in our house, sometimes not. One needed coins to be slotted into the back and I remember my mother's joy when the company emptied the meter and gave her some money back.

Many a night while she slept, I would sneak in and put the telly on low, sit up close to hear it and frighten myself half to death watching Hammer Horror movies. With irregular meals, I was often hungry but I'd found a hidden stash of cake decorations on a high shelf in the pantry. Another sugar high! There were hundreds and thousands and little steel-coloured candy balls left over from the cake my mother had made for my birthday party and I would sit in front of the telly and treat myself to them, thinking each time that I'd taken few enough for it not to be noticed.

One day after school, another man knocked at the door and I sneaked a glance out of the window the way I usually did. William Urquhart stood there, wearing a trenchcoat just like the Betterware man did. Following my mother's instructions, I opened the door to him straight away. He and his coat were certainly not as smart or slick as the Betterware man. Seeming much older, he had sunken cheeks and must have been about 50. One of his eyes was opaque blue-grey without a clear pupil, which aroused my curiosity. He did have the same fixed grin but his foot-in-the-door was no polish tin; instead, it was boxed and foil-wrapped Easter eggs, which he said my father wanted my sister and I to have. Seven years old and obviously innocent, I was delighted. My father had remembered. From then on, William Urquhart became a regular visitor to our home.

One Saturday, my mother took Cathleen and me into town for a day out and William Urquhart 'bumped into' us. He took us to a café and bought me my first knickerbocker glory. Looking back, I think the meeting must have been planned. Soon, he started visiting my mother at night. I wonder, now, if he brought her any alcohol. I know I never saw him drunk once.

Spooned in bed with Cathleen one evening, I heard him go to the toilet and then my bedroom door opened. My mother wasn't in bed, so I assumed she was lying drunk in the living room, the way I'd often seen her. It was dark in the bedroom and my sister was sleeping beside me. The light from the hall shone a single ray into the room. From this single ray came the shadow of William Urquhart. He was wearing his stained trenchcoat. The smell of his sweat and neglected clothes arrived at my bedside before him.

I didn't know what he wanted but I knew straight away I didn't want him there. None of the men who came to see my mother came into my bedroom. Why did I not shout for my mum? It would have been pointless anyway.

Even though I was silent, he put his hand over my mouth and then William Urquhart raped me. I only remember feeling my left arm, which I had extended to push my baby sister as far away as possible.

'Shh!' he said and I knew I couldn't escape. I just focused on my left arm. I thought about his bad eye and I knew he would be looking at me through his 'good' one. I remember he smelt awful. I've tried to think what the smell was. I think it was unwashed. I think it was long-term unwashed.

I looked at my wee sister Cathleen, her tousled hair, her eyes that thankfully remained shut. He whispered in my ear, telling me how much I had wanted this. I forced myself not to cry as he was hurting me. 'They'll take you away from your mother,' he said. 'And if they don't, I'll kill you. Don't forget: I'll come and get you if I think you've been telling.' After he left, I rose from the bed and cleaned myself up in the toilet. Staring at the wall in front of me, I tried not to look down.

My dream that night placed me in a dark-grey cell, holding a small child protectively by my side. There was a door and there were bars on a small window in the door and I was waiting, terrified. A man was coming to the door and I was trying to be so quiet so he wouldn't see us or know we were there.

The morning after the first time Urquhart raped me, I woke up and sat on the couch in front of the fire and stared into the flames. I was in pain, like I had been bruised, and I was terrified, but I was still alive physically, though I felt my life would never be the same again.

At school, I have only one memory of primary two and it's from around this time. As the better weather came in, we were allowed to go outside to sit on the grass for an art lesson but I was left sitting indoors at a table on my own because I'd wet my pants. I hadn't been allowed to go to the toilet when I'd asked the teacher. I remember the humiliation, taunted by my classmates' whispers.

My mother sent me down to Urquhart's house to collect money from my dad every wages day. She shouted at me when I didn't want to go, so I went. I waited in the close, hoping my dad would answer my knock. One time, it was Urquhart and he pulled me into his bottom-floor flat. He pinned me against the wall in his hallway then molested me.

When he had finished, I heard my dad shouting, 'Who's there?'

I stepped forward and saw that he was sitting in Urquhart's living room, drinking.

The flat was squalid, littered with old newspapers and congealed food on dirty dishes. There were piles of stinking clothes and the furniture was grimy. I refused to go again. I don't remember rowing with my mum about it or telling her what had happened but I think she must have suspected something. For some reason, she and I took to waiting outside my father's work instead, to catch him before he could 'lose' his wages.

At that time, my father was working in the bottle works in Shettleston. Soon the factory was to close down and it became a great place for a child to roam. I wandered through the yard, imagining I was raking through treasure and that all the pieces of different-coloured glass were actually jewels. Emeralds and rubies and pearls. What would I do if I had all those jewels? It was a fantasy that took me away from my life.

Urquhart continued to visit my house and, a child in bed, I couldn't avoid him, awake or dreaming. The visits were random and went on for almost a full year. I'd stay awake, waiting, falling asleep only to snap awake at any noise. My bed was placed against the outside wall of the house, next to the front door, and I could hear footsteps arriving before the door would be knocked. Would it be tonight? I would fixate on the pattern on the wallpaper as he crawled in beside me. It only stopped when my mother came into the room while he was in bed with me one night. By now, I was eight years old. I don't remember the excuses he gave her for being in my bed: I can only remember the way I felt and the anger that spilled out of her towards me. Standing at the side of my bed, she shouted at me, 'You wee whore,' and then immediately spat out, 'Why did you not tell me?'

Soon I was to hurl the word back at her. Getting out of bed to go to the toilet one night I found my mother already there, drunk and having sex on the toilet with her friend Agnes's son, William. Our eyes met when I opened the door but I turned and went back to bed.

The next day, angry, I paced the living-room floor while she was in the kitchen. She snapped at me through the open kitchen door, 'You still here? Get to fucking school.'

'Why should I listen to you?' was my seething response. I called her a 'whore', shocking myself for swearing at my mother. The shock cost me valuable time.

From the kitchen, she launched herself at me with a wooden sweeping brush in her hand. I turned to run but wasn't quick enough. The brush came down on my back and I fell to the floor in agony. I lay there as she beat me like a rug. In slow motion, I came to. As I began to rise from the carpet, a cold controlled fury filled my brain. I slowly turned and faced her.

'You dirty, fucking, fat whore – I fucking hate you!' I screamed. 'Fuck you! Fuck you! I know all about your men.'

As I spouted the obscenities at her, my rage was realised and our eyes locked. The intensity perhaps stopped her violence. I even called her a lesbian, not knowing what it meant.

It was over. Both our chests were heaving; I had let her know I was not the only whore.

Disgust festered in me. I had no one to tell about this new way of life I'd been inducted into and I was too afraid. I remembered what Urquhart had said. How could I forget it? Something terrible would happen to me and it would be my fault. I thought I must have deserved it anyway.

My father returned home after this at some point. I don't know if he'd found out what had happened between his daughter and his friend. He never said. I like to think that maybe my mother pushed for a reconciliation in order to remove Urquhart from our lives. I do know the drunken violence escalated. He would rage at my mother and he would rage at me, flinging cups, bottles and even chairs if he was drunk or exasperated enough, then he'd pull on his boots and slam the front door on his way out, leaving the dog barking and all of us quaking. If Cathleen was standing howling, her mouth open and her nose streaming tearful mucus, I'd grab her up and take her into the garden or into bed in our front room.

My father was back and he was strict and old fashioned. He wouldn't allow cards in the house, calling them 'the de'il's game'. He didn't take kindly to make-up and I remember having my face scrubbed after I had applied some – either my mother's or a freebie given away with a comic. My mother scrubbed my face on my father's instructions and I wonder now if they thought I had somehow attracted Urquhart because I'd been allowed to play with it.

The house, meanwhile, became slowly and painfully shabbier, and the atmosphere in it grew heavier. My mother continued her not-so-secret 'house drinking'. By this age, I was becoming even more conscious of it and was developing a sense of my surroundings. I remember being put out the back door to play by my mother and tasting my first sense of pity. Two grey-haired ladies with the surname of Kelly lived next door to us with their brother. As I stood outside with a skipping rope, one of the ladies appeared and handed me an apple over the hedge. Our eyes locked for a second. I accepted the apple and thanked her but I felt awful. A crumpling happened inside my stomach as I realised she must know what life was like for me at home. I didn't know the name for what I was feeling but my shame was revealed in that moment of eye contact. I felt a profound and solemn sadness. I was also terrified about just how much people might know and I vowed never to be caught out again. Something terrible was bound to happen to me, I was sure, if anyone knew the truth about what Urquhart had done to me.

At school, too, my life was affected. Often enough before that, I'd played innocent games of chases in the playground. One game was called Kiss, Cuddle or Torture. In this, a group of half a dozen or so boys linked arms and tried to surround and trap one individual. We usually ran squealing for safety into the girls' toilets. Some of the girls who were caught chose the easy route, asking for a kiss or a cuddle, but every time after Urquhart, if I was trapped, I chose torture. I preferred to endure all the boys in the group punching or kicking me than face the shame of asking them to kiss me or cuddle me. More likely, I ran even faster to get away from them, simply to avoid the spirit of the game.

There were better times. In the early days after my father came back, there were more treats at home. On wages night, he would bring home a meal from the local chip shop. I nearly always got a chicken supper with a pickled onion and a bottle of ginger, with a Turkish Delight to finish. My mother would get Fry's Peppermint Cream or Fry's Fruit Cream. We'd feed Cathleen mouthfuls of ours or give her individual chocolate drops to suck, she and I sitting on the floor in front of the fire with the guard and all its washing moved away to let more heat out.

Everything was good on these nights. My father enjoyed bringing this treat to my mother and me, and I had my comics, too. However, as the weekend progressed, so did the drunken rages. My mother would be left hiding behind a chair or the couch; I was usually in the middle of things, shouting at my father to stop. On many occasions, I remember him rampaging about the house, furniture being flung about and my mother cowering. As usual, he'd be shouting, 'Get those adopted bastards out of here.' If it wasn't flying furniture hitting me, it would eventually be one of my parents.

Despite the violence, I think I felt safer knowing my father was there and, though I was always on guard whenever there were men on the same side of the street as me or visiting the house, slowly I settled from my state of high anxiety to one of background uneasiness.

Perhaps it was because of the turmoil in my real life that I immersed myself in reading. I would ask for books for my birthdays and Christmases. I collected all of the Nancy Drew series and the Alfred Hitchcock mysteries. I was proud of my collection of books. I wanted to be like Nancy Drew: clever and full of life.

Thursdays and Fridays were comic days. I would get my pocket money and collect my comics from 'the wee hut shop', also known as 'the burn shop' because it was small and situated next to a burn. I would wait in great anticipation for my next instalment of *Look-in*, *Jackie* and other comics. Sometimes on a Friday I'd sneak an extra comic in when I was sent to pay off the 'tick': this was the shopping bill that had mounted up, occasionally over several weeks. Sometimes, though, my mother came with me. I would usually have taken along my doll's pram and that acted as a great shopping trolley, very practical for carrying the drink my mother had written down on her list. How the shopkeeper would compliment me to my mother, on my speech and politeness. I was a good girl. I had to be. My mother had told me, a year or more before, when the social workers visited us, that if I was bad I'd be sent away.

The burn next to the shop was a great place to play in this industrial part of Glasgow – a little oasis of wilderness with its tree swings over the water and tall weeds to wander through. A great game I played with my only real friend Beth, who was a year younger than me, was to tie pieces of grass together with the agenda that the next person to stroll along towards the shop would get their feet caught in the trap and fall over. I never saw it work. More often than not we were the ones who tripped up and we ham-acted the falling over ourselves.

Beth and I were friends almost right through to the end of primary school. Her house bordered the wild burn area yet only once do I remember being inside it. I grew up thinking I wasn't welcome. Never wanting to go home, not even to go to the toilet, we would relieve ourselves in the tall grass or behind a tree. We were free and neglected in this aspect, feral and unfettered.

Peeing games weren't just reserved for the boys. On the banks of the burn, we would position ourselves so as not to get our shoes or trousers wet and see who could pee the fastest and who could direct the spray the furthest. I still associate the bindweed, with its delicate white trumpet flower that entwined everything that grew there, with the smell of pee.

When I did go home, I knew there'd be mint imperials partly hidden down between the cushion and arm of my mother's fireside chair. I enjoyed occasionally stealing one. She would get so angry. I thought at the time it was because she couldn't catch me doing it. Maybe it was partly that and partly because I had uncovered her secret. She thought no one noticed her drinking because the mints disguised the smell on her breath but by now her behaviour was too erratic to be concealed and any public respectability she'd once had was long gone.

When I wasn't avoiding home by going out roaming about the burn and surrounding area, I was alone in the library. Having read all the books in the children's box, I moved on to the shelves. I'd read anything. Nature books about the sea and books about other lands opened up a fascinating and desirable world to me. Sometimes I would take a book home, read it and return it the same day so I could borrow more. A book about grampuses, or Risso's dolphins, became my favourite and I just couldn't bring myself to return it. Thus began my career of 'borrowing' books permanently.

If I wasn't reading a book I would be lying in front of the fire with my comics. One evening, my mother was sitting in her chair, knitting and sucking her mint imperials. I lay devouring my comics, which were sprawled in front of me. I flicked through page after page, enjoying the articles and familiar characters in the stories. My eyes scanned the pages, top to bottom, side to side. I was lost in storyland, hook line and sinker. I dug my elbows into the carpet and slid myself up closer to the pages.

From nowhere, my mother's voice rasped at me. I looked up and her face was bent down towards me.

'I know what you're doing.'

I was horrified and frightened. I knew instantly what she meant, as her mouth twisted.

'Stop it.'

Had I grunted or gasped as I slid myself up towards the comics? I can't remember. I was full of shame at myself and fearful disgust at my mother. I knew by the tone in her voice she meant I was simulating sex. So obvious was my mother's interpretation that my own shame deepened.

5

Lullabies

Away from the house, the atmosphere around me was lighter. En route to school in the mornings, my friends and I would sing songs, picking more people up on the way. School was only ten minutes' walk from my house.

> Holy Mary I am dying,
> Just one word before I go.
> If you see a German soldier,
> Stick a bayonet up his . . .
> . . . Holy Mary I am dying.

This was sung to the tune of 'What a Friend We Have in Jesus' and was so melodic; it sounded so happy and inoffensive that you couldn't help but join in.

In the playground or after school, you just had to have a set of balls! Two round balls, swirling with colour. It was a girl thing. And a wall, you had to have a space on a wall to demonstrate your coordination skills. A ball in each hand, each one in turn bounced on the ground onto the wall before being caught in your other hand, the balls switching from hand to hand simultaneously. As you threw the balls, you'd sing:

Alka Seltzer
Speedy Alka Seltzer
Alka Seltzer
Takes the pain away!

No sweet nursery rhymes, just a reference to a tonic drink for hangovers. In our house, it was Andrew's Liver Salts rather than Alka Seltzer. I loved it and sneakily drank it like juice. I remember the fizz in the water before it went down my father's gullet so he was fit to go out and start drinking again. Bed and food were all a home meant to my father: somewhere to eat and sleep between drinking and working.

To join the big league at balls, you had to master the art of using them one-handed. It was a natural dexterous progression. Many school playtimes were chorus-filled with rows of girls lined up facing the concrete corridor wall, singing, bobbing up and down with their arms twirling.

And if it wasn't balls, it was elastics. This was another way of getting position in the primary pool and creating friendship groups. This game must have been the invention of a post-war rubber-band company looking for new markets. Elastic bands of different colours were looped together like a daisy chain and all linked up into one big circle. Two girls would enter the circle, making an elastic rectangle form round their ankles. Then it was, 'Jingle, jangle, ingle, angle, you are out!' as each player took her turn of dancing in and out. Next, the bands were moved up to knee height, then thigh, then waist, shoulder, neck, and the fittest girls were performing handstands to be able to pull the elastics down when it was their turn. Great exercise and good for teamwork. The girls were focused on the game; the boys in the playground were focused on the knickers that flashed when the girls jumped.

I remember getting a sugar cube from a nurse at school as we all waited in line. This was my polio vaccination. On another of her visits, I was given a letter to take home to my mother. At home, I could see my mum had been drinking again but I had to give it to her: I was a good girl and did what I was told. My mother read the letter and I saw the change coming over her. The letter said I had nits. My mother was so angry with me. She said I'd brought shame to her door. I was walloped for that and felt dirty for days until my head was treated.

Another time in my class at school, we were getting ready to paint Easter eggs when the class door was knocked. All eyes went to the door and as the teacher opened it, I saw my mother standing there. I sank into my chair, thinking please let her be sober. It turned out I had taken an uncooked egg from the kitchen to paint at school. My mother had discovered this as she had tried to boil my previously boiled egg. It had exploded all over the kitchen. The teacher met my eyes and gave me a smile as he called me out to take the new egg, but rather than feel grateful to my mum I was furious with her for embarrassing me by coming to the school smelling of drink.

Her alcohol dependency was affecting my life outside the house more and more. For a while, I went to classes at the youth club hall to take my bronze badge in tap-dancing. I loved my red tap-dancing shoes. The teacher's voice would resonate throughout the hall as I danced my heart out. 'Shuffle, hop-step, ball change, girls.' 'Shuffle' sounded like '*Shuffool*'. I loved the uniform sound of the tap shoes striking away against the floor. All the gear needed for the class had been bought on tick – evidence that my mother did try her best for me in the early days.

The tap-dancing show at Wellshot Hall in Shettleston was the highlight of the year's work at dance classes. I was in the teddy bears' picnic scene. Dressed in a chocolate-brown taffeta cape and hood trimmed in pink, I danced and sang in the back row, 'If you go down to the woods today'. As we danced, we watched and copied the movements of our teacher, who stood in the wings, coaching us.

In the next scene, our capes and hoods came off, then the poignant Lulu song 'I'm a Tiger' played. Out we'd come, tapping away in our little white tutus. The lead girl was dressed in tiger skin. My mother came to see me take to the stage but that made me feel anxious instead of excited. My mother wasn't like the other mothers. While I was up there, I was afraid she would be sitting in the audience drunk; perhaps the mint imperials masked the alcohol on her breath but they couldn't mask her swaggering body movements. And when there was no longer the money to pay for me to go, this class was another loss: another uncompleted part of my life.

My father slept in the back bedroom for as long as I can remember. In theory, the back room was supposed to be my bedroom. All my pop posters taken from my comics were on the walls there. I had a wonderful psychedelic poster of Marc Bolan with lots of snakes entwined in his hair. A little second-hand shelved cupboard with glass doors was my library and it sat in there, too. I played in there when my father was at work, now either on the railway lines or on the buses as a 'clippie' – a fare-gathering bus conductor. One of the reasons I was given for my father sleeping in my bedroom was that he had rheumatics from working outside in the winter. It's only looking back I realise how their marriage must have been an incredibly unhappy union.

So my bed was the marital double bed, which I shared with my sister. My mother slept in the single bed in the room with us. In winter, these steel houses were freezing. We'd roll up newspapers along with sheets and towels to keep the draughts from creeping in under the doors. Newspapers would also be very useful for wedging shut doors that would otherwise fly open in the wind and for keeping the kitchen cupboard jammed closed. When the need arose, the *Evening Times* was further used as loo roll, doubling up as reading matter.

Moving from my place in front of the living-room fire into a freezing bed at the end of the day was misery. With no central heating, there'd be icicles on the outside and inside of our windows, made, my mother said, by Jack Frost. He was the winter's bad man. The bogeyman and the bad fire were used as a threat against us all year round. I rebelled against believing any of this nonsense even as a child and chose to believe in nothing I couldn't understand or see. However, I was afraid that other people seemed to believe in the superstition. I asked myself if it was me who was stupid or them, and, as they were adults, surely it had to be me? Anyway, I had experience, now, of my own bad man. And whether Jack Frost was real or not, those icicles were and they were chillingly cold.

My mother would boil kettles of water so she could fill up ginger bottles that she'd wrap in towels to heat up the bed. Sometimes the glass would crack and the bed would be drenched. I remember lying in bed shivering from the cold till I was warm enough or tired enough to fall asleep. My sister I and sought comfort and heat from cuddling up together. When she was old enough to talk, she'd ask me to sing to her. I knew lots of songs, as I used to fall asleep with my radio under my pillow, listening to either Tiger Tim or Radio Luxembourg.

Increasingly, it was I who was taking most care of Cathleen. As soon as I came home from school, she was my responsibility, to feed and to look after. By this time of the day, the drink would be taking its effect on my mother: she'd be too drunk to look after Cathleen and too drunk to cook us dinner.

'Mum,' I said, so many times. 'What are we having for dinner?'

She'd be slumped on her chair. I'd go into her purse, looking for money to buy bread and milk, or more often than not I'd take Cathleen to the burn shop to buy it on tick.

One evening, I pulled back the blankets to help my mother into bed. Her hearing-aid box had come loose and was hanging by a wire from her ear. Its piercing whistle seemed to grow louder the drunker she became. I caught the box mid-swing, she removed the earpiece and I sat it on the mantelpiece beside her bed. As she crawled into bed, I noticed and was repelled by the bloodstains I could see on her underwear. Embarrassed and angry at her neglect, I said to her as if I was her mother, 'Why don't you wear sanitary towels, Mum?'

She replied without embarrassment, 'I'm allergic to them.'

Heaven knows how I knew about them. I don't remember having any sex education when I was at school and it certainly wouldn't have been something she'd have told me about.

Sometimes, though, if Cathleen was watching telly or had gone out somewhere with my mother, I could do what I wanted after school. That's when I began to rove further afield. Once, I wandered down to Budhill Avenue, where I met some kids I knew from primary school. I stood at the corner, watching them playing 'kerbie'. Some had skipping ropes. Someone shouted, 'Let's play hide-and-seek.'

Ella and Charlotte looked towards me. 'D'you want to play, Eileen?' one of them said. Glad they'd eventually noticed me, I smiled and walked towards them.

The game commenced. Like marbles on an uneven surface, children scattered everywhere looking for places to hide. There was a big yellow skip at the bottom of Budhill Avenue. Ideal, I thought. They'll never find me in there. How could they? I was barely big enough to see in it myself.

Up on tiptoes, I levered myself up with my two arms hooked over the top. Throwing one leg up, I rolled over the lip, landing inside on my back on a pile of cardboard boxes. Smug that I'd got probably the best hiding place, I lay waiting, quiet so as not to give myself away, and looked around inside the skip.

Shocked, I discovered I had company. There was a pile of soft sandy fur with black tips lying beside me. Then I saw the pink tongue hanging out of its mouth: a big, dead Alsatian dog! Game over. I jumped out and ran home.

Another time, I remember springing through the grass field beside the burn next to Beth's house on the long inclining Hollowglen Road. Rummaging around, looking for beasties, swinging on the tree swing, Beth and I played the usual games like hide-and-seek. Then my sister Cathleen appeared. Our house was only five minutes up and round the corner and, forced into early independence just like me, she skipped into view. She said she had money and diverted into the burn shop for sweets for us all, then, joining us, we all played together until Beth was called in, the shout coming from over her high hedge. Cathleen and I shouted our goodbyes and 'See you later,' as I knew we weren't invited to her house. Then we two sisters toddled home.

As I pushed open the door, I was blasted with, 'Where the bloody hell have you been?' My mother was in a rage, all round red face and flopping curls, coming at me, demanding, 'Where's the milk?'

I stood frozen.

'Where's the bloody milk? I sent Cathleen with the money for you to get me milk,' she raged.

I heard Cathleen say, 'I gave her the money! We were playing with Beth.'

I stood paralysed in fear of my mother and in confusion over my sister's explanation. Then I understood: Cathleen's sweetie money.

Stuck between a rock and a hard place, afraid of my mother's anger and preconditioned into not being able to 'grass' on my sister, I spluttered out, 'I lost it down the burn.'

My mother wasn't convinced. She chased me and smacked me on the head with a hairbrush. Crouched in a corner of the kitchen, I took my punishment. Later, my arms pulsed with the bruises from the blows she showered down on me. However, I took the thrashing and went for the milk for her. On the way there, I sang to myself to divert my mind from the pain:

> Tell tale tit,
> Your mammy cannae knit,
> Your daddy cannae go to bed,
> Without a dummy tit.

It was considered a great humiliation to grass. So I didn't. This gave my pain some pride and stemmed any rage I might have otherwise felt.

Somewhere along the timespan here, I found that I despised my mother. As well as despising her, I hated myself for it. The shame I felt. This feeling was encapsulated first in an incident I witnessed. It was on one of the rare occasions when she'd gone by herself to the local shop. I was standing in the living room, picking at the putty in the windows with the curtains behind my back, when I saw her on her way back, coming up the street towards the house. She waddled up, fat and so frumpy, yet she was still a young woman, I realise now. She wore a dark, heavy, big-buttoned overcoat and little, flat, black granny ankle boots with fur round the top, and she was swaying. I realised she was completely drunk and time froze for me. She was in full view of all the neighbours; in her hand was her old black-leather shopping bag with the fraying handles. The window must have been open, because I could hear the clinking of bottles. I shrank back onto the wall, pulling the curtain round me to hide, and watched in horror. My mother opened the garden gate and proceeded up the path towards the door. Then she fell flat on her back, so drunk she was, her little fat legs flailing in the air. She wobbled like a Weeble, a rotund and irritating popular toy.

I found her disgusting. My greatest pain, which stays with me still, is the guilt I felt for not going to my mother's aid. I left her there. I could cook and clean, put my mother and sister to bed, but I couldn't help my mother when she needed me most.

The guilt at despising my mother was crippling. I only understood these emotions later in life. Back then, I just knew I was a bad girl.

This vision of her came back to me later. I'd been down to Sunday school in Annick Street, home of the man who'd promised to kill me. Annick Street was a short street with no gardens, just the severe four-storey tenements whose sandstone walls had been blackened by the city's industrial smut and soot. I ran through Annick Street with my friend Beverly Reid, whose mum, May, was my mother's main drinking pal. Across the road from us was the familiar dismal close I'd had to visit to collect my dad's wages in the months when he'd left home. In one of the ground-floor flats would be Urquhart. Did he see me? I couldn't look directly at his flat. I couldn't acknowledge his existence, even to myself. Out of the corner of my eye, I followed his window line until I was at the church door. It was almost straight across from his flat.

I had worked my way through the church's children's organisations. I had been in the Rosebuds, then the Brownies. Now I was growing up so much I'd become a Girl Guide. My mother used to walk me to the Eastbank Church Hall at the corner of Annick Street and once she'd dropped me off she'd go to the local pub along the road. Was she meeting up with men like Urquhart?

Inside the church hall, the other girls would be jabbering excitedly. I loved the buzz of the Guides before the leader called us to be quiet. Most of the girls would be in uniform or have some aspect of it, like the sash for all the badges, or the blouse and necktie, but not me. I suppose there must have been little money left for Guide uniforms once the wages had been spent in the pub. Maybe my mother just didn't care any more as the alcohol sapped her drive, her pride and enthusiasm.

I'd had bibles presented to me for my attendance at the Brownies and the Guides. I also received religious education through the school, not forgetting my father's vitriolic rants, launched irrespective of whether he was sober or drunk. The East End was infested with religion, violence and drink. We were the same as so many other people there, yet we were different. It was the industrial east of the city, with its works and its trains cutting through it, yet in ways it was a village. Everyone knew my father was Irish. They also knew that Cathleen and I were adopted and that my mother was a drinker. These things labelled us: everyone knew who we were.

Leaving Sunday school that day after a small meeting in which we'd been drawing, Beverly and I were crossing the street when a woman about my mother's age fell in the middle of the road. Her skirt blew up from the back, revealing a massive pair of white bloomers. Beverly and I dissolved into constrained hysteria. Even in the '70s, bloomers were funny and seemed very dated. Then conscience pricked me. Embarrassed at my mickey-taking, I helped the woman to her feet and gathered up her shopping for her. I felt disgusted at myself and I didn't want to laugh any more when the woman went on ahead and Beverly prodded me, still enjoying the joke. It no longer seemed funny.

At school, in primary six, I was moved into a class with some other children who were older than me. It must have been what we now call a composite class. Our teacher was prone to throwing the blackboard duster around the room and whacking unsuspecting pupils with it. It wasn't long before I witnessed his complete nervous meltdown. He began to throw the duster and soon other objects followed. Several of the children began to taunt him and the tension rose in the class. It was verbal and physical chaos; everyone was shouting and objects were flying. He ran from the room, quite hysterical. I felt complete sorrow for him as he fled. Maybe I recognised him as a fellow victim. I didn't rationalise it. All I know is that in the hubbub of the class I stood quiet.

6

Darwinian Chimp

My mother didn't have much in the way of cooking skills and as time went on she must have lost interest in this, too. She once had an argument with her friend May, who was cooking ribs in her kitchen at the time.

'Eileen doesn't eat much. She's not keen on ribs,' my mother said.

Always starving, especially now that I was over ten and growing, I stared at my mum, chewed my hair and didn't contradict her.

May immediately replied, 'Eileen? Eileen *does* like ribs. She eats them at my house. Don't you, Eileen?'

Looking from one woman to the other, I shrugged. What could I say?

Embarrassed, my mother remained silent. Probably she told her I didn't like them as a way of excusing herself for not cooking. Tinned spaghetti and tinned Granny's star soup with loads of bread were our usual meal, though she did occasionally make lovely homemade tomato soup.

Often my mother was too drunk to cook. Finding myself hungry in bed, I'd wait until she fell into a drunken sleep. Once her breathing slowed, deep and wheezing as she lay on her back, I'd peel myself away from Cathleen, push back the covers and sneak out into the kitchen to rummage for something to eat. Small wonder that the doorstep slice of the loaf, toasted with a lashing of butter, seemed such a deliciously luxurious eating experience to me. And one I could prepare myself.

Even without the alcohol, my mother's health was poor. She had suffered from fits as a child, had lost her sense of smell, wore a hearing aid, used inhalers and had attended the 'special school'. When she couldn't breathe because of an asthma attack, I had to go and get someone. She would sometimes turn red and purple, and the veins in her neck would stick out. That was the image that pounded in my head as I ran to someone's house for a doctor or other help. We didn't have a telephone.

Her illnesses frightened me. There were fewer and fewer times that we shared together. She still enjoyed playing with Cathleen, as she had me, when Sunday bathtime came round, and I did, too, splashing Cathleen with water or helping to wash her hair to avoid soap going in her eyes.

I also remember enjoying wringing out the sheets with my mother, taking them from one sink to another and squeezing them amazingly flat with the mangle that was screwed between the kitchen sinks. The water would pour out one side as we'd turn the iron handles, feeding each sheet through the mangle's rollers. It would come out the other end into clean, rinsing water in the second sink. This was repeated back and forward until each sheet was well rinsed and wrung almost dry. Then they were hung out.

By now, though, my mother had become more insular and aggressive. She was increasingly violent to me and rarely went out. Her loneliness must have been immense, something I couldn't appreciate fully at the time. Her mother, who had been a nurse, had died when I was around a year old and only once do I remember visiting my grandfather as a child. He had remarried. She had a brother, Edward, whom we saw occasionally, and a sister, my aunt Helen. Helen had distanced herself from my mother, however, so I rarely got a chance to see her. But we did stay with her when my mother had to go into hospital. I loved it there because it was homely and I had the company of my cousins. Their house seemed to me to be in a state of constant organised chaos: we would be jumping up and down on beds, squealing with delight, though we had to do family tasks as well.

By now, Aunt Helen and her family had moved from the tenements in Budhill to a new flat. It seemed then to be miles away, and a great walk, with a great swing park. It had a huge chute with a wooden box at the top. This was next to a chicken farm. I'd hear stories of how the chickens ran about after being strangled but no matter how I secretly wished to see them I never did.

I remember visiting my mother in two hospitals in Glasgow. One was the Belvedere on London Road and the other was somewhere in Duke Street. Many years later, I discovered that Belvedere was a leading hospital in respiratory care and Duke Street was regarded as progressive in psychiatric care for alcoholism. For a while, my mother had her bed placed in the living room; I think it was on one of her returns from hospital. I assumed it was for the heat from the coal fire. She did have a few visitors then and I remember her being happy and not drinking. I was happy that she was happy.

By now, as well as working as a clippie on the buses, taking the fares, and sometimes on the railway on the lines, my father had also taken a job at night as an usher in one of our local cinemas, the State Picture House at 1311 Shettleston Road, and my mother started sending me with him. Perhaps, again, this was a preventative measure, to combat his drinking, children not being allowed in pubs in those days, and to try to ensure he'd refrain from drinking on the job. Or maybe she wanted some free time.

I was quite happy. I would be sat up in the back row on my own, usually with a free ice cream, while my dad did his ushering. I saw many of the Disney movies there, even *Bambi*, at which I refused to cry, as I knew my father would tease me if he caught me. Like most people of that era and location, my mother and father disliked open shows of emotion and would tell a crabbit child, 'I'll gi'e you something to greet for.' Crying or complaining was weakness and my father in particular hated it. My mother mainly used the phrase to shut me up. Sitting in the cinema in the darkness, my throat muscles would be aching as I tried to control the tears at the realisation that Bambi's mother had actually been shot.

I loved *The Sorcerer's Apprentice* but *Jungle Book* was my favourite. It was the ending of *Jungle Book* I loved – the feral child who finds his natural place among his own kind – though at that age I never knew why. My mother got me a beautifully coloured circular jigsaw one Christmas. It showed quite a few of the Disney movies all running into one another around this circle. I remember so clearly the enjoyment of piecing together the exotic landscape of the jungle, with Baloo lying on his back in the water and Mowgli sitting on his stomach, and the fantastic colours of the magic in *The Sorcerer's Apprentice*. The jigsaw was so unusual it was like having a treasure. I loved the way it had no apparent end.

My father's love of teasing was at full throttle during the then deemed adult movie *One Million Years BC*. It contained the famous clip of Raquel Welch wearing a fur bikini. The movie seemed to be intensified by the unique lack of dialogue. As the characters evolved through grunts, and tension mounted, I leapt from my isolated row in the cinema and ran into the foyer to hide under a burgundy-coloured velvet couch. The scene when the person was being eaten alive by the dinosaur had become too much for me. My dad roared with laughter at my distress but I refused to go back in to watch the end of the movie.

In 1974, all my friends were talking about a new music movie. It was Gary Glitter's *Remember Me This Way*. By now I was 11 and, although I was a glam rock fan at that age, I felt he looked like an old man even then. This was to be Gary Glitter's farewell to his public. I was more interested in Marc Bolan and David Bowie but my father took me to see it. For some reason, he disappeared during the movie, leaving me alone with my ice cream. I have no idea where he went, as it was a different cinema from the one he worked in. Sitting alone, Gary Glitter's overt sexuality and the effect he had on his throng of pre-teen followers mesmerised me but the whole experience left me feeling isolated and sad. This was a time before the word 'grooming' became widely known.

By now I truly was living up to the Mowgli image of the feral child. With my mother often ill or drunk, and my father working or disappeared on another alcoholic binge, I wandered rootless and wild.

One time during the summer holidays, my cousin Lena came for a visit. She was my aunt Helen's daughter and she was six months younger than me. We were close in age and close friends. We met up with my cousin Edward, my uncle Edward's son, who lived round the corner from me.

Budhill's library was a small hut of a building, sitting right on the corner of Hallhill Road next to my primary school. Across the road was one of two parks in my local area. We were hanging about, innocently enough, outside the library, chatting and laughing the way children do during the long school holidays. I think we were monkeying around the red public telephone box, probably causing a bit of noise, when we were approached by two policemen on the beat. We didn't see them at first, so intent were we on each other's company and because the box was obscured partly by a big oak tree that hung over it like an umbrella.

Suddenly the police were there and they put us through the drill. I sensed they were toying with us, asking each of us our name and address. I gave mine and Lena gave hers. They asked her why she was in the area, given that her address was quite some distance away, and were satisfied by her answer that she was my cousin and staying with me.

When our young cousin Edward was questioned, he blurted out his name and address all in one panicky breath like a soldier in an army drill. His eyes were as round as his face. By now I had moved to the side of the policemen and, out of their line of sight, was bending my knees up and down and whispering, 'Evening all.' I was trying to make them laugh but my poor cousins – especially Edward – thought they were going to be arrested. We left, collar unfelt by the law and me giggling. Edward's summer glow had vanished, leaving him pale.

Another day, I was out playing with my two cousins and a new friend from Moredun Cresent in Larchgrove. I have no idea who this friend was, where she came from or where she went that day, but I do know we had crossed the Old Edinburgh Road to reach the Cranhill-Ruchazie side, still in Glasgow's East End but quite a distance from my home. Long summer days meant we had plenty of time on our hands, so we wandered into the grounds of the Stepps Hotel.

The hotel and its gardens were enclosed by old grey-brick walls and there were quite a few well-established trees. Sensing that we were shut off from the rest of the world in this leafy place so close to the city's streets, we spread out to explore. I couldn't resist climbing one of the larger trees. Its trunk was rough with plenty of footholds but the others wouldn't join me. Darwinian chimp that I was, I wasn't put off and soon climbed up higher than their heads and beyond. When I reached branches I could sit on, I was delighted, having achieved my mission. The leaves were swooshing around me. I called to the rest to join me but they weren't curious like me: it was too high for them and they wouldn't.

Through the trees, I could see across the Old Edinburgh Road towards my grey steel house. To the left was Larchgrove – the tough scheme that stood higher than the rest. Behind me was the hotel with its red sign running round the walls. Beyond that was Ruchazie. I could see the water tower with its tall columns like some piece of elegant classical architecture. Cranhill was to the right; Easterhouse was to the left. The Old Edinburgh Road split the schemes, running through them like an equator. Then I spotted Lena, Edward and the new friend running away. Bewildered by the fact they had left me, I shouted after them, 'Where the fuck are youse going?'

Then I heard a voice saying, 'That's no way for a young lady to speak.'

Looking down through the branches, I made out the black pancake top of the hat that belonged to a policeman. I was horrified! I never swore in front of adults. The real me had been caught and now they had proof that I was bad. My heart began thumping and I'd no option but to climb down. Alone, I stood in front of him. This time, I wasn't so brave. I couldn't meet his eyes. He asked my name and address, which I dutifully told him with head hung, feeling anxious to get away. I must have appeared to be remorseful, because he let me go with a simple chastisement. Maybe he even laughed as I streaked down to the Old Edinburgh Road.

At the Old Edinburgh Road, the traffic was rumbling past, both ways. I waited for a break then dashed across. Up ahead, I could see my two treacherous companions, my other friend having disappeared.

'Wait!' I shouted. 'Lena!'

She turned to look and they slowed down, waiting for me to catch up. I thought I saw her scanning beyond me for any signs of the policeman following but he was well gone.

'You all right?' Edward asked me.

I made him wait. 'I'm all right,' I said. 'But we're in trouble.'

He stopped. 'How? What d'you mean?'

I waited till a truck went past, buying me time to fabricate the details of my story properly. Then I told them both: 'The policeman made me give him all our names and addresses. He saw you. It wasn't just me.'

Edward's face had blanched again.

'He's going to see your parents. We're being charged with trespassing.'

I stuffed my hands in my pockets and strode on, letting them stew in it. Feeling suitably compensated, I didn't tell them the truth for hours.

7

Trampoline

In primary seven, my last year at primary school, I had a teacher named Mr Stuart. He was reported to like a drink at school. One day I vividly remember, he was reading Scottish poetry to the class. As he read, he was banging his fist on his upright desk and spitting as he recited. I don't remember the poem but do remember being entranced not only by his behaviour but also by the passion in his words. Overawed, I was amazed that poetry could make you feel like that and, though I couldn't articulate it, it made me aware that there could possibly be more to life than the experiences I'd had so far.

As Christmas approached, this feeling would intensify. My mother took Cathleen and me to see the lights in Glasgow's George Square followed by a visit to Goldbergs store in the Merchant City, where Christmas was bought on tick. Goldbergs' decorations were so beautiful, it seemed such a magical and sophisticated place, and this too stirred up my restless longing for something I couldn't have: cleanness and beauty.

My mother always liked to make a fuss over us at this time of year, even though it got her further into debt. Caught up in the excitement, I looked forward to Christmas but it was always such an anticlimax, partly because I would find my presents early. My mother would be too drunk to hide them properly and instead just left them in the bottom of the wardrobe in our bedroom. I would wake early on Christmas morning and sneak another peak while Cathleen was still asleep, before taping them up again. My mother would be too drunk from the night before to get up and my father, as always, would be somewhere unknown. Despite this, I always pretended I was seeing my presents for the first time on Christmas morning, which delighted my mother.

For Christmas that year, I received a guitar, which I already knew about. I'd been up during the night and had eaten half the pickled onions and glacé cherries from the hidden hamper tucked behind the coats and other clothes in the bottom of the wardrobe. Me, I was always hungry and there was never much of a Christmas dinner to speak of. In fact, I never remember having a family Christmas dinner.

As school started back after the Christmas holidays, I enrolled for guitar lessons. When I arrived at the class with my guitar and sat down, I was told by the teacher, whom I only remember as being a woman, that she couldn't teach a left-handed child. I had to get up and leave. Home I went, dragging my guitar, and I never did learn to play it.

Things were definitely changing. I was changing. Now 12, the only prominent bumps on my body were my ribs and knees but I was more and more conscious of the life I was living and couldn't help comparing it to the lives of others around me. This I did more and more as the deterioration at home got worse and worse. Other people had clean windows and ironed clothes but my mother took no pride in her home at all. My father had lost interest in gardening long ago and, as the house fell into disrepair, the back became overwhelming and unmanageable. I did try to weed and tidy the front, desperately trying to maintain a façade of normality. I felt it was all my responsibility and my fault, and I knew I didn't measure up. The frustration of not being able to do anything about it festered in the middle of my stomach. My mother was always drunk or shaking, my father was increasingly violent or absent, and Cathleen was my responsibility.

In spring, in preparation to go to the 'big' school, Bannerman High, my mother took me into town in a taxi. She never took public transport any more, even though we could get cheap tickets as my father was back working on the railways.

Fishers, just off the Gallowgate, was a department store that allowed you to buy goods on tick and pay it off on a weekly basis. This meant it was more expensive than other shops and it wasn't very fashionable, but I liked the place. It was here that I had learnt from one of the sales assistants how to tie my laces, my mother never having bothered to teach me. It had several floors and always meant a good day out. This time, my mother and I had lunch together and she bought me shoes and other clothes.

Though I enjoyed the day out shopping with her, I was soon on the way back to the East End. How I wished I could be transported to places I knew existed either because I had visited them – like the world of plenty that Fishers and Goldbergs seemed to represent – had seen them on television or had read about them in my books. Somewhere with no cares and no shortages. My mother and I were now ever more frequently hiding behind the couch when the debt collectors came to the door. My father's regular claim that he'd 'lost' his wages in some street, somewhere, meant that this happened a lot.

Adding to my gloom at this point was the fact that I had also fallen out for the first time with my friend Beth. I was going to a school disco, I think, which was to be the last one before going to the high school. My mother had promised me a new outfit for the disco if I stopped picking the scab at the top of my nose, caused when the boy in the corner house who owned Bruce the dog had thrown a stone at me. I constantly picked at that scab. I also chewed on my shoulder-length hair incessantly. It would stand by the sides of my face, hard with dried saliva as if it had been starched. My mother tried to stop this by scraping the sides of my hair up and tying an elastic band with a bobble or ribbon in it. I hated having the elastic bands removed, as when the hair fell back into place the movement hurt my scalp, so tightly had it been brushed up. I also bit my fingernails and toenails, sometimes till they bled.

My new outfit was a burgundy denim trousersuit with big steel zips that had round rings on the ends. My mum was supposed to go into town every week to make a payment on this suit until such time as it was paid for, and she nearly always made it. I stopped picking my scab as I'd been asked and I got the outfit. On the night of the disco, Beth met up with me. She had bought the same suit. I felt like she was my twin sister as we walked through the local park together. She was my one true friend. Then she told me she couldn't see much of me any more and spoke about a new friend she had made. I am ashamed to say that in anger I grabbed her by the shoulders and swung her round. I don't remember what I said to her. I felt the same way I did when I was lying on the floor after my mother had broken the wooden sweeping brush over my back. Everything was happening in slow motion and I was only aware of the anger inside me. Trembling, I was very frightened and ashamed by this feeling. I ran home and waited for something terrible to happen.

That summer before I went to the big school, new houses were being built on Hollowglen Road to replace the old prefabs that had gone up on the cheap during the war. Beth and I had taken Cathleen there and wandered about the now derelict homes. I relished doing this. It gave me a silly sense of exploring people's history. We even found a large animal tongue lying there among the ruins. It seemed so out of place. How could a fresh tongue end up here in the ruins of an old building in the East End of the city? I remember standing, eerily fascinated, and poking it with a stick.

The new houses were bright and modern and in my eyes very good looking in comparison to my own. At night, after the workies had gone, we would enter the houses. They smelt great. Silly things stay with me, like the fresh smell of the putty used for putting the windows in. I would always find a lump of fresh putty to take home. It was much better than Plasticine, I thought, even though it wasn't coloured. Maybe I liked it because it was pinched but it did smell so good. In some of the houses, the toilets were plumbed and we could use them. It was so clean. A blank canvas. The favourite game here was to climb the stairs, up and down stairs – such space – and if the floors hadn't been laid, we would jump straight through the beams onto sacks full of fibreglass down below. We paid for it in a way, as it itched terribly if the sack burst. I never once considered myself to be breaking and entering, just exploring.

People began to move into the houses almost as quickly as they were built. I met a girl one night as I was wandering around the square at

Shettleston train station. Her name was Jean and she was new to the area, having just moved into one of these new houses in the area that was now called Greenfield. She was to become my best friend for the next few years.

On one of the last occasions Beth and I spent together, I felt a horrible sense of foreboding. As we walked from her house round the corner towards mine, I asked her, if my mother died, could she ask her mother if I could live with them.

'All right,' she said.

I was relieved but didn't believe her. Feeling strangely remote from her yet not wanting to let her go, I fixed on the cars passing along the road.

'I might be moving away,' I said. 'My mum's been to look at houses in Easterhouse and away out in Hamilton.' I rattled on about this in the same nervous, ham way she had rattled on to me about not being able to see me any more. 'There's a young boy called Joe who lives there. He wears glasses,' I said, tempering my imagination by adding glasses so it didn't seem too good to be true, 'and he's the same age as us.' I wanted a reaction and I was hoping for jealousy. I got it but I was left feeling frustrated and sad at my actions. I didn't understand them.

Most of it was made up but, curiously, my story came true. My mother did go to look at houses in these areas and there was a boy who wore glasses, just as I had told Beth.

My first year at Bannerman began. My new uniform seemed so grown up: purple and blue, it was. I had a registration teacher called Mr Reid, who also taught trampoline after school and I became involved with this. I loved it. I felt so free, soaring up through the air. He asked me if it was true that I'd never been on a trampoline before and I was so proud: he obviously thought I had a natural talent. I also saw sewing machines for the first time and used them. In cookery, we were taught how to turn a cooker on: me that had been left hungry many a night and had had to cook for Cathleen and myself.

I satisfied a hunger of a different type with my new best friend: one that took me away from the squalor and discord at home. As my father had alternated between working on the railway and the buses when I was younger, I'd often travelled with him on the green and white corporation buses for free. All the clippies had known me because of that and most of them let me on for nothing even if he wasn't there. My father's job, therefore, opened up a gateway that allowed me to roam.

Now, if I had been given pocket money, the first thing that I would want to do was go and find a bus I had never been on before so I could go to a place not familiar to me. Sitting on the bus, usually with Jean, was freedom. We'd go all the way to the terminus and back. These trips might not have been exotic by any standard but to me they represented an adventure into the unknown, a chance to see new sights and discover. When I ask myself as an adult what I was hoping to discover, the answer is hope. I seemed to need to see space and new places: the greener the better. I remember getting off the bus once, as I wanted more time to be free in this adventure. We disembarked from a bus with the word Cardowan on it and I have a memory of seeing a colliery. Having gone all the way there, we weren't too impressed, as there was not much to see at the terminus and we didn't know what to do other than turn back round and come home. I was just disappointed that the journey itself had ended.

Jean and I would travel to school and back on the train together and arrange to meet up at night. We also went to a youth club in Cranhill together. And I remember that it was around this time that I got my first bra. My mother bought it for me and, curiously, she got a black one. So much for innocence. This at a time when all good girls wore white bras and ecru tights. Only good-time girls wore black ones. I never wore black tights until after I left school.

Jean's house was so different from mine and, unlike Beth's, I was allowed into it. She had lovely ornaments and it was clean and bright. She had a big sister called Linda, whose birthday was the day before mine and whom I liked, and she had a wee brother called Edward. With her shiny black hair, her mother looked so glamorous, too. They seemed to have lots of friends and I was part of a group. One night while out with Jean, I bumped into Beth. I remember introducing her to Jean and feeling awkward, barely being able to keep eye contact. Beth and I never spoke again.

With Christmas just past and on the eve of the New Year 1976, I was 12, about to turn 13 in the February. My mother and father had gone out for Hogmanay and had left me to look after Cathleen; I don't know if they went out together or if my father just didn't return from work.

The Bells drew closer as the evening wore on. Apart from the area close to the fire, our steel house was freezing. I gave Cathleen some toast then put her to bed, giving her a kiss before I left the room, as if I was her mother.

There was no sign of my parents. Kneeling in front of the coal fire, I tried to keep it going. My thoughts turned to food for myself but there was no bread left and by now the Christmas hamper was empty. My feet froze on the kitchen floor, even though I walked on tiptoes to minimise exposure to the cold lino. There were some potatoes in the pantry. Lifting a few, I folded them into the hem of my jumper and picked up the sharp knife. I took them through to the living room and placed them at the hearth. After a dash to the toilet, I went to check on Cathleen then settled at the fireside. Hogmanay celebrations danced about the channels on television: men in their kilts and women in white gowns with tartan sashes. Excitement and happiness illuminated the screen. My attention turned to the potatoes I began peeling. The white wet starch slid down the shaft of the knife onto my fingers. I loved raw potatoes.

There were voices outside and then the front door opened. I stood up from the fire. In came Beth's brother and another man, supporting my mother. She must have been in their house drinking to celebrate the New Year. I hadn't even realised she knew Beth's mother.

The men were virtually carrying my mother. They avoided my eyes, which I was grateful for. Then they sat her down, paralytic drunk, in her chair and left. I sat back down in the hearth and studied my mother. I'd never seen her quite as drunk before. Her glasses hung skewed on the end of her nose, her hair was unkempt and her mouth hung open. No party clothes. I was embarrassed by her public behaviour. It framed a picture in my mind.

I watched and kept the fire going. On television, the bells were ringing and all the people in the programme were linking arms and singing.

> A guid new year to ane an' a'
> An' mony may ye see,
> An' during a' the years to come,
> O happy may ye be.

Through the glass of the living-room window and the hollow steel walls I could hear party noises from people who were celebrating, going first-footing to neighbouring houses, bringing them luck. Still I sat, watching my mother. She was slumped in her chair, folded in on herself. She'd never been quite so drunk as this. There was a stillness about her and I watched to see that she was breathing. There was a strange sound, then urine poured out through the bottom of her chair and onto the carpet. I could hear it and smell it. She disgusted me.

Now the television was quieter and so was the street. My mother remained motionless. At some point, she appeared to change colour in front of my eyes. I felt as though the room had changed mood. It was cold, still, despite the fire. Thinking back, it was me who was freezing. I reached out, terrified yet guessing what I was going to touch. I couldn't stop myself; I had to know.

I touched my mother's hand. It was cold. It felt dead. I had sat and watched my mother die. I circled her like a frightened lamb too afraid to bleat a whimper, then I retreated to the hearth. I stayed there, waiting, peeling potatoes with the large knife and eating them raw. The whistling of her hearing aid whined. In a while, I got up and made sure that the living-room door was jammed shut with a newspaper, so that if my wee sister woke up she couldn't come in. Then I went back to the hearth and didn't leave it, even to go to the toilet. I did the toilet in a newspaper and wrapped it up, placing it on the embers of the fire. It took ages to burn. I felt the heat of the fire ablaze on my cheeks as I willed it to burn, afraid it would be discovered.

8

Competitiveness of Pain

1 JANUARY 1976

The night passed.

Maybe I dozed but I've no memory of it. In front of me, stark in the electric light, was the same grim scene that wouldn't go away. My mother remained motionless in her fireside chair, her lips blue. The whistling of her hearing aid had stopped. There was no warmth left in the fire but still I huddled as close to it as I could and waited. The curtains had remained open through the night and as morning eventually came, its light was as grey as the steel house I lived in.

Hanging in the room was the pungent scent of stale alcohol and my mother's urine, which had darkened into a pool under her chair. I remember easing my legs, uncurling them from where they'd been folded under me in my attempt to keep warm and to keep my distance. The fire had all but gone out and I was cramped with sitting on the cooling hearth for so long. My eyes were heavy from lack of sleep and they were glazed from lack of tears.

A noise in the hall made my heart rush. Cathleen was only six; I couldn't let her see Mum like this. I ran across the room to stop her coming in, closing the living-room door tight behind me. But it wasn't Cathleen. It was my father, drunk, trying to put his key in the front-door lock.

All the fury sprang out of me and I came to life. Gripping the handle, I pulled the door open and screamed at him, 'You killed her, you bastard. My mum's dead.'

He stepped into the hall, screwed up his eyes and stared at me, still reeling from his New Year celebrations.

'She's dead. You killed her!'

He shook his head, too drunk to take it in.

I tried to keep my voice under control but I was shuddering with fear and cold, and my voice was cracking. 'She's dead,' I said. 'I watched her.' All this time, I was conscious that Cathleen was sleeping just through the wall from where we were standing. She'd be wrapped in our fluffy white and pink candlewick bedspread, her hair rumpled on the pillow, but she might not be sleeping deeply without my warmth beside her. I didn't want her to wake up and find our mother.

I waited for my dad to do something. I knew what the scene was like through the living-room door behind me and I wanted him to take control.

But he didn't. He just stared at me. 'Jesus Christ,' he said, mumbling. 'Jesus Christ.'

I was used to his hands trembling. Now they were juddering and it seemed outwith his power to stop them.

'What are you going to do?' I pleaded.

He braced his hands on the walls of the hall with his body leaning forward, the spume of his alcohol breath spilling out towards me. He swayed and I thought he'd fall.

'Jesus!' he said, and wiped a hand across his mouth. He started nodding, then, looking at me and shaking his other hand towards me. Then, without a word, he turned and ran back out of the open front door. Up the street he went and left me standing.

Deeper shock must have set in once my dad ran away, probably because my words had made it real. I could have been in the Goldbergs' fairyland; I could have been spirited away by aliens; I could have been anywhere in the atlas and it wouldn't have meant anything to me. For the following few hours, my mind is a blank.

The next thing I remember is sitting on the bed in Auntie Joyce and Uncle Edward's house. He was my mother's brother and they lived in the next street to us. I don't know how I got there. I don't even remember where Cathleen was but I know I was dressed by now and there was a policewoman in the room with me. 'Give her tea with sugar,' she kept saying, even though I told her time and again I didn't like it with sugar. 'Give her tea with sugar,' she'd say. I don't think she knew what to do with me.

What turmoil I had inside me. I was angry, trapped, terrified – I suppose because I didn't know what was happening or, more correctly, what was going to happen. The one constant that supported me was that I knew my mother's sister was coming over for me.

I loved my auntie Helen. I knew everything would be better when I was with her. I held on to the cup of tea they gave me (with or without the sugar), just as I held on to the knowledge that Auntie Helen would soon be there. Auntie Helen wasn't like my mum at all: the oldest in my mother's family, she was capable and loving, holding down a job as well as being mother to a large family of her own. I'd feel safe with Auntie Helen.

And that's how she did make me feel, the anticipation building as soon as I heard the car. There was her voice in the hall, she opened the bedroom door and reached out for me, no questions asked. It was a primitive thing: as she pulled me in against her dark fur coat, I knew safety.

My next memory is of being in Pitt Street in the centre of Glasgow, to be interviewed in the main police office there. I don't know how I got there or who took me. What did a 12 year old know about police interviews and statements? My memories are freeze-frame and tape loops. All I remember is that they sat me on a table, not even in a separate room, and a policewoman and man asked me about the knife they'd found in our living room. The knife in the hearth! I'd used it to peel myself potatoes to eat but they thought it might have been involved in my mother's death. I quickly realised they suspected my father and, for all my rage against him at first light that Ne'erday morning, the more they probed the more protective I became of him.

The policewoman even went so far as to look at me directly and ask, 'Did your father ever do anything to you that you didn't like?'

'No,' I replied adamantly. And all the while at the back of my head I begged her to ask me who did.

Ask me who did. Ask me who did, a wee voice was saying in my head. Urquhart's name was balanced on the end of my tongue waiting to be spoken.

But I was never asked that question.

My father was eventually cleared of any involvement when it was confirmed that my mother had died after inhaling her own vomit. I didn't find out for years that this was what had happened and continued to torture myself that it was somehow my fault.

For a while I felt safe at my aunt's house. Cathleen and I slept in my cousin Lena's bedroom, in one of several beds squeezed in to line the walls.

Though I was relieved, there was a constant niggle of insecurity. It became clear to me that Auntie Helen couldn't keep Cathleen and me but she didn't want us to go back to our father. I sensed even then that the council's Social Work Department weren't coming up with money or practical help. In the house, the phone would ring and doors would be shut to exclude me, and all of this made me anxious. I knew the calls concerned me but no one would tell me what was going to happen. In addition, my cousin Lena was probably feeling out of her depth about how to comfort me and maybe jealous, too, that she now had to share her space with me. I felt an uneasy mixture of being awkward and ungrateful. Family dynamics are strange: Lena wasn't mature enough to understand what my sister and I were going through and neither were my other cousins. Auntie Helen's house was quite big, with no carpet on the wooden stairs. One day I fell down those stairs. I felt confused and was seeing double but my cousins thought it was funny. Theirs wasn't a malicious laugh and, cock-eyed, I even joined in, but I do wonder now if I might have had a concussion that, with all that was going on, went completely overlooked. One incident that demonstrated the tensions in the house happened while I was playing schools with one of my older cousins, Helen. She belted me hard with the buckle side, presumably – consciously or unconsciously – taking out her anger on me for the way I'd disrupted her family. I was no cry baby but that belting made me cry.

When we were alone, Auntie Helen started confiding in me. She said she'd told my grandmother that my mother was unfit to adopt a child. So desperate was my mother for a baby, my aunt said, that my grandmother had gone so far as to ask my aunt Helen to give her sister her youngest child. I was too young and traumatised to cope with this information but I was ashamed that I felt that way, so I would sit and listen. Maybe my aunt thought by telling me this I would understand that even before I was born she had tried to protect me; maybe she unconsciously needed to salve her conscience – though the inadequacies hadn't been hers. I never became angry at the things she said. That was for two reasons. First, I totally believed her and, second, I didn't want to be put out. I knew that Cathleen and I were dependent on her and that I had to walk this kind of tightrope to keep us safe. But I'd try desperately to see through the ferns etched into the opaque glass separating me from Auntie Helen as she took yet another official phone call; I was desperate to know what was going to happen.

I wasn't even allowed to go to my mother's funeral. Children didn't go to funerals in those days, perhaps because it was too painful for the adults. The adults were making decisions for me and I wasn't part of it.

I didn't go to school in the short while I was there and I certainly didn't miss my dad. I remember playing in my aunt's garden, trying to be a happy child so she wouldn't let anyone take me away. Then the day came when a social worker, Nigel Watt, arrived to take Cathleen and me home. I cried then. I cried hard. I remember thinking, if I cry, he won't take me. In his car, wearing a red polo-neck jumper I didn't recognise as my own, I watched as the houses and gardens in my auntie Helen's street faded away and I told myself I'd never cry again because crying didn't work.

Unbeknown to me, but not surprisingly, in the few weeks I was living with my aunt, my father had been sinking deeper. The winter bills hadn't been paid. He owed money for the rent; the insurance to pay for my mother's funeral hadn't come through; the Co-op was calling for an outstanding bill to be paid; and on top of all that he'd had a letter saying the electricity was about to be cut off. Nigel Watt had tried repeatedly to meet up with him at our house while I was at my aunt's, without success. It was one of my father's friends who phoned the social worker to tell him my father was temporarily living elsewhere. When Nigel sat down with my father to talk over how he was going to cope, being a single parent to two children who weren't even his own, he quickly formed the impression my father was afraid of the responsibility. He just wasn't convinced my father actually wanted us but the belief at the time was that children should be reunited with their parents.

Thanks to the social worker's intervention, the Co-op agreed to wait for their money. The electricity people took a harder line but eventually the power was restored. When he realised my father would be out at work from seven in the morning till almost five at night, Nigel Watt contacted the home-help department of the council and was told he would have to make an appointment. Even a neighbour who had originally offered to help look after my sister and me changed her mind, no doubt when she realised just how huge the task of being go-between was likely to be. No other measures were put in place to ensure that we would be looked after properly but, despite the obvious problems, on 31 January 1976 I was taken in the car back home to 40 Hermiston Road. My mother had been dead for four weeks. I was scared of how I would feel going back there but I was looking forward to seeing my friend Jean again and to going back to Bannerman High School.

My father had tidied up and built a huge fire for us but, even so, the house was cold, damp and dismal, mirroring my feelings. As she sat in front of the fire, Cathleen seemed lost in oblivion and so young. She was easily cheered, however, especially when my father promised that he would take her out for a walk soon to buy sweeties. I had dried my tears by this time, and pretended I was fine, but when Nigel Watt left and the door closed I felt the first tremors as my world began to collapse about me.

In the end, I was only to spend three days in the house. With my father at work and with my six-year-old sister to look after, living in this house that roomed the memories of Urquhart and fear of his return, as well as the ghost of my mother, was to prove too much for me.

One of the good memories I have of those three days involved meeting up with my friend Jean again. The movie *Jaws* was on at the cinema and we decided we'd go to see it. It was a certificate 12, so we knew we could get in; however, I had to take Cathleen with me. With little money, and her not being of age, we had to figure out a way of smuggling her in. We hit on a foolproof plan. One of us would go up to the counter and pay for two while the other would go to the toilet with Cathleen sneaked in behind her. It worked. We found our seats and Cathleen sat on my knee in the packed cinema house.

The hype surrounding the movie had been successful. The tension was electrifying and the hush and screams throughout the movie amused me. I never screamed; I was proud of never screaming. The only time I got a fright was when Cathleen jumped up off my knee at the infamous scene when the severed head fell out of the boat. Not once do I remember thinking about what would be waiting for me back at the house again.

After the movie, we sauntered home suitably thrilled. We'd spent all our bus fare on sweets but chattered excitedly during the long walk. The chink in my delusion of fearlessness came after we said goodbye to Jean, and Cathleen and I turned for home again. Fear came in the form of having to check the toilet and being as quick as possible in case a shark should bite my bum, and then staring at the plughole of the bath, waiting for an enormous snout with an eruption of teeth to crash up through it.

But there was more to be afraid of than that. Three days was long enough for my father to behave. He came home drunk that night and shouted at us.

I went to bed and dreamt of my mother.

The bed where Cathleen and I slept was damp, with no ginger bottles filled with boiled water from the kettle to warm it. My mother's single bed in the corner lay as empty as my stare. I awoke from a dream with the sensation of someone sitting at the bottom of my bed; I heard my mother calling me in the dark and I heard her cough. I reached out in the cold and the sensation disappeared. There was no one there. My dream disappeared and the reality was a nightmare.

In the darkness of the bedroom, with my wee sister sleeping beside me, I was terrified of what I had experienced and only in hindsight do I realise I was traumatised. To this day, the memory of that night and the following day remains one of the very few times I recall with a blanket of unconnected nothingness. I have no memory of crying or not eating, no memory of hunger. Only the dream places me personally there.

Nigel Watt wrote in his social work report that I wouldn't get out of bed, stop crying or even eat for the whole day. My father had gone to him to tell him. He didn't know how to cope with me and the fact I'd told him I didn't want to stay there. As a temporary measure, Cathleen and I were removed from home and sent to an emergency placement for two nights at Cairnvale Children's Home in Glasgow.

In the stories I'd read, Heidi went to Switzerland. Me, I spent a couple of nights at the children's home before being moved on to another children's home on the west coast. I wore the red polo neck then, too. Throughout the journey, grief made me empty. I *must* have been grieving for my mother but mostly I remember how low I felt to be leaving my aunt. I remembered how my father would shout at my mother to 'Get those adopted bastards away from me.' Now the voice in my head insisted, 'Nobody wants those adopted bastards.'

In the car on the way up to the children's home, Nigel Watt pointed out a big house in the distance. 'See that house? That's where you're going. That's Clydeview.'

As a child, the size of Clydeview oppressed me. I found the house cold and massive. I walked, that day, through a long, echoing corridor, on a journey I hadn't chosen. A social worker opened a door and left me in a large room filled with rows of chairs and a TV at the far wall. I sat there, with Cathleen sitting on my knee and cuddling into my red polo neck. As soon as the adults left, the other children crowded round. Who are you, where are you from, they wanted to know. What happened to you? Cathleen and I were a bigger draw than whatever had been on television. I think of it as a pain competition in which certain qualifications were required if you wanted to compete. Like me, these were mostly Glasgow children – it was a council-run home – and they all had similarly painful yet different stories from mine. I was reluctant to say anything other than that my mother had died.

Clydeview was my home for the six months after her death. Cathleen and I were in the same dorm, she in a single bed and me in the top of one of a set of four bunk beds. Other than one shelf in a shared cupboard, that bed was my only personal space. At night, I'd lie listening to the sea howl and the trees lash in the coastal wind. That was great: it matched my feelings, took me out of myself; it was my ethereal escape.

I had one poster on my bit of the wall. Though in the outside world girls my age might have been screaming for the Bay City Rollers, I had a poster of Andy Williams with his twin sons. People said I looked like him, with my blonde feathered haircut. Apart from that I had my clothes – including a pair of the latest black wedge-heeled shoes I'd brought with me that the other girls envied. I'd pestered my father for the money, as Jean had a pair.

My aunt had given me money and stamps so that I could keep in touch with her – this being before the days of mobiles and instant messaging. We weren't allowed to use the phone or receive any calls. To keep the money and stamps safe, I climbed up to my top bunk and eased the stopper off the tubing of the old-fashioned black metal frame. But they fell right down to the bottom. I was scared to tell my aunt the truth and she was cross with me when she didn't receive any letters; it added to her enormous sense of frustration. I'm sure she felt I should have kept my mother's house together. She wanted me to take on the responsibility, perhaps because I seemed more grown-up than the 12 year old I really was, due to the way I controlled my emotions.

In Clydeview, we had communal sleeping arrangements; we also had communal showers, all the girls in the dorm taking their turn in the ritual of institutional cleanliness. Self-conscious and aware of my ugly, skinny body, I hated this. I especially hated the worker who'd supervise us. 'The Shower Lady' wouldn't let me close the shower curtains and I'd feel her eyes on me all the while the water was running. I used to turn my back on her and hurry to wash and dry myself so that I could get back into my clothes again.

Cathleen and I were enrolled at the local schools while we lived there. I suppose it's round about this time that I should have had the inoculation against rubella but I didn't get it there.

In the February, close to my 13th birthday, I had another chest cold and it aggravated my asthma. Alone in the top bunk while the others were at school, I became aware of the dorm door opening and the Shower Lady coming in. I knew she was coming for me. I'd been interfered with by Urquhart and though this was a woman I picked up the same signals of the predator I'd recognised in him. Feigning concern, she came over to me and asked me how I was. Her hand reached up under my covers and she began to rub my chest, then moved down to my stomach, then lower. I lay sickened by dread. I knew this day was going to come. I was the new girl. I'd seen the way she'd been watching me. I was her new prey. There was a click from the door and the handle turned. Quickly she snatched her hand away from between my legs. Her eyes shot me a look. She'd only stopped because another residential social worker had come into the room. I think the other worker must have been suspicious of her, or maybe that's wishful thinking on my part.

Soon it was my birthday and Auntie Helen, my uncle and cousins came to visit me. It was a nice day out for them, I suppose, but I felt such despair when they left. I wished they hadn't come. In my distress, I felt they could congratulate themselves for having done a good deed then go and carry on with their lives outside, while for me it brought all the sadness and isolation back to the surface again as I watched them leave. I ached when I saw them go, knowing they were leaving me behind. It was a reminder of everything I'd lost and the situation I now found myself in.

Headstrong by nurture, I struggled to bow to the routine of the children's home. For example, the first time I was served liver I refused – full stop – to eat it. I could smell it yards away and it made me feel sick. The next day, it was put down in front of me again. My frantic mind came up with a plan. I wasn't allowed to leave the table till I'd eaten it, so I cut it up into tiny pieces and tucked it inside my sleeve while no one was looking. Then I put my knife and fork together on the cleared plate, asked if I could be excused and went to the toilet. I shook all the rubbery greyness out of my cardigan and flushed it away, boaking and angry at having to resort to such deceit.

There was a big army base near the home and, as part of their interaction with the local community, the troops would take groups of children from the home to give them tours of the base. The children would come back with sweets and sometimes even cigarettes. That set my alarm bells ringing. I didn't ever want to go, sensing there might be more to it. I'm not accusing any of the soldiers, of course, but after my experience with Urquhart and the Shower Lady I was alert to these things. My suspicions were aroused and I hid under beds or out in the trees whenever they arrived at the home. And I didn't get into trouble, strangely, for hiding.

I suppose some people become involved in child care through a deep-rooted instinct to care for and protect children but I'm also in no doubt that some join the profession for other reasons. On some occasions I had direct experience of this; on others, it was just a vague threat. One of the workers at Clydeview was an ex-Navy man. Jock Sutherland was a large, imposing figure and kept a ferret on a long chain leash. In April, he caught my little sister eating some of her chocolate Easter egg when she should have been going to sleep and he lashed her with that chain. It was a chain we all tried to avoid. Even now I'm resentful and ashamed when I think about that event and the way I was impotent to prevent it.

The Easter eggs must have come from Auntie Helen. Now and then we were allowed to go to her house for the weekend and I remember how a social worker would go with us. The need for us to be escorted meant a day out for them. We'd be driven there in a black Princess car. Even then I was aware of the irony: the council – Strathclyde Regional Council, as it was then – could afford this big car and chauffeur for us but they couldn't afford to pay my aunt to keep us. Despite my general suspicion of adults, I thought the driver of the black Princess was very nice and I felt he was like me: he had a flaw but he could still function. He had a false hand but it didn't interfere with his driving. He used to chat with us throughout the journey. However, the contrast between this chauffeur-driven car and me with my plastic carrier bags of clothes made me feel small and dirty, shrunken in size. The beauty highlighted my poverty. My previously white socks, now grey, hung round my ankles as the elastic had perished. My fingers with their bitten nails sneaked repeatedly to pull them up. I tried to tuck my legs behind the bags as I sat on the luxurious polished seats.

Soon I'd be back at Clydeview, unhappy and uneasy. Even a simple action like going to the local sweet shop had uncomfortable resonances, as I didn't like the man who ran it. I went there with an older girl, Katherine Masters, who told me as we arrived at the shop door that he would give us free sweets if we sat on his knee.

Plastic rainbow streamers fluttered in the doorway; Katherine separated them with her arm and I thought it was too late to change my mind. He put his hand up my skirt and I never went back.

With this constant feeling of unease and fear of abuse, it's no wonder I wanted to leave. Everywhere I went, I thought about it: at my school desk when I was supposed to be reading; in the dense foliage of the house's gardens; in my high bunk with Cathleen and the other girls' breathing filling the dark. As we were sent to bed early, a shaft of light from outside would slant on to the wall near my head, drawing a line of yellow down my Andy Williams poster.

I told the social workers I wanted to go back to my father. I said I was missing him, which was a lie. I just wanted out. I was afraid that someone like Urquhart was going to turn up there and I'd be killed, just like he had threatened. And so, in July 1976 at the age of 13, I left Clydeview Children's Home, pretending to be happy.

9

Back Home

My desperate decision to lie to the social worker Nigel Watt in order to get me out of Clydeview Children's Home and back home to my father had worked. Smiling on the outside, I returned home with Cathleen.

I didn't want to be back home but it would remove me from the danger I sensed in Clydeview. Once there, I would just have to deal with what came my way. It seemed like my only option and at least I would be in familiar surroundings, able to go to school with my friends, not miles away should I have to find help, though where I actually thought I would get help I don't know.

While we had been in Clydeview, my father had been offered an exchange of house. Under the circumstances, it probably seemed to him and others a good idea. A new house with no memories would be a better place for him and for us children. However, the exchange was to a flat in the worst possible area. It was in the optimistically named Larchgrove area of Springboig, next to the infamous St John's School for 'troubled boys', as they were called at that time. There wasn't a larch tree in sight, only some broken and mutilated rowans. My heart sank as we arrived in the social work car. The area, with its graffiti-covered walls, looked dismal but I never let on how I was feeling, afraid that one flinch would give the game away and Nigel would know how unhappy and scared I was. Instead, I maintained my happy façade.

Our new home was a flat above a corner shop. The flats round about us were built in a big circle, all three-storey blocks with entrance closes that led from the street through to the back gardens with their washing poles. I could see the gardens from the back windows of our flat, and the small play park set in concrete in the very middle of the circle. A path ran through, breaking the circle; this allowed easy access from one end to the other and to the local shops.

Our building was closest to the path. We lived in the middle flat with one above us and one below us and the shop block at the side. I could climb out of my bedroom window onto a veranda that gave access to the roof of the shop. There I would sit, watching the world go by, safe in the knowledge that while I could see them, no one could see me.

Internally, the house was sorrowful. The decor was stark, a dull, dated, dank brown, with no cheer or homeliness about it. The once white paintwork was now yellow and peeling. My social work files acknowledge that, in retrospect, this move was not a good one; my father was gullible and had been easily manipulated into the house exchange. The only thing I remember having from the previous house was my bookcase. My books had been the only possessions I'd asked for when I was sent to Clydeview but they were taken from me for 'safe-keeping' while I was at the children's home and I never got them back. Here, in Larchgrove, my bookcase was empty of my collection.

Cathleen and I had a double bed in the main bedroom and at nights I'd lie and sing to her. She thought I knew all the songs in the world; anything she asked me to sing, I could. She would ask for the Carpenters' song 'Top of the World', to which she'd add her own version of the next line, 'looking down on Coronation Street'. Many nights I would lie awake while Cathleen slept snuggled up beside me. The small windows in the flat afforded little light, day or night. I'd lie there, feeling ashamed at being ashamed of my surroundings. I felt at some level I should be grateful.

My father's drinking continued. I'd lie in bed and hear the familiar words of 'The Sash', punctuated with loud shouts of 'I'm an Irishman. A UDA man,' as he walked towards our close. His shiftwork at the railway continued, too. Frequently, he'd disappear for the night only to return looking rough and wretched from a combination of drinking and heavy physical work: frighteningly wretched.

Our toilet was shabby and bleak. We struggled to have a bath, as my father's work overalls were always put to steep in the bath – a wash in the twin tub didn't seem to remove the heavy dirt he picked up on the tracks on the railway. A layer of scum floated on the surface. I hated having to go to the toilet after my father, as the stench was almost unbearable; this was due to his diet of cheap wines like Old England, Lanliq and Eldorado. It was bad enough to make me gag and the smell filtered throughout the house. No amount of bleach could clean the bath or toilet nor mask the smell. Smells always made me feel sick.

I told my social worker, whom I had to visit every week, that my father was drinking heavily. It was noted in my files as early as the July when we returned. It was noted as something that had to be checked out. Another part of the arrangement that was supposed to be put in place for our return was that my best friend's mum, Mrs Collins, would help out with Cathleen and me, but for whatever reason this never happened, though I resumed my close friendship with her daughter, Jean.

My file records that social workers came to visit the house on 10 August, at which time they recorded that they thought my father was coping well. He claimed he was settled with us and that there were no major problems, although my father confided I was staying out late. A double asterisk next to one sentence by social worker Nigel Watt says, 'a close watch must be kept on these children'.

My father never brought his drinking friends or any others home, though that remained my constant fear. He did, however, disappear with Cathleen to go to see friends. Sometimes he left me money on the mantelpiece above the fire for food, sometimes not. He must have thought I was independent and capable. And I was happy in the house by myself, though I was afraid of having any outsiders there.

A greying memory I have of this time concerns unexpected visitors. A bang woke me; our front door had been kicked in. Hearing many gruff male voices, including my dad's, I jumped out of bed to see uniformed policemen dragging him away. Our house was raided but the details of why have disappeared from my mind. Was it irritation or malice from the community, provoked by his sectarian singing and slogan shouting? No charges were ever filed against him.

The only person I allowed into my new house was my friend Jean. As well as being fearful of having others in the house, I was too ashamed to let anyone else in. Jean had such a lovely house compared to mine, with its duvets, ornaments, colour, freshness in the decor and nice clothes, homely noises and TV. Despite this, she never made me feel anything other than her best friend.

At the end of August, Cathleen and I returned to school. I went back to Bannerman High School and Cathleen to Budhill Primary. It was important to me that Cathleen went to school and I would make sure she was up and ready every morning, but motivating myself to go was often a problem. On my first day back, when I arrived in my geography class my first boyfriend Allen Reid, who'd asked me so romantically if I'd heard about 'shagging' when we were six, and his friend Brian, with whom I'd previously played football, asked me if I was now an orphan. This stung! I was in classes with new people, too, and felt very isolated. I began to stay at home or go for long walks, returning home at the same time as if I'd been at school. By September, only weeks after the term had begun, I had already played truant several times and could easily forge my father's signature for my letters and truant card. I had given up speaking to the social worker about my father's drinking, as he had seemed quite cross with me for telling on my dad. The East End sentiment of keeping stumm prevailed even in the Social Work Department.

I spent hours in the local graveyard when I was playing truant. I loved it there. On one occasion, Jean, another girl called Kim Bain, two boys and I decided to play truant in Kim's house since her parents were both at work and it was somewhere different to go. One of the boys was a local policeman's son. While we were there, we realised how suspicious it was that we were all off school at the same time. We decided one of us should phone, pretending to be a parent, so we could excuse ourselves from school. The problem was that Kim didn't have a phone. Her next-door neighbour did, though. All that was needed was for one of us to climb through the window at the back door so we could use the neighbour's phone.

We stood around the door, checking to make sure we weren't seen. Since I was the smallest (and gawkiest), I had to be the one who climbed through the window. Anyway, I had plenty of experience of climbing out of my own window onto the shop roof. Kim told me where in the kitchen the back-door key would be hidden. So, with a lot of pushing and shoving from behind, I wiggled my way through the small top window till I fell onto the worktop inside the kitchen.

Success! I opened the back door and we all piled in, made the phone calls, felt we had covered our backs and were very pleased with ourselves. We lounged about on the big couches, high on bravado and talking excitedly. Not satisfied with that, the policeman's son decided to take a look around and we followed. I ran my hand on the wood of the swooping banister and gazed up at the high ceilings in this gorgeous house, breathing in the scent of cleanliness and lavender polish.

'Hey, look at this,' the policeman's boy said and I heard the sound of bottles clinking. He was taking drink from a cabinet. We were all caught up in the adrenalin rush of the situation – a mixture of excitement and panic. We crazily thought if we took a few things we were again covering our backs – it would look as if some unknown people had broken in with a view to theft, rather than just to use the phone.

Back in Kim's almost as grand old house, the rush began to settle and I panicked. I really panicked. I felt reality biting, as though the whole thing was entirely my fault. I knew, I knew with certainty, that somehow the blame would come to rest at my door. I was the one with no strong parental back-up. Someone would be looking for a scapegoat and who could be better than me? I decided to run away.

Jean and Kim made up their mind to come with me.

We headed down to the graveyard and hid the stuff we had taken from the house. I don't know where the boys went but we headed off to the train station with no real plan other than to run. We dodged all the fares on the trains and ended up miles away in Gourock. Dunoon was the place we headed for, as it was the furthest away place any of us knew. We managed to get on the ferry without paying the fare, too. After the short journey, we landed in Dunoon with just a few pounds and some Polo mints between us.

For a while we wandered around and looked at the sights. Then we settled on the beach for a rest, but it was autumn: the wind off the sea was harsh. Cold began to set in and in an unbelievable attempt to keep warm we set a fire on the beach using our lovely coats from Rita's in the Glasgow Barras ('the place to buy') for fuel.

By now it was getting late and, hungry, we gave up on the idea of staying on the beach and headed back to the pier. Our money ran to a shared bag of crisps and a drink. We stole another packet of Polo mints and ate them in the dark down by the water, the streetlights from town glittering on the waves lapping around the boats. The embers from the fire were still glowing.

It was getting late and we'd nowhere to go. The toilets on the pier were still open as the lights twinkled in the distance. Cold, and with no coats, we drifted towards them. Not wanting to be seen at that time of night we locked ourselves in a toilet. We huddled together on the floor, keeping our feet up on the door so that people returning from the pub and looking for a place to take their winching partner couldn't get in. By morning, Kim had had enough. To be honest, we all had but neither Jean nor I wanted to break rank and be the first to concede.

Kim phoned her parents from the public phone box at the pier and shortly after that the police arrived. We were arrested – arrested – taken to the police station and spoken to. We confessed to the housebreaking. Much later, we discovered that the policeman's son had been found lying on his living-room floor unconscious from too much alcohol.

Soon we were back on board the ferry with an escort and we were met by police at the other side, to be questioned again about the break-in.

As a result of my misbehaviour and my aunt complaining to the Social Work Department about my father's inability to look after Cathleen and me, my social worker was having long talks with me, trying to appeal to my reason. I had too many secrets to hide, so I became more accomplished in giving people the answers they wanted to hear. My memories of this time are supplemented by my social work records, which I applied for a few years ago under the Freedom of Information Act. On numerous occasions, it was written in my files that a close eye had to be kept on us and that people would be assisting us. But this didn't happen and, with my mother no longer around to be used as a punchbag, I was now the sole target of my father's brutal, frustrated rage.

There was rarely any food in the house, so I would often have to steal money from him just to buy essentials for myself and Cathleen. One morning, I sneaked into his bedroom early and fished around for his trousers. The air stank. The trousers lay on the floor, crumpled and filthy. As I had done many times before, I crept, cat-like, towards them, lifting them carefully so that the change in the pockets wouldn't jingle and alert my father. My gaze shifted quickly between him and his trousers till they were securely in my hands. But on this occasion I was careless. He caught me.

'You thieving wee bastard,' he said, springing from his bed.

I didn't get time to run.

'I'll teach you no' tae do that to me!' His Irish navvy hands knocked me to the floor.

I found myself face down on the carpet. All the change from his pockets spilled out. He kicked me again and again with his bare feet. The kicks landed on my stomach, head and side till I curled up, tightening my grip on his trousers. They stank of urine. I took the rest of the kicks on my back.

'We need milk, Dad,' I shouted. 'We need milk.'

I refused to cry. Anyway, the pain was irrelevant; I was more concerned at seeing my father naked. I averted my eyes and watched the pennies rolling away from me under the bed.

Later, he gave me the money. We did need milk.

I was living a semi-feral life. Unattended. Left to my own care and trying to work out the rules of the environment I found myself in. I'd always been ashamed that my poverty was evident in my dress and then I heard about 'snowdropping' – a term used in Glasgow's East End to describe the act of stealing clothes hung out to dry on other people's washing lines. One day, Jean and I were bored and happened to wander to Inveresk Street in Carntyne. I was quite excited to be straying and, away from our home ground, we decided to give this snowdropping a go, not without some anxiety. We wandered around the back of some three-storey flats, passing an eye over the lines of washing and inconspicuously – we hoped – inspecting the gardens left and right. Eventually, we'd built up enough gall to grab something from a line. I'd spotted a likely looking cream top and after snatching something each we ran out of the gardens towards the park, through it via the bowling green and up to the entrance that took us to our neck of the woods. My chest was straining with fear and exertion. We threw ourselves into the bushes, peering out to make sure no irate housewife was giving chase. Then we held up our acquisitions. On inspection, I didn't like the top. Once the thrill disappeared, I felt dread and guilt. It brought me no joy and I never wore it.

On another occasion, Jean and I decided to go and see *The Exorcist*. Although the movie was certified as an 18, we got caught up in the hype and were determined to see it. We set about the task of making ourselves look older, and after finding the highest heels we could to wear – after all, height equates to maturity – and smearing on red lipstick, we tried to figure out what else we could do to ensure our easy passage into the movie. Toilet roll became our next ally to deceit – carefully folded, moulded round and tucked into our teenage bras. So there we were with our heels, red lipstick and disposable implants. As we sneakily teetered out the door, handbags over our shoulders, I paused. One last idea came to mind. Sunglasses. Sunglasses made you look cool and sophisticated.

We set off by train from Shettleston and arrived at Queen Street Station, convincing ourselves by the time we had sauntered up to Renfield Street in the city centre that we were indeed the business. We could not fail.

As we arrived at the Odeon in Renfield Street, we did a stock check: lipstick, fine; hair, fine; and only then did the sunglasses come out of our bags. With enhanced busts that matched our confidence, we swaggered (or perhaps staggered) through the doors of the cinema and breezed up to the kiosk counter to pay for our tickets. When we asked for tickets for *The Exorcist*, however, we were promptly asked to leave, and within a few seconds we found ourselves back on Renfield Street, all dressed up and nowhere to go. Thank goodness for those sunglasses that shielded us from our humiliating exit. We dared not look back at the staff in order to leave some part of our injured pride intact. How they must have laughed.

My files show that my father was spoken to about his drinking and he admitted he had a problem. Our social worker was attending Alcoholics Anonymous meetings with my father and the notes make it sound as if he was there to support my father and for that reason alone, but some neighbours informed my aunt that the social worker himself was an alcoholic. Maybe it was a malicious rumour but maybe it explains why I never felt he took me seriously: maybe his sympathies lay with my dad.

Despite this apparent effort, in the space of two months, the situation at home had broken down to such a point that the Social Work Department was contacted independently. On 19 November 1976, a representative from the Royal Scottish Society for the Prevention of Cruelty to Children came to my door. My father had been picked up for being drunk and disorderly the previous night and was charged with several offences. Neighbours reported that he deserted the home at the weekends. I was questioned by the authorities and we were once again removed and sent to my aunt Helen's. It was noted that the Larchgrove house was filthy and that there was a suggestion of bruises on me. Ironically, when a social worker contacted me at my aunt's, I was quite happy, but that's because this was where I wanted to be.

By 30 November, my father was back in the AA. Nigel Watt met up with my aunt and recorded his view that she was terribly uncommunicative. I can imagine my aunt seething with anger and frustration, not only because of my home situation but also because of the relationship between her and the Social Work Department. She wouldn't have seen the reports that accused her of being troublesome and of poisoning our minds against our father. But she would have had a good idea of how she was being represented. In my file, Nigel Watt recorded his unequivocal support for my father, while stating that my aunt had not returned his calls. He recorded how he was still accompanying my father to regular AA meetings and noted his pride at my father's first sober fortnight in years. Within a week of that entry, however, my father had begun to miss his appointments with the social worker.

By now, my aunt had received a cheque for fifty pounds towards the expense of keeping us. I was safe in the knowledge we would be spending the festive season with her. Anxiety gnawed at me, as I knew that this could all be shattered after the holidays were over, but at least I could breathe for a while. For this Christmas and New Year – one year on from the time I'd witnessed my mother's death – we would be included and safe. I didn't know what was being planned for us; I only knew I was still tiptoeing that tightrope, the sad wee girl smiling.

Once again, we had to change schools, but by 16 December, the social worker contacted my aunt as he had been informed that we were not attending school. My aunt explained that there were two reasons for this: we had colds and we didn't have adequate winter clothing (well, I had burnt my coat!) The response was that she had to send us to school as quickly as possible. The mistrust and tension remained between them. It was personal.

My aunt worked hard, as did my uncle, but with a large house, four kids still at home plus a son-in-law and a grandchild, and now with us to look after as well, she needed any financial help she was entitled to. Yet she was accused of trying to make capital out of the situation by asking for money towards our keep. The slant on her is appalling, as is the way the department lost sight of the interests of Cathleen and me. My aunt suggested that if my newly married cousin could be allocated a council house of her own, there would be adequate room in my aunt's house for us. Annette had a new baby and my aunt's house was very overcrowded. The Social Work Department felt this was unreasonable and further exacerbated the rift. She was accused of trying to pull strings to get her daughter a house in a good area.

On 17 December, a social work conference was held in the then headquarters at Osborne Street in Glasgow. My father had become concerned about the lies he felt my aunt was telling about him and it was now decided that it was not in our interest to stay with her any longer, to ensure our minds would not be further poisoned against my father. I wonder what I would have said to this social worker if I had known the lengths he was going to in this vendetta. I just knew not to trust him but to play sweet – a basic survival instinct to avoid antagonising the one who held all the power.

None of those affected by its rulings – my father, Aunt Helen,

Cathleen or I – were allowed to attend this conference, at which the war between my aunt and the social worker resulted in a decision being made that we should be taken into care. And for the first time the possibility was raised of Cathleen being fostered out without me. On the same day, Nigel Watt contacted Uncle Edward and Aunt Joyce, who lived round the corner from our old house, to see if they would take us, such was his dislike of my aunt Helen. But they said no.

If I wished for anything that Christmas, it was for us to stay in the safety of my aunt's house. I knew no one would harm me there – she wouldn't allow it – and though she was not emotionally demonstrative, she was wonderfully feisty. My aunt had used the money that was collected after my mother's death by neighbours not for flowers for the funeral but for basics such as vests, pants and other items for us. She now gave me money for a pair of badly needed trousers but by the time I got into the city centre, my purse had been pickpocketed. So terrified I was of going home without them, I eventually went into Chelsea Girl and stole a pair. My racing heart as I walked out of the store was nothing compared to the fear of letting my aunt down. She worked hard for her money and I was worried that even if I told her what had happened, she might not believe me.

Nigel Watt noted that he'd had a phone call from my aunt on 23 December in which, he said, she was irate, furious that he'd told my father the department had given her money to look after us. She believed it was no concern of my father's. She also asked Nigel not to tell me and Cathleen that they were going to take us into care again until after Christmas.

My father didn't want us to be sent back to Clydeview and was happy to sign under Section 15 of the act that governed voluntary placement with parental control. So in the new year, a social worker from Braeview House on the outskirts of Glasgow arrived at my aunt's house to visit us before we were transferred there. Our reaction is recorded in the files in one word: tearful.

By 25 January 1977, we had moved into Braeview and I was enrolled at the nearby high school – my third school in the year or so since my mother's death.

Having visited the home previously, Nigel Watt anticipated no difficulties for us settling in. His empathy with my father continued through the pages of my case files. He recorded my father's 'tremendous progress', said my dad was happy visiting the girls at Braeview, and that Cathleen and I seemed happy.

In contrast to Clydeview, Braeview House was a more intimate setting and had a homelier feel as it was made up of small units. Staff members lived in the same house as us and we were also part of the community. I shared a room with an older girl called Rena Walker. It should have been a good time for me, a chance to start putting my life together, but I couldn't settle completely. In retrospect, I'd been through too much upheaval; I'd lost any kind of stability. I wanted to be with my aunt Helen but once again I'd been removed from her and placed with strangers. I wandered the grounds on my own, isolating myself physically and once again finding some kind of solace in a garden.

That's not to say there weren't funny moments. Like the time we had an open day with entertainment hosted by TV children's presenter Glen Michael. We kids had no privacy – now we were on display to be gaped at by voyeurs from the local community. I climbed a tree to stay out of their way. My turn to watch. Far from this being an opportunity to showcase the 'good girls' in the school, the locals were instead treated to the sight of me stuck up a tree. My attempts to hide from everyone were thwarted.

I also enjoyed the company of other girls my own age, such as Rena and Danielle, and I even had my first snog with John McDonald, one of a set of twins. That was a terrifying and near vomit-inducing experience but I couldn't lose face, so I went through with it. He told my new friends that I was a great kisser, and Rena passed it on. I never let on it was my first real kiss. It was such a relief to get it out of the way and for kissing to eventually become a normal experience. However, in the background, my worries continued.

Soon it was my 14th birthday and my dad came to the home to visit me. He never missed my birthday and always brought me a cake, though not always in one piece. More often than not, by the time it reached me the icing would be smeared over the transparent top of the cake box and the candles would have burrowed deep into the sponge.

One minute my dad was visiting me at the home and giving me pocket money, the next I was to appear as a witness against him at court. His trial date was set for 23 March 1977, on charges of abandonment and neglect. All I can remember is borrowing a hooded denim zipper jacket from Rena to wear and standing on my own in the witness box, terrified. I'd only just turned 14. All his in-laws stated in court that our house had been filthy and that Cathleen and I had been starved and poorly clad – something that Nigel Watt disputed. I had to point my dad out in the court, acknowledging him as my father. I also remember my father's lawyer questioning me when it was said we'd been left hungry. 'Were there not eggs in the house?' he said, sternly.

Defensive, I replied, 'I don't like eggs.' Why I said that I have no idea, except that I was trying to tell the truth.

The truth was that we were hungry on many occasions. I had even eaten potato skins from the bin but I was too ashamed to say that in court. I was angry at the suggestion that I wasn't being truthful when I claimed I'd been hungry. I said in court that I didn't want to go back and live with my father. I felt so ashamed at having to give evidence against my dad and at the same time I was feeling frightened and guilty. I also seethed with anger towards his lawyer for humiliating me in his attempt to get my dad off. My dad must really have felt that I had let him down. He was found guilty of the charges and fined forty pounds.

Nigel Watt's main concern remained my dad. In the case notes, he made a list of bullet points about his plans for our family. All of them related to my father. The first of his aims was to get my father off the drink, after which he hoped it would be possible for us to be reunited. As it turned out, this would be his parting statement. After that, Nigel Watt moved on. My life, after all, was only his work.

I didn't want to live with my father. I was terrified of the idea but back at Braeview my feelings were a turbulent mix of loyalty, guilt and shame. Not that I was aware that that's what I was feeling; at the time, I just felt utter confusion and concern – a sense of being trapped. My greatest fear was that I would be in town with my friends and we would pass him lying drunk in the gutter. What if he approached me? How would I react? Yet another part of me was afraid that he too was going to die. I felt I would somehow be to blame. I should have been able to take care of the situation and I couldn't work out why this wasn't the case.

10

Nothing In, Nothing Out

My father was still the person the Social Work Department wanted me to be close to. But his visits were erratic. Dutifully, I would wait for him to visit me at the home, watching out for him walking up the drive, my nails bitten down to the quick. On one occasion, I remember he appeared looking smart in his suit and tie but he was drunk and had had his head shaved. I still remember how frightened I was for him. I thought he must have been in prison.

I always did my duty when he came to see us and was left alone with him for the duration of his visit. Cathleen, being younger, would take the pocket money and run. I'd make him tea and sandwiches. I can still see him, sitting paralytic and sneezing mucus down his tie and shirt. His suit trousers would always be wet when he came back from the toilet and there'd be traces of previous stains, too. More often than not, his zip would be left down. Yet the social workers would tell me I was lucky: he was my father after all and other kids didn't get visitors. Inside, I endured these visits but my face, with its mask of pleasantness, concealed a heart that was cold and resigned and a head that was brimming with resentment. And as ever I felt guilty about my embarrassment. The feeling wasn't dissimilar to how I'd felt when I'd hidden behind the curtains at home after witnessing my mother falling drunk onto the garden path.

At Braeview, as at Clydeview, I felt a sense of wonder at all the features in the old building, so typical of many children's homes, and the large expanse of grounds where I could roam around. The grounds painted a picture of a healthy place to grow up, with their wide-open spaces and established trees. Whilst I enjoyed this picturesque snapshot, I knew it wouldn't last, though why, I had no idea. I couldn't understand why I could feel so old, yet know nothing. At night, in the room I shared with Rena, I could hear staff members and their boyfriends having sex. Occasions like these evoked memories of Urquhart. I wanted it all to go away so I could go home to my own bed, my own books and my own garden.

I knew there was no way back: my life had changed and I couldn't understand how to accept it. I wasn't stupid: I knew my previous life had been unhappy but this was worse. It was shit but it was unfamiliar shit – no comfort in that. I missed saying the name Mum; I missed someone telling me that they loved me. Even though it was said mostly in drunkenness, it was adult–child affection. I could at least have a cuddle, be told I was loved and hear my mum singing to me, 'Have I told you lately that I love you?' even though it was me putting her to bed. Here, now, I was lost, with no idea where I was going or where it was all going to end. I just wanted it to. I saw life like a running river, a stream of consciousness, with me a paper boat, left and forgotten, half sunk at sundown. Ashamed at this secret sentimental self-pity, my dialogue with myself was harsh and unforgiving. 'I'll gi'e you something to greet for,' I told myself so many times. My secret motto became 'Nothing in, nothing out'. Give nothing away and let nothing in. Emotions were destructive. Surely, I told myself, I could work out what was happening if I just thought everything through and never let on. My stubborn streak came to the surface. I'd find a way to protect myself from all the emotional pain and weakness.

All of this was set against a background of ordinary childhood physical knocks, of course. At Braeview, we were arranging to go on holiday for a week to a caravan park down the west coast at Saltcoats. We kids were high with anticipation and I remember running around outside in the sunshine at Braeview wearing the new red bikini I'd got specially for the holiday when I was challenged to a fight by a known hard girl from the local scheme. All my excitement abruptly vanished as the attention telescoped in on me. This girl was notorious: I was scared rigid.

The other girls stood back and waited, eager to see what I'd do. My heart was thudding. What could I do? Well, all I did was stare her out – not because I was challenging her back but because I was frozen. Maybe it made me scary looking, as, for whatever reason, she backed off. I was still stiff with fear. With everyone watching me, I slid upright, like a white chess piece, back to my unit.

I joined the kids at the door of our unit. There was hilarity, the packing nearly done. My wee sister ran after me, laughing, chasing me with a bucket of cold water. I ran away, trying to outrun her, turning round to gauge if she was catching up on me, and heard a shout. I turned to the front and ran straight into an open window. It felt like I had been struck by a hammer – a dull cloth-covered hammer. But there was no pain. I looked across at the gardener who had shouted a warning. His lips were moving but I couldn't hear anything. I put my hand to my head and stood, noticing the metal-framed window reverberating, then I felt the warm gush run through my fingers. When I took my hand away it was covered in blood, and blood had begun to run down my face, drip off my chin and down between my small breasts.

Half an hour later, I found myself wrapped in a towel and sitting with Janice, a staff member whom I quite liked, in the casualty department at the Victoria Infirmary in Glasgow. It must have been a Saturday afternoon, as there were a few football casualties and I remember being embarrassed because I was still only wearing my bikini under a blanket.

The medical staff shaved the front of my head and I was quietly upset at losing my nice feather cut and worried about how it would affect my approaching holiday. I had an injection into the wound to numb it and it was stitched up. Thinking my ordeal was over, I was then taken into another room and told to lean over the sink. My bikini bottoms were lowered and another injection was given into my buttock. I was told it was a tetanus jag, to make sure I wouldn't get a lockjaw infection. It was agony: my whole buttock and leg muscle went into an intense cramp. Back at Braeview, I rearranged my hair parting to cover the bald patch at the left side of my head.

I was really looking forward to this holiday. Janice and Margaret, another young staff member, accompanied us. Margaret helped me with my hair and shared make-up with me. I enjoyed the beach and the closeness of the unit in the caravan. One day, I took some of the younger children to the caravan-site shop and recognised the man working there. He was the owner of the burn shop from Springboig. I faltered, wondering what on earth he'd think of me and if he'd remember how I used to go to his shop to buy my mother's drink on tick. He did recognise me and asked how I was. Embarrassed but polite, I pushed the money for our sweets towards him but he wouldn't take any, from me or the other children. He probably thought he was doing something nice for us but I felt stung by it, remembering the pity in the eyes of my next-door neighbours when they gave me handouts, too.

After a few nights when all of us had gone out together, I met a local boy. His name was Cammy and he was going to join the Army. The staff allowed him to walk me home but halfway there he stopped to kiss me. I kissed him back. It became clear to me that he was looking for more. I struggled to break loose from him but he wouldn't let me go, holding on to my shoulders as I stood literally with my back against the wall. The pebbledash imprinted itself on my shoulder blades. I bought time by chatting to him and asking all about the regiment he was going to join.

He allowed the chat for so long before returning to kissing me, with one hand above my head against the wall. His other went up my skirt and pulled at my underwear. I pushed him away with all my strength and then ran. I got lost and wandered about the site till eventually I found our caravan. The staff gave me a real dressing down and said my behaviour was questionable! They'd been about to call the police. I said nothing about what had happened.

On return from holiday, I was introduced to my new social worker. Hannah was an older woman, genteel and middle class. I confided in her how much I loved reading and art, and as a result she took Cathleen and me out for the day to Edinburgh, to the art gallery on Princes Street. I loved it. We spoke of things other than me and my situation. We spoke of normal things on a trip to an art gallery, like what I thought of this or that painting, and we went out for lunch, too. Although I was having a wonderful day, I kept waiting on a trick question about myself, my aunt and my feelings about my dad, but, happily, it never came.

For quite a while, my father didn't visit, so Hannah wrote to his work to ask for permission to interview him there. I'm sure she would have reminded him frankly of his responsibilities. My case file states that my dad was very anxious during this visit and would have agreed to anything to get this woman away from his work. She reported that he didn't see the need to have anything to do with me and Cathleen when we were in care, because we were being safely looked after. I wondered if he was still hurt about the things that had happened in court – the things I had said. There I was, his daughter, publicly betraying him. Possibly even the fact that he couldn't have us at home made it too painful for him to visit us. Or was I – am I – trying to make excuses for him? My father was obviously incapable of being a father for many reasons and I was incapable of saying I didn't want to maintain this relationship with him; after all, I needed a link to the past and I had been told how lucky I was to have him.

His responsibilities were impressed upon him, as mine as a daughter were impressed upon me. I couldn't understand why I wasn't listened to when I asked repeatedly to see my aunt. It was obvious that being cut off from her distressed me, as did my father's erratic behaviour. I didn't know what else I could do. Talking, asking and waiting till the next social work visit left me feeling impotent. All I knew was how frustrated I felt about my situation, with pressure building up in me.

The exploding point came when I was accused of stealing a cake – a Swiss roll cake – and although I knew who had done it, I wouldn't allow myself to say. As punishment for the theft, I was denied my pocket money from the home, so I ran away.

It was 10 July 1977, full summer and the school holidays had already begun. I wandered down to the park at Braeview and met a girl I knew from school. She was there with a few boys, drinking cola with aspirin. The mix was supposed to give you a high. I hung around for a while and tried a few sips to pretend I was going along with it, though it did nothing for me. Then she took me home to her house in Duke Street, across the road from the Great Eastern Hotel, which was Glasgow's infamous 'model lodging house' for homeless men. Soon my father would become one of its residents.

This friend lived with her mother, who was out at work. When she came home, I stayed hidden away in the bedroom and settled down that night feeling strangely safe and cocooned. For a short while, Urquhart, all the social workers in Scotland and my father had disappeared.

Curiously, in this house I had a strange, spooky experience. I woke up very early the next morning to the sound of chains clanking and horses' hooves. When I peered out of the window, there were only cars and buses in the street far below, so where the sounds were coming from was a mystery. Later in the day, I asked my friend about it and she told me that the flats had been built on an old prison site, but I've never checked that out.

Speaking of prisons, my liberty didn't last long. Very soon, the police came knocking on the door. I was taken back to Braeview House and an emergency social work meeting was set up. This resulted in my being put on probation for one month at the home: any breaches of behaviour and I would be removed. My social worker, who I felt was well meaning but fairly ineffective, attempted to contact my father on several occasions at this time without success. However, the month passed with just a minor breach near the end and the staff at the home decided to let me stay.

I'm not sure where the initiative came from but it was next proposed that my father should take Cathleen and me on holiday to Ireland, to visit his sister. We set sail on 11 August, to stay for a fortnight. I felt very anxious about the trip. I was scared, waiting to see if my father would drink and if I would therefore have to be responsible for him and once again risk being humiliated in public. My memory of the voyage itself was that I was very tired and my father got Cathleen and I a bunk. I even felt guilty that he didn't get one for himself. The boat lulled from side to side, with loud rumbling noises coming from the engine room.

Once in Donegal, I was introduced to the daughter of a neighbour, Niamh, and sometimes I played with her and her brother Dermot. They invited me to go to see a band called The Boomtown Rats with them but I wasn't allowed. Most nights, my holiday consisted of going to the pub with my father, his old friends and his sister. On one occasion, I was introduced to a man in a club we went to. He asked me to dance. At 14, this all felt very grown up and initially I suppose I was flattered by the attention, but I quite quickly began to feel uneasy. My aunt whispered in my ear that he liked me and told me he wasn't long released from prison for political reasons. She said he was a 'good man'. He bought me a drink, took me aside and began chatting to me about myself. The next night, he was there again.

This persistent attention from an older man scared me – I knew his type. The atmosphere in the place became oppressive; I resented the invasion of my personal space, so I escaped from the club early and walked home to my aunt's house along the dark roads alone, only to find the door locked. I wandered around in the back garden till I was fed up and then huddled up on the back doorstep. At my back through the door, I could hear the dog snuffling, wanting to be let out. The sky darkened and it began to rain, and I wanted to be let in.

With no sign of my father's return, I crawled into the dog's compact kennel and slept there for the night, curled up shivering on his rough square of carpet while he was warm in the house. The next day, I could see the family considered me unruly and best ignored. I sat for the rest of that day in a musty drawing room, reading newspaper cuttings about Elvis's death. This seemed such a big deal to people. I couldn't understand its significance. I decided to take the cutting with the headline 'The King is Dead', fascinated by the picture of his face in death. I craved something of significance. There was no proof of my mother's death anywhere. My anxiety was rising again and I wanted to go home to Scotland. On our return home, it was noted in my file that the holiday was so successful and we'd enjoyed it so much that we planned to return over Christmas. I never mentioned to anybody the incidents with the 'good man'.

Rena, with whom I'd shared a room, had been moved to the hostel block at Braeview while I was away, so I came back to find I was now sharing with a young girl named Linda, who had been shoved through a glass door and had permanent damage to the nerves in her arm. I mention this just to show the extent of the lack of continuity in my life and how powerless I was even to keep the same room-mate.

Although I grew close to Linda, this change unsettled me even more, as had my holiday. My relationship with my father had disintegrated further, as I'd witnessed him drinking heavily again. How could I find some constant stability? I craved it. My thinking was that if I appeared happy and grateful, maybe the social workers would let me see my aunt. When I confided my fears that my father was drinking again to my social worker Hannah, she picked up my anxiety about him and gave me permission to go home on evening and sometimes overnight visits to Larchgrove, to see him and my friend Jean. Cathleen didn't want to go.

I hardly saw my father during these visits as he was either out drinking or doing shift work but I didn't tell the staff that and neither did he. It meant I could continue to see my friend Jean and be free for a while. I was floating between the children's home and my father's house. I had friends in both places but didn't really want to stay at either. I asked constantly if I could see my aunt and cousins, missing them painfully and the safety I felt there. I wanted to be sitting by my aunt's chair, listening to her talking to me. It was the nearest thing imaginable to the closeness I used to have with my mother. But I was denied access to my aunt and she to us in a separation that was sanctioned by my father and my social worker and which ran completely contrary to every wish I expressed for my well-being. The social workers insisted the right thing for them to do was to work towards reuniting Cathleen and me with my father but soon his weekly visits stopped again. He wouldn't take responsibility for us yet he was allowed to deny us contact with other family members.

At last, during a visit from my social worker at the end of August, I was told that we were allowed to see my aunt for afternoon visits, though not for any overnights. Delighted by this, and thinking maybe this social worker was going to be on my side, I was shattered when she then announced she was leaving. This left me facing even more upheaval. I cursed myself for raising my hopes and investing my faith in her, and my secret motto played in my head again: 'Nothing in, nothing out'. She made arrangements to visit me in two weeks to bring my new social worker to meet me.

'Is it a man?' I asked, my old fears never far from the surface.

'Yes,' came the reply.

The day before they were due to visit me, I ran away again. I said I was going to visit my father. Instead, I wandered about Braeview, sleeping one night in the park, curled up in the bushes, alone in all that darkness and feeling sorry for myself at this situation I had got myself into. Though part of me was cold and afraid, another part rejoiced at my sudden autonomy. Looking back, I'd compare it to the feeling as an adult of locking the door, shutting the curtains, unplugging the phones and having a duvet day.

The next night I spent in a flat that was frequented by girls in the home and occupied by a guy we called 'Super Serge' owing to the name on his filthy fridge. I didn't really know him but felt fine so long as there were other girls around. On my own with him overnight, I felt more insecure than I had in the park. That night in the flat, I hardly felt safe enough to close my eyes. I was picked up by police the next day while wandering about the local area.

The bosses at Braeview House, whom I had never spoken to, decided that they could not tolerate behaviour like this. I was not to be returned there. However, my new social worker, Hamish McColl, whom I hadn't even met, negotiated for me to stay for one last night. Nine months I'd been there, but for me, with all the emotional trauma I'd gone through, I guess this just wasn't enough time to find someone to trust. And nobody asked why. Now my behaviour and their lack of understanding – their failure to empathise – meant I would have to be moved on.

Yet the sadness among the care staff at my unit was clear. They knew I'd shot myself in the foot. And how could I tell Cathleen? Who would look out for her?

There had been good times for me in the unit. I still retain special memories of the younger children: helping the staff delouse them; talking to them about their feelings; cuddling a lovely wee baby who had cigarette burns; eating round an intimate table and feeling that Cathleen and I were almost absorbed as part of a family there. There was the fondness I felt for my room-mate Linda, too. I had even been allowed to visit Ina, the matronly member of staff, at her home in the next street and had become friendly with her daughter. But I'd proved too difficult and thrown it all away. I tormented myself. Why? What was wrong with me?

Yet while I felt that way, part of me was glad to be on the move again. 'Nothing in, nothing out.' That last night in Braeview I gnawed my fingernails till they bled.

11

Kidron House

My first impression of my new social worker, Hamish McColl, was that he was a tall, hairy hippy who smiled a lot. I would go on to discover that this big man would show me more compassion and unselfish care than any of the many social workers and care workers I'd ever met.

During that final night he had arranged for me to spend at Braeview, Cathleen avoided me. I think she must have been angry with me for causing so much trouble. Older than her, I understood that she was shutting down to avoid any further emotional hurt. Later, I sadly learnt that the only question she'd asked about the whole situation was, 'Do I still have a sister?' My wee Cathleen with her squinty eye and her blue National Health specs. My special song to her had been a version of David Dundas's one-hit-wonder, 'Jeans On', only I substituted specs for jeans and sang to her, 'When Ah wake up in the morning light, Ah put on ma blue specs an Ah feel all right.'

The next day, I was collected from Braeview and sent to the social work offices in Osborne Street in Glasgow to await my fate. There was no crowding of staff and children chattering at the door to wave me off. It might have been too painful for all concerned, this sense of failure. There was just me and my new social worker.

'Got your bags?' he asked, standing jingling his keys, ready to open the boot. I raised my arms to show him. All the possessions I had were packed into a couple of carrier bags. I took them into the back seat beside me, then we drove off. I left showing no emotion.

The social work office was like any other I'd been in. Phones were ringing; people were waiting. I sat on a metal chair in the waiting room, aware I was on the fringes, in some kind of no-man's-land, observing other people.

A place was offered to me, as if I was in any position to make choices, in a young women's hostel. It was called Kidron House and had a strict Presbyterian ethos. It wouldn't be available to me for a week, though.

Hamish *asked me* how I was feeling and how I felt about my family members. I told him I didn't want to go to my father's house and that I loved my aunt. Unbelievably, Hamish decided to ask my aunt – who up till now had been shunned by the Social Work Department as a bad influence on me – if she could keep me for a week. My aunt agreed.

I was delighted by the decision to let me go to my aunt's, secretly hoping that she would keep me for ever. It couldn't have been too much of a secret, though, as I learnt from my notes that Hamish discussed it with her. At this point, she said, she felt she couldn't take us. I was certainly proving too much trouble, the way I'd run away twice, and my cousins may have resented having to squeeze up for us. Hamish decided not to tell me this, afraid I wouldn't settle and instinctively knowing I deserved some simple happiness with the aunt I'd longed to be with and who obviously loved me.

When as an adult I read what Hamish said about me, I couldn't cry but not crying physically hurt. At 14, I thought I had hidden everything from him but his sensitivity in dealing with me, his anger at my treatment and sorrow at my past is very clear in the words he wrote. I regret that, although I liked him very much and trusted him, I couldn't tell him how I was feeling and what had happened in my life. I think I was afraid he would turn away from me in disgust and something terrible would happen to me if the truth came out. Urquhart had to remain history. Yes, Hamish was a social worker who cared. But it was too late for me.

Hamish came back to visit me at my aunt's house and the three of us sat and talked. It was agreed that Hamish would take me to visit Kidron

House two days later and he and my aunt explained that though she loved me very much and would continue to offer as much support as she could, she wasn't in a position to be able to take care of me. 'Nothing in, nothing out.' According to the notes, I appeared to take what the adults said on board and seemed quite positive about my aunt's love for me. The reality was that I was heartbroken. It was me that was the problem, I thought. No wonder she didn't want me.

I kept my outwardly positive attitude up as we visited Kidron House. Gloomy and austere, this was another impressive house that wasn't a home.

A big staircase climbed in front of me as I entered the building. I breathed in the sober smell of polish and dutiful plain cleaning, aware that, here, everything would be in its place and it would be no place like home. I did the usual: articulate speech and politeness as we wandered round the no-nonsense house, my eyes scanning under the radar for signs. Signs of danger or safety.

I was shown my bedroom, which contained five beds, a wardrobe and several cabinets. The high walls were bare and a white that was colourless in a way only old paint can be. Functional curtains draped the bay window, which looked over to a Catholic chapel. My head filled with memories of my father singing 'The Sash' loud enough for the Murphys, who lived upstairs from us, to hear. I used to wonder why the Murphy girl went to a different school from me. It did feel ridiculous that I wasn't allowed to play with her on religious grounds.

Miss Dunnett, the sensibly girdled and shod matron, was visibly impressed by my fine speaking voice and manner, and I'm sure she had designs of crafting a fine, decent Presbyterian young woman out of me. This was a correct establishment, which would pave the way for a girl who was wayward and needed a guiding light. As part of the Kidron House ethic, I was to be cut off from my aunt and the rest of my family. From now on, I was a Kidron House girl and would have to abide by Kidron House rules. I knew I was bad and these people were good. Why, then, did the rumblings of fear start and an internal contempt for them begin to build?

＊ ＊ ＊

Hamish made a conscious effort to see me every week at Kidron House. I was lonely, separated from Cathleen and the friends and staff I'd come to know in Braeview, so I looked forward to his visits. He was so alive in contrast to this deadly place. On several occasions, I went out with him and once we visited his house. This too was a grand house with beautiful gardens but it was one I did find impressive. It was a split-level conversion house – something I'd never heard of. I found this sharing of grandeur from a previous age a very socialist division of wealth!

I met Hamish's wife and his son and daughter. I was delighted at being in his house and as I stood in his living room looking at a painting on the wall, Hamish asked me what I thought it showed. Terrified and desperate to pass this test, I said that I thought it was a bull and cart. My memory is vague on the details but I do remember the way Hamish made me feel: this strange realisation that maybe I could be clever. Even more basic: that I was entitled to have an opinion and express it without fear of derision. No one had given me that confidence before. How lucky you must be to have a 'good family' life, I thought.

We wandered down to his basement, me still tentative, but I was amazed. There in front of me was a pinball machine – a testimony to this family's ideology the way some people keep a flash car in the drive. Hamish's basement was a place for play, a whole space in the house dedicated to having fun. The walls in the basement were covered in brightly painted murals done by the family. I remember purples and reds. I really wanted to stay there. I wanted to be his daughter; I wanted this family. They were feelings that scared me. I was afraid for myself and ashamed of having such a deep-rooted need. I also knew my wants were impossible to fulfil.

Hamish had a car but it was a kind I'd never seen before. It was colourful, too, with a sense of playfulness. It was a bright yellow Citroën Diane. It made me laugh inside when I was out in it.

I asked Hamish if he could get me my photo album from Clydeview. I had made up an album at my father's house and it had been brought to me along with my books. Like them, though, it had been taken from me for safe-keeping and never been returned. Hamish was good as his word and brought me my album but he told me my books were lost. I looked through my photos frantically before Miss Dunnett took the album from me and put it in a filing cabinet 'for safe-keeping'.

So I'd lost my books but there was a library not too far from Kidron House, which meant I was within reach of as many books as I could wish for. The local library was big and ornate; I loved it. It was filled with light and was always peaceful. I spent hours there, reading nature books, history books, war books and, of course, poetry.

Starting at the local secondary school was difficult as usual, with new faces and teachers and friendship groups already established. But I soon worked out the routine at Kidron House. On Saturdays, we were allowed to go out to the shops to buy our toiletries and we had to prepare Sunday lunch. On Sundays, we'd go to church then return to the home and do a Bible reading in the drawing room. We also had to go to services on other days.

When it was my week to prepare and give the reading, I chose a passage from Corinthians 1:13:

> If I speak in the tongues of men and of angels, but have not love, I am only a resounding gong or a clanging cymbal. If I have the gift of prophecy, and can fathom all mysteries and all knowledge, and if I have a faith that can move mountains, but have not love, I am nothing. If I give all I possess to the poor and surrender my body to the flames, but have not love, I gain nothing.
>
> Love is patient, love is kind. It does not envy, it does not boast, it is not proud. It is not rude, it is not self-seeking, it is not easily angered, it keeps no record of wrongs. Love does not rejoice in evil but rejoices in the truth. It always protects, always trusts, always hopes, always perseveres.
>
> Love never fails. But where there are prophecies, they will cease; where there are tongues, they will be stilled; where there is knowledge, it will pass away. For we know in part and we prophesy in part, but when perfection comes, the imperfection disappears. When I was a child, I talked like a child, I thought like a child, I reasoned like a child. When I became a man, I put childish ways behind me. Now we

see but a poor reflection; then we shall see face to face. Now I know in part; then I shall know fully, even as I am fully known.

And now these three remain: faith, hope and love. But the greatest of these is love.

God, like Santa, had died in my bedroom at home with the Narnia wardrobe; however, as I had no choice but to read something, I chose this passage for its sentiment. The combination of the content and my delivery so impressed one particular member of staff that she followed me about all day, asking me questions about myself. I was deliberately vague. She began to give me playful slaps on the buttocks. This made me uncomfortable. I'd noticed she wore a brooch of the fish emblem and I stopped her in her tracks by telling her what her brooch meant: that it was a secret symbol of Christianity.

She looked at me in awe. 'How on earth do you know that?' she said, the implication being that unfortunate circumstances must equal intellectual poverty.

I didn't argue. I knew this kind of dutifully dressed woman from before: she had come to me in the shape of the Shower Lady. Although I'd understood this feeling – what this woman was symbolic of – I could not put a name to it, far less vocalise it. I just tried to avoid being in the kitchen with her, as she seemed to enjoy running round the kitchen table skelping me with her 'playful' slaps.

At Kidron House, we never did any housework on a Sunday. Sunday was a day for contemplation. I did my contemplation at other times in the week, too. Washing the sheets from my bed and wringing the water out of them by putting them through the mangle, the effort of turning that big handle, was just one of the things that took me back in my mind to when I'd done it with my mum.

At night, we were locked in our bedrooms, supposedly to comply with fire regulations. I shared the room with one other girl. She was opposite me and all the other beds were empty. Apart from the two lumps in bed, the room had no other signs of life.

One day I was getting ready to go to school when I noticed my navy-blue school skirt was badly ripped. A gaping hole had appeared at my hip, with threads threatening to unravel the entire seam: how it happened I didn't know but I did know I couldn't go to school like that. I went downstairs to show Miss Dunnett. She was in her office, so I knocked the heavy wooden door and waited for her to call 'Enter.'

Inside, she was already at her desk, looking through some papers. I waited for her to look up, conscious that I was running out of time to get to school.

'Miss Dunnett,' I said, holding the torn edges of my skirt together at the zip.

She looked up and frowned. 'Yes, Eileen? Are you still here?'

'My skirt's torn,' I said, and waited.

She put down what she was reading and sat back in her chair. 'That was careless. How did that happen?'

'I don't know.'

Her lips were pressed together. 'Skirts like that cost money. You should know better. You can sew it as soon as you come home. Now, hurry up or you'll be late.'

'But, Miss,' I said. 'I can't go to school like this.' Every time I moved, another few stitches of the seam loosened. From the hallway I heard the sound of the front door closing as the last of the girls left for school or work.

'Have you not got anything else to wear?'

'No.'

'Put a pin in it, then.'

'Miss Dunnett,' I said, 'a pin won't do it.'

'Yes, it will, dear.'

'I'm not going to school like this!' I said.

She rose from her chair. 'Yes, you are, girl.'

'No. It'll fall off me,' I said, stepping backward.

'Nonsense. Now get on with it.'

'No! I'm not going. I'm not going like this!' I was as adamant as she was.

Eventually Miss Dunnett had to phone Hamish and tell him I was acting up and refusing to go to school. I went upstairs to my room to get out of her way and to wait for what would happen next.

Hamish had to intervene to calm Miss Dunnett down; he even had to come in person to sit with us and negotiate peace. Though he might not always have believed I was right, Hamish always gave me a sense of not being wrong. In other words, I might have been wrong but I had a right just like everyone else to state my feelings, and gradually I began to half-believe that.

That didn't necessarily change the way Miss Dunnett and the other staff regarded me. The old building at Kidron House was musty, particularly in my bedroom, and, more than once, that and the stresses I was under triggered an atmospheric asthma attack. I remember one time vividly. I lay in bed, struggling to breathe, my inhalers having no effect. My chest hurt and the veins in my neck and hands became more and more prominent. As my breathing became shallower, a doctor was called. Like a vacuum-packed bag of wheezing bones, I waited in that cold room for his arrival, knowing from past experience that the injection he'd bring would give me almost instant relief. Exhausted, and with no involuntary physical resistance, my body accepted the injection. The doctor left.

This time, the relief didn't come. My lungs siphoned at the air to no avail till the room was grey and indistinct around me and I was sure I was going to die. I almost accepted it, just looking to the window and trying to keep breathing. Soon I was barely aware of my surroundings.

My hearing still alert, I heard the door click and became vaguely aware that Miss Dunnett had come into the room. She leant down beside me and I looked up into her eyes, needing some support. Instead, she whispered in my ear, 'That's your badness coming out in you.'

That brought me back; it seemed like a switch had been flicked in my brain. The ambulance arrived and in its sanctuary I knew at least I wouldn't die with her for company.

12

The Trick is to Keep Breathing

I was admitted as an emergency to the hospital and was immediately placed in an oxygen tent. Having lived with asthma all my life, I wasn't afraid of it because I always recovered. I did know that this attack was more serious than any previous one but I didn't know it could kill me. I felt safer here than I had in my bedroom at Kidron House. At least I stood a chance here.

I was exhausted but in my head I was vitally aware. Through the plastic tenting I could make out nurses coming and going, and all the time I forced my chest to rise and fall. Breathe, I said to myself. Breathe. Rise and fall. Breathe.

The plastic rustled and a young male doctor appeared. He was annoyed at the medical staff attending to me. Lying there in this old building with its high ceilings and uniform colourless decor, I heard him say, 'I didn't want her in the oxygen tent. I wanted to try something new.'

On top of everything else, this made me nervous and I was relieved that I'd been put in the tent before he got to me. I didn't want to be someone's guinea pig. You're on your own, Eileen, I told myself. As always. I knew there was no back-up. No parent to take a firm line and say, 'No, this isn't happening. You're not doing this to my daughter.' I was at the mercy of another stranger making a decision that might not be wholly in my interest.

Soon I was transferred to a ward, out of the tent but with all my inhalers. A nurse injected me with a drug and told me I'd soon feel better, but almost immediately I started to shake. It seems I had a bad reaction to it. I made a conscious mental note to myself to remember the name of that drug – Septrin – and I tucked it away in my memory in the same way I had done with the name Annick Street, the address of Urquhart.

After a few days, I was feeling better and went along to the day room, desperate for a cigarette. What an irony! I was already addicted at 14. Another patient gave me one but the doctor wasn't pleased. He told me I'd be in a wheelchair by the time I was 30. I thought he was trying to scare me – I'd never seen or heard of anybody in a wheelchair because of smoking.

The relative safety of the hospital ward was to be over too soon and I was returned to Kidron House. I hadn't told anybody about the incident alone in my bedroom with Miss Dunnett. It was too awful. If I told someone, it would mean I would need to accept that it was a reality. And anyway, who would believe me? Badly shaken, could I deal with the consequences of telling on this woman and knowing that she could do that? A girl like me didn't stand a hope in hell.

So, I returned to Kidron House feeling very frightened. Unbeknown to me at the time, Hamish had stated in my file that Kidron House was not a good placement and I could not rely on Miss Dunnett for support.

On 23 November 1977, I was locked in my bedroom at night once again, supposedly for fire safety reasons. I lay awake talking to Jane, the girl who shared the room with me. We had sneaked some teabags up from the kitchen because we'd heard you could smoke them, so we burst the bags and made our own roll-ups with sheets of the home's hard toilet paper. It was fruitless, of course, and funny. Yet the timer switch in my brain flicked again that night. I knew I had to get out of there; it was almost a panic reaction. Was it the snib on the bedroom door locking? Again, I couldn't explain what triggered it but nothing was going to stop me, not even myself. I scanned over the room, taking in the wall fitted with an old wooden wardrobe in which I had a drawer; the high ceiling with its stale wedding-cake cornice; the off-white walls, large windows and empty beds.

'I'm out of here,' I said to Jane. I pulled on my clothes and stripped one of the spare beds of its stiff white sheets.

Jane watched me knot them together. 'You're mental,' she said, then jumping up from her bed she announced, 'I'm coming with you.' She started to get dressed. 'I'm not staying here on my own.'

I tied one end of the sheet rope tightly to the large metal radiator and then opened the side window in the room, threw the bundle of sheets out and climbed down from the window, two storeys up.

I had to jump the last few feet and fell into rose bushes, but I was high on adrenalin and don't remember being scratched. I looked up for Jane. She was a big girl; I watched her large frame coming down the sheets. Then we were off, leaving the sheets flapping about in the wind like sails on a moored boat, hoping that, because it was the side of the building, no one would notice till we were well out of the area.

A false euphoria kicked in as we ran. Once again, running was the only freedom of expression I thought I had. We kept the pace up till we reached the lights and traffic of the city centre. Then, as quickly as the euphoria came, it left us. Where would we go? On this still busy street, which way would we go? Freedom sure is another word for nothing left to lose.

We had no money, no food. It was cold and dark. As on other occasions when I'd run away, it was a case of choosing somewhere that we knew, somewhere that was *familiar*. I came to the conclusion that my father's house would be safe, as he would be either too drunk to notice us or he would be at work. We walked for miles, me hoping I had got the direction right. As we headed towards Parkhead Cross, I remembered being in Parkhead at the dentist, having gas as an anaesthetic. My mother's friend had let me take her daughter's doll as a comfort. As the gas mask covered my face, I'd started to lose consciousness and I felt the doll slipping from my arms. In the distance, I heard it repeatedly calling, 'Mama'. May had come with me, as my mother couldn't take me.

From there, Jane and I headed to Westmuir Street and on to Old Shettleston Road, where my father had worked in the bottle factory – my place of treasured stones. On we went, through Urquhart's Annick Street (though I didn't tell Jane about what he'd done), up past Budhill's Springboig Library on the corner of Hallhill Road and Hermiston Road. I can't remember if I passed the house I'd lived in when my mother died.

It's not just criminals who return to the scene of the crime, as I did constantly, convinced it was me who was in the wrong. Here I was returning to my old streets like some kind of forensic investigator trying to make sense of everything. This became a lifelong behaviour, lest I forget.

What did Jane and I talk about on the journey? I have no idea. Possibly unrealistic goals of where we were going and what to do when we got there. But more probably that would be ignored, reality being too huge to contemplate. No doubt the long walk would have included the swapping of our personal histories, though, as ever, there was much I'd have kept to myself. We created a solidarity with references to the circumstances that brought us both to this place – the sharing of the pain.

When we eventually reached the familiar outline of the row of shops and the looming flats with their verandas, I knew I'd reached my father's flat in Larchgrove Avenue and I must admit that I felt quite proud of having found my way. Why, I don't know. All these emotions, like little memory islands, stray away from me like flotsam and jetsam, with no concrete connection to them.

We climbed up the two flights of stairs, our steps echoing in the stone stairwell. As we climbed the stairs, Jane was puffing beside me and I was planning what I was going to say when my father opened the door. But he wasn't at home. No cock-and-bull story was going to get us into the house.

'What are we going to do now, then?' Jane said, standing against the wall, leaning on her hands.

I crouched down and looked through the letter box. The house was in darkness; there was my dad's familiar pungent smell of drink and overalls. 'I'm thinking,' I told her. I straightened up and tried shaking the handle but the door wouldn't move. From the flats above and below us came the sounds of TV shows' canned laughter, dogs barking, a woman singing.

'I know,' I said, and started off down the stairs again, Jane following me. I'd just climbed down the sheets at Kidron House. Now I came up with the idea of scaling the drainpipe onto the adjoining shop roof, over the veranda and hopefully in through my bedroom window.

The plan went well up to a point. The shop was shut and there was no one around. Jane was too heavy or scared to climb. I was this scrawny, skinny kid, wild as a cat. And like a cat, I climbed the drainpipe and up over the brick veranda but my bedroom window was shut and I couldn't get it open. I thumped the frame with my fist in my sleeve to try to knock the handle off the latch but it wouldn't work.

From the street, I heard Jane's voice. 'Eileen – did you get it?'

'Shh!' I whispered. In desperation, through tiredness and fear, I decided to break the window. I found something heavy on the veranda – a brick or some rubble. I looked round over my shoulder to check there was no one in the street – no police or anything – then I tapped the brick against the glass, hoping to minimise the noise. If I just cracked it, I thought, I could push the glass in and no one would hear it.

'What are you doing?' Jane called up.

I looked over the veranda at her, one floor down and half hidden by the privet hedges. What could I do? I turned round and smashed the glass, climbed into my dad's flat and let Jane in through the door.

We slept in my bed. It was damp from months of emptiness but held a certain safety and we had no fear of intrusion. No one knew where we were. We awoke to knocking on the door, which we ignored. Later it came again and I answered it, knowing it would be the police. I was afraid to ignore them and perhaps by now we realised the futility of the situation. We were taken to Tobago Street police station and put in a windowed cell. The police gave us a drink and I remember them being very kind to us. I was sure it wouldn't last; I was waiting on the twist from their side – that they would charge me with breaking and entering my father's house. Thankfully, that never happened.

As we sat in the cell, Jane and I resisted any talk about the possible consequences. We listened to the music coming from a radio in the police office. Bored, I suppose, and as a distraction from facing our own music, we began to sing and dance to the tunes being played. This was until we heard laughter coming from the room next to us – the office. I looked at the cell window and realised it was a two-way mirror and the police were laughing at us. Apparently, we'd been entertaining them. Embarrassed at our apparently carefree attitude to our situation, we sat down on the bench and shrank with shame. Soon, a policewoman came in and returned us both to Kidron House.

I don't remember what happened to Jane. I was kept off school as Hamish McColl was coming to see me. While I waited for him in the silence of that big house, with the staff ignoring me, I sat alone with the sheets I had tied together for my escape. I was to hand wash them as my punishment. The staff stayed down in the basement kitchen. I was angry. I wanted to lock them down there. I wanted this to the extent of even staring at the door lock and having a fantasy of doing so and then swinging from the sheets which in my daydream I had tied to the top landing banister.

The doorbell rang. I stood at the bottom of the large staircase. The dark wood made the place so gloomy; the beautiful stained-glass window halfway up the staircase behind me afforded no light on my circumstances. The door seemed so far away and on the other side I knew it would be Hamish. Maybe he would save me from this or maybe he would be angry.

I wanted to run to the door to reach Hamish but Miss Dunnett came up from the kitchen. I was frozen to the spot as she passed me; I sought out his eyes as she opened the door to him but he was professional and gave me no clues.

Miss Dunnett, Hamish and I went into the office. I sat looking at the filing cabinet that I knew contained my photo album and tuned out. I was brought back into the reality of the room when I heard Hamish trying to persuade Miss Dunnett to allow me my regular visit home to my aunt. Why should he have to persuade her?

It was to be a further punishment for me. My strictly limited access to my aunt was to be curtailed even further and it was my own fault.

Miss Dunnett stated that this was the only appropriate punishment for me. I became slightly tearful, mostly through anger. I think my tearfulness pleased Miss Dunnett, judging by her face and the way she held me resolutely in her gaze.

Yet hearing Hamish arguing my case to be allowed to go evoked a feeling in me that, yes, I had done something wrong by running away and having the police involved, and, yes, I was only 14 and these people were adults, but I, too, had rights. Hamish was lighting a fire in me, which on reflection I know was already kindled: a sense of self and self-worth, but I'd no idea how to use it. I therefore felt reliant on him to show me.

Hamish asked for a few moments alone with me and Miss Dunnett left the room. I wanted to explain to him how I felt and why I acted the way I did, but I found it impossible to talk about my past, particularly about the visits from Urquhart, as I felt he would be disgusted. I couldn't even bring myself to tell him about the way Miss Dunnett had acted when I had the asthma attack, as I felt I would be causing trouble and I feared he might not believe me. I wanted Hamish to respect me. I wished I had a father like him; I wanted him never to leave me but I feared he would, just as other social workers had left me. This was why I fought to control my emotions and appear composed, and why I always agreed with whatever he said.

Miss Dunnett returned but she remained unmoved by Hamish's argument. I was afraid to let Hamish leave Kidron House without me but was also confused about what to do. He spoke about coming back for me the following day to take me somewhere else. He said, possibly to buy time, that it might be like going from the frying pan into the fire. I was tired. I wanted a home but there was no home to go to. Such was my terror of this woman and this institution that I told him I wasn't staying there. In his notes, Hamish wrote: 'For her [the fire] must be like a furnace.' He knew. He knew. And I didn't know how he'd seen my fear.

My aunt was phoned and she agreed once again to take me. I asked for my photo album and was refused.

13

Leaving Kidron House

My aunt was called upon to take me in again and she did. Just how angry my latest antics of running away from Kidron House had made her became apparent when she informed Hamish at one of his regular visits to see me at her house that she wouldn't be able to cope with me if I played up.

The truth was that I was interference in her household, 'the cuckoo in the nest', interference that wasn't needed or understood. Hamish was afraid that if I was there for a long time we would become alienated from each other. For my part, I was sure she would stop loving me because of the trouble I'd caused. She and my cousins were the only link I had to the past. They were the proof that I had existed back then and if I lost contact with them – if I was to be without love of any kind – I was sure I would somehow be killed, so vulnerable and unprotected did I feel. Urquhart had made sure I would think like that. That illusion, that scrap of illusion I could cling to, that I belonged to a real family and was only in care temporarily was what gave me strength.

So desperate was I to please my aunt that one day when she sent me to get some fish for the family's dinner, I ran the two minutes to the local fishmonger and chose the biggest pieces I could get for the money she gave me. On my return, I was subjected to incredulous looks, followed by hoots of laughter when I explained my choice. The massive fish was obviously too big for the plates. 'Whales,' my aunt said.

After we had been with her for about a month, Hamish found a children's home nearer to where my aunt lived. It would be ideal for both Cathleen and me. I would once again be at the same school as my cousin and within walking distance of my aunt's home. It sounded perfect or, if not perfect, the best I could expect.

So once again I faced a move to another home, another school, with more new sets of rules and people's politics to adapt to. Before I could be accepted as a resident at Fernlea Children's Home, of course, I had to visit and meet those in charge.

Hamish and I sat in the office at Fernlea with the matron, Elspeth Muir, towering above me. I knew I had to make it work at this home; everything inside me that was contaminated – including what Miss Dunnett perceived as my badness – I had to hide.

Elspeth Muir reminded me of the Queen, the same queen I'd thought was the queen of the entire world because as a child I'd studied her face on money and stamps. Her hairstyle was modelled on that stiff, slightly swept back, curled look and her body looked as though it was encased in a no-nonsense girdle, designed to support a good set of child-bearing hips. Her blouse and Presbyterian burgundy check skirt, teamed up with the sensible Marks and Spencer shoes, made her seem like a formidable character. My immediate reaction was that I didn't like the look of her. The rigidity of her appearance scared me. My experience had taught me that the aura she gave off was one of snobbery, churches, puritanical zeal, piety and hypocrisy; however, I had no choices left and I knew it.

Hamish lolled in his chair, legs stretched out, while I was being interviewed. Casually dressed, often in corduroy and with that hairy hippy look, he always came across as relaxed. Ever since I'd met him, Hamish had been encouraging me to express myself, to be myself. He was trying to instil a sense of self-worth and confidence in me. Now, during the interview for Fernlea, I was conscious of him watching the formality of my performance as I further developed my persona of the polite and articulate young woman, while all along I was internally guarding my thoughts and watching my words. It was important to me that I give these people what they wanted, while constantly watching that nothing slipped out that they could trip me up on. I was sure the truth would repel people and confirm my badness to them.

I must have given a pretty convincing performance, as at one point during the meeting Mrs Muir looked up and gave me a warm smile of approval. It felt to me as though there had been a fleeting moment of recognition from one female with a steely resolve to another. I had clinched it.

I was given a tour of the building and shown the room I would be given if I were accepted to stay there. And here came the main, instant delight for me at Fernlea – I would have my own room. A bedroom all to myself! The walls were orange, the quilt and curtains contrasting orange and black stripes. I had a wardrobe with a mirror that lit up, with several drawers under it. The room was tidy and clean, small and warm. It felt homely. The window wouldn't open wide, as it was a safety window, so none of the children could fall out. There'd be no sheets down these windows.

'Call me Aunt Elspeth,' the matron said after she'd shown me the room. 'We expect all the children to refer to members of staff as aunt or uncle.' She looked from me to Hamish and added, 'We're a family unit.'

I was accepted and, yet again, I had to undergo a medical. Every time I was received into care or left care I had to have a medical, though I don't remember ever being asked about my vaccinations or any possible medical conditions. A typical examination consisted of my nails, hair and ears being checked to make sure I wasn't harbouring anything contagious that I could pass on to inconvenience someone in the home. I always had to strip down to my underwear for these medicals and at Fernlea there I stood yet again, feeling dirty inside and out, despite the fact that I bathed as frequently as I could and hated to wear anything that was un-ironed, ripped or had marks on it.

The other kids in the home were mainly younger than me, ranging from some still in nappies to others in late primary school. As at Braeview, I enjoyed this created family. I enjoyed the responsibility of helping to look after the younger children and often I would take my wee favourite Stephen out in an old rickety buggy. I would visit my aunt and wander the streets at a slow pace, feeling more normal than my normality. Now and then we'd even come back with money in that buggy as a result of Stephen or me unintentionally charming some passing citizen into generosity. They knew we were from the children's home.

I began to feel needed and wanted at Fernlea and I loved the privacy of my own bedroom as well as being attached to my family of strangers. I thought everything would be all right as long as I could keep up my persona. Nothing in, nothing out. My relationship with the staff would be superficial and I could steel myself against any probing.

Soon a relationship developed between the matron, whom I was to call Aunt Elspeth, and myself. It was a relationship similar to the one I had with my aunt Helen. Possibly because I was a few years older than the other children, or because I gave off an impression of maturity, she started to confide in me. Mostly she confided in me about her views on her own life as well as her views on the other members of staff. I soon discovered there were two camps in the home. One camp was headed by my 'aunt', the matron, and the other by Lillian, who was second in charge.

Their relationship was very tense. I realised I was going to have to choose between the two groups and this would determine how I was to survive the people-politics of the staff. As my aunt Elspeth was the one who seemed to choose me, my choice was made for me. I was her protégée. My allegiance was to her. Yet this would cause me great stress and lead to a certain amount of payback when she or her cohorts were off duty or away on holiday. But such was my situation.

The practicalities of this relationship affected me differently from my relationship with my aunt Helen. She and I had a shared history and I needed to feel loved by her, so my relationship with her remained really important to me. Now I was allowed to visit her from Fernlea and I'd go round regularly. She was everything to me: up on a pedestal. She was my link to my self. As I had done with my mother, I would sit with her on my own and listen to what she had to say. I never challenged her and I accepted everything she told me.

She had an innate anger at my mother. I often heard the tale of how clean my mother's house had been compared to what it had become. How my mother could not cope without her own mother: she was a weak person, I was told. The way she spoke about my father's drinking habits and urinating in the close all painted the picture of how much she had opposed my adoption into the family. Before my adoption, her own mother had suggested Auntie Helen give up one of her children to my mother. It felt like the whole mess was my fault. Often I would lose concentration and be lost in the gas flame in front of me as I sat on the floor at her feet.

I didn't know why she was telling me all she did. Whatever her intention, it had the effect of confirming to me that I was inherently bad and weak. Anything that happened to me would be my fault and complaining would make me the same as that awful mother of mine. In contrast to my mother, my aunt took pride in her appearance. Her tongs and make-up were a permanent fixture in the kitchen, where she used them before rushing off to work.

I drilled into myself that I had to be strong but I was very confused by a question Aunt Helen would ask of me often over the years: 'Should we have just let you go?' I always replied to this by saying no, I loved her. That was my panic reaction to her question. I thought I was doing the right thing in giving her this answer yet it always left me feeling a strange confusion, as if this was a puzzle that I couldn't solve. The resolution always eluded me. Was she looking for reassurance that she had done the right thing by me?

My relationship with Hamish, meanwhile, was good. As long as he didn't know too much about my personal history or how I felt about my present circumstances, then I believed he would continue to respect me. I was always on my guard in case he tried to get too close and trip me up, but within those confines I was happy. Any time he visited or we went out for lunch, I was my usual outgoing, chatty self, trying to impress him with my knowledge and actually enjoying having someone listen to me about my teenage thoughts on books, poems, art and the world around me. I felt I wasn't always under the microscope with Hamish. My every movement wasn't interpreted and written down in a daily book; he didn't examine me medically and file the result; I didn't see him discussing me at conferences. Hamish was not oppressive. He was interested in me.

My father would visit on the odd occasion but more often than not he wouldn't turn up when he was expected and I'd be left waiting in one of the visitors' rooms for him. This was particularly difficult for me if the opposite camp were on duty. I felt humiliation at their mostly unspoken pity or, worse, their smirking pleasure.

On one of these occasions when my father didn't turn up, I felt particularly vulnerable and asked a member of Lillian's staff if I could go and stay at my aunt's for the night but she refused. I clearly wanted refuge but I wasn't allowed to go. Once again, my family of strangers legally had the right to refuse me access to my legal family. I added this rejection to the shame I felt that my father had let me down but I deemed it my responsibility to deal with this pain by myself.

The situation brought out my stubborn streak. I wanted to go to my aunt's house and I tried to stick to that. Eventually, Hamish was called to deal with me and I didn't get to my aunt's that night. He explained to me that the staff were looking for a breakthrough whereby I would go to them with my emotional turmoil. They expected that everything I had contained to preserve my dignity during my short life should be spilled to relative strangers who had the power to have me ousted and moved should their self-interest or prejudices desire it. To me, it seemed that the mass volume of strangers I'd met in all the children's homes, the changing social workers and police that had passed through my life in such a short space of time were all asking something of me that I couldn't give. I couldn't. It would kill me. I wanted a resting place, a place to forget and develop. I didn't want to be the guinea pig on the receiving end of some recent training course or current trend in social work theory.

The filing cabinet in the office at Fernlea always reminded me I was just that and the daily handover diary in which my behaviour and anything I said were written down reinforced my adamant intention to keep myself intact.

As I was hanging out of the toilet window one night, having a cigarette out of the reach of anyone who'd try to prevent me smoking, I thought it through. We weren't allowed to see what the staff had written about us, which seemed very unfair to me. A history was being written about me by strangers, to which I had no access or means of redress. I tapped the cigarette packet on the window ledge and planned a way of breaking into the filing cabinet. I was going to read my files to see what it was they were writing about me. And it would have to be done right under their noses.

If a social worker was visiting, we were allowed to remove our files and hand them over, then later we were asked to put them back. We weren't supposed to open the files and look at them. After Hamish's next visit, I stayed behind to return my files to the cabinet after everyone had left the office. I held them in my right hand. In my left hand, I held a piece of card I'd torn from my cigarette carton. It was folded into a small square. As the staff returned to the office to chat over their work, I pushed the drawer back and slipped the small piece of card in the side of the drawer so that it would block the catch. To all intents and purposes, it looked as if the cabinet was locked.

Later, I picked my moment. I walked quietly along the corridor, listening as the voices coming from the kitchen and other rooms faded with each step. At the office door, I paused and listened again to make sure no one had noticed I was missing and was coming to look for me. Quickly and smoothly, I went into the office and crossed to the filing cabinet. I opened the drawer, removed my files and hurried back to the privacy of my own room to read them. Repeated reference was made to a phrase that Hamish had introduced to the staff: I was apparently afraid of further rejection. This angered me, as it seemed to put all the blame for any problems squarely on my shoulders. On reflection, I needed them to help me open up. I needed them to talk with me and help me to explore my feelings, and in the absence of the adults instigating this I remained as detached from the staff as they were from me. It was all trendy theory that was not put into practice. As a result, I wrote my poetry; the staff wrote their reports. Once I'd read the files, I followed the same procedure to replace them.

I checked up on what they were writing about me on a few occasions after that. It made me feel I was one step ahead of them. If something was brewing for me, I was going to be prepared and would anticipate it, rather than let it be a bolt from the sky that might crush me.

14

Good Places for Bad Children

From my notes, it would seem that the only issue I raised with Hamish concerning my feelings about going to Fernlea in November 1977 was about having to return to school. Fear expends a lot of mental energy and the sheer effort of trying to hide my past, and my confusion about it, were grinding me down. The thought of having to attend yet another school – the seventh move in such a short space of time – was exhausting. Always being the new kid is enough to put you on guard to start with. Adding to that the fact I was from a children's home certainly aroused people's curiosity. Once they found out about me, I could see them visibly backing off into the safety of their own perceived respectability.

I didn't play the game of hiding my circumstances. What was the point? They'd find out sooner or later. My attitude was that I should keep up my veneer of honest respectability: my 'This is who I am'. In order to survive, I had to hold my head up high while trying to find my way round unfamiliar school buildings, attempting to make friends and getting to know what point each class had reached in the curriculum. As long as I appeared pleasant, smart, clean and interesting, I could get by on the surface.

The exception to this was that I didn't know how to explain my return to people who had previously known me at this school near my aunt's and this worried me. I'd been there briefly after my mother had died in January 1976. Two years had passed and, now approaching 15 I felt tired and anxious about returning.

The grand sandstone exterior of the school led into an echoing corridor that little light seemed to penetrate. I entered it with the same reluctance, jostled by the other pupils, who seemed like a uniformed swarm, threatening my isolation.

I did settle to a degree this time, and even began to enjoy it. Hamish McColl visited the school and spoke to my guidance teacher, Mr Stein who, Hamish wrote in his notes, 'demonstrated a certain amount of understanding and cooperation'. It was felt that I was adapting well though I enjoyed some subjects more than others. Art and modern studies classes, for example, seemed to afford me a feeling of normality and acknowledgement of self-worth. In particular, I enjoyed English How I loved the permission an English class gave me to read and explore writing and writers. The texts not only resonated with my adolescent feelings but also gave my confused emotions about my past a secret home. The power of words. I could hide behind poems, words, fiction and fact. Poems were like Elastoplasts for my turmoil: a quick fix for my needs.

Words were clever, they could identify the range of emotions people – in particular, I – went through in many different ways yet they could also be protective and only reveal what the writer wanted, to the people who could hear. An adolescent girl, say, could write a poem about a tipped-over dustbin with its rubbish discarded, and it was really about herself and her opinions. This truly amazed me. How clever this all was and what a wholesome, intellectually and emotionally nourishing place for my head to live. I began to love adjectives, adverbs, conjunctions and sonnets.

Although I had been reading frantically and obsessively for years, I began to feel alive inside. I no longer cared if anyone called me nuts crazy and off my head. I began to voice my opinion more frequently I was reading voraciously for class and I lived for the discussions over the text. In Fernlea, I read alone in my room for hours, as I had done as a child but now with a certain amount of hope, waiting for my next English, art or modern studies class.

I was reading Kafka, Shakespeare, anything I could get my hands on, and still stealing books from the school or local library. I would read about any subject that resonated with me and worked my way through many anthologies of poetry. I had moved on to reading contemporary poets such as Edwin Morgan. I still felt stupid because I interpreted this new-found hope that reading gave me as something everyone else had, which I had missed out on. I thought I had a lot of catching up to do. When I read something I didn't know how to explain by a commentary, I felt dense because I understood what was being said yet couldn't explain it in words. I sensed what Kafka was saying but I couldn't fully express what I sensed.

When I came across words I had never heard before, again I felt inadequate for having such a limited vocabulary, yet I understood instinctively what they meant in their context. I couldn't discuss this with other people, because I didn't want to appear stupid. I could use them in their appropriate place when writing but sometimes couldn't pronounce them as I had never heard them spoken out loud before. So I took to reading dictionaries. When I discovered a thesaurus, my heart soared. It was food for my intellectual and emotional hunger, for my cultural and creative starvation. Books replaced my broken-glass gems from the bottle works. I gloried in them, sated myself in them. They were my secret treasures. It never occurred to me that I couldn't say the words because they were not used in my environment.

I'd joined the school in third year and found myself with an English teacher called Victor Lamont. He reminded me in appearance of a light-haired Freddie Mercury and, what's more, I really liked him as a teacher. Some of my classmates knew this, and teased me. I laughed at this. Although I knew they suspected a crush, this was not the case. I'd never had a crush on a teacher, as I thought it was too girly a thing for me.

When we were studying a play in class, Mr Lamont would pick one character that he would read aloud himself and he'd allocate the other roles to different pupils. Together, they would read the play aloud while the rest of the class listened and followed the text in their books. I still remember when Mr Lamont chose me to read the part of his wife. I could see my classmates from the corner of my eye as they suppressed their giggles behind their schoolbooks. The blood was burning in my cheeks but I rose to the challenge. I stood up and played my part, reading commendably well at the same time as holding off the giggles that were building up inside me while my friends sniggered and nudged each other. The feat of suppressing my amusement while entertaining my classmates was probably more admirable than my acting and diction. I detected from a slight glance that Mr Lamont felt that way, too.

I began to write in secret, mostly in code. Anything I had written down before, I had immediately destroyed, terrified it would reveal the crimes of which I was guilty, crimes such as:

allowing Urquhart's visits,
not getting help for my mother,
not keeping my mother alive,
not being able to run a household,
grassing my father up in court and to social workers,
letting my wee sister down,
feeling I had not protected her enough,
letting my aunt down,
failing to keep myself out of trouble,
being bad, stupid and crazy,
not keeping my virtue intact.

I was afraid that people would find me guilty of the above crimes, deem I was insane and have me locked up. Let's face it: they had the power to do so and I knew it.

Gaining enough confidence, I wrote a poem for a class exercise. It was called 'Human Rat Race': a poem about poverty and depression. Having invested a lot of my private emotions in it, I was anxious it should meet with approval. Picking my nails at the desk while he distributed the marked papers, the worst-case scenario I could imagine was ridicule. Mr Lamont reached my desk. I couldn't look at him, fearing derision. He placed the poem on my desk and I thought I saw him smiling as he turned away. In front of me was the sheet of paper with its blue lines and red-ruled margin. My eyes searched the page, looking for his comments. I had got a B. This delighted me, as did his very encouraging feedback. I wanted to jump up and shout 'Yes!' One of my dreams was to be a writer. Maybe I could write, just maybe.

Exam time came round and he spoke to us about what would be required to pass and gave helpful pointers about what to do and what to avoid. He told us to avoid doing a poem, as nobody got an A in poetry.

My ears pricked up at this information. Not being able to help myself and on the back of the B I had already received, I rose to this challenge. I wrote a poem. I got an A.

Another two incidents at school had an impact on me at this time. One day, a girl who sat near me in the English class passed me in the corridor. I'd never spoken to this girl before, never having had any reason to. We were on our way between classes when she stopped, looked me straight in the eye and smiled at me. I hesitated and looked straight back at her. Then she said to me, 'I saw you this morning.'

I stood waiting.

Still smiling, she continued, 'Yes, you were skipping along the road to school.'

Panic and then anger flashed through me. The panic was caused by the fact that someone had witnessed me in a private moment. I was panicked by the fear of accusation or even ridicule. The anger was directed internally for letting myself be revealed. Was she going to sneer at me? What was she going to say? However, these feelings only lasted for a second as she stood there smiling.

Slowly I smiled back, realising her sincere joy at my moment. She was happy for me. What an impact that had on me: the impact of positive perception. And there was nothing I needed to worry about. She taught me that compliments didn't necessarily mean a payment would be taken.

The other incident involved a pupil who had entered the English class later on in the term than I had. I didn't really know him well. He was dark in features, scruffy and very quiet.

One day, he was sitting subdued in the corner of the classroom while we were busying ourselves in discussion. A sound made us turn casually to look at him. He began to foam at the mouth and fell to the floor, and the whole class froze – even Mr Lamont, who just looked down at him. I stood up to go over to the boy but Mr Lamont told me to stay where I was and sit down. He left the room and returned with another member of staff and we were dismissed. The whole class seemed drained of energy. Still. As if all the energy was hurling about inside the boy. We never saw him again. I remember to this day the pang I felt at my inability to help him and it upset me that we never received an explanation about what had eventually happened to him.

With no choice I forged on, making the most of attending school and living in Fernlea. Making the most of it yet at the same time fearing meltdown from exposure to what was in effect a much more intimate setting, complemented by Hamish's sensitive human interest in me.

Fernlea was very different from Kidron House in the respect that we had our own cook and cleaner and that all our washing was done for us. In other words, living there was more like being cared for in a home, without that capital 'H'. I was still enjoying the contact with the younger children and I loved having my own room, with my own bed: my own space that felt safe enough, surrounded as I was in the evenings by the emotional support of my books. But part of me still didn't like the night.

Glorious Technicolor. Biff. A slap stung my cheek. Wails shrieked through my ears. I was running, being chased and not getting anywhere. Howls and blackness. Dampness. Words, tastes, sounds and numbers flashed through my brain. The nightmares that I'd suffered from as a child continued. I remembered them in extreme detail. If I was struck, I felt the pain; my senses were being assaulted. My brain was registering the images as real. I would dream of murders; of running, being chased and not getting anywhere. I dreamt of being crushed by trains, which would come at me in slow motion. Inevitable. There I'd be, trapped, shouting at the bystanders to help me. Nonchalant and untouchable, they'd ignore me until the train hit and was a wreckage. As steam rose from the carnage, the bystanders would tut and walk away. By now, I'd be watching the scene from an observer's viewpoint and see myself climbing from the tortured wreckage.

Continually exhausted by these nightmares, I was too afraid to tell anyone about them, partly because I thought dreams of this severity must happen to everyone. Partly because I thought I might be mad. Or would be taken for mad.

Either way, I knew it wasn't a good idea to say.

Having clean clothes and food on the table is surely all you need to live. I had those. All my functional needs were catered for. The law saw to it. So why did the nightmares not stop? Why was I always so afraid and alone?

Round about the same time as I moved to Fernlea, I had begun to listen to punk music, including the X-Ray Spex and the Sex Pistols. I had pinched a pair of lab specs from the science department at another school I had attended, customised them by colouring them and wore them around town. I also bought a pair of metallic-silver skin-tight drainpipe trousers, which I adored. I would never go to school or leave my room without my make-up, no matter how late it made me. The staff at Fernlea hated this get-up and I was deemed unladylike and troublesome, especially by the staff members my 'aunt' didn't favour.

Again Hamish came to my rescue. He spoke to the staff, discussing with them how they should be aware of their own prejudices and bias. He said all I wanted to do was express myself. I suppose, in a way, I was trying to find myself.

My aunt Elspeth seemed to warm to Hamish, considering him a learned and respectable middle-class man. He impressed merely by steadily speaking his mind with his constant compassion. As long as I had Hamish, and my aunt Helen's house to visit, I had sanctuary of sorts. Yet this seemed to irritate the staff in Fernlea, who voiced over and over again their concern that I wouldn't open up to them. I didn't realise then that people react in a very self-protective way. They can be afraid of the person who appears in control and this fear can be even worse when it's a child. I might just be revealing their fallibilities. I could be dangerous to them. I tried to talk to them about the things that interested me, such as art, politics and religion, but they seemed to take this as a kind of challenge, as though I was trying to provoke an argument. Now I can see that many of them didn't have the knowledge to engage in these kinds of debates.

The issue of my having family outside the home raised its head repeatedly but Hamish recognised this and again spoke to the staff about their behaviour.

I was smoking steadily by now and the little pocket money I got, plus the money my father gave me, afforded me this. Some of the staff smoked. Phil in particular, if he was short of cigarettes, would ask me for one on the fly and when I had none, I'd take one from his packet. This was a silent arrangement. If I got caught, I had to say I stole from him, which on rare occasions I did. When this happened, I had my pocket money stopped. I had a similar arrangement with a staff member called John.

John and Phil were of a similar age and really only a few years older than me. By now I was 15, John was 21 and Phil not much older. John was tall, very slim and liked punk music. He lived locally. Phil, too, was tall but he was dark and more muscular. His tastes were more catholic and he came from a nearby town.

Aunt Elspeth had taken John under her wing. He didn't have a good relationship with his mother, though he still lived with her. He seemed to prefer his father, who was separated from his mother.

John first made his appearance at Fernlea shortly after I arrived there. I remember my introduction to him. It came when he popped his head round the door and flicked me with a tea towel. I wasn't having that. I chased him back and slapped him. We both laughed. I refused to call him or any of the other staff aunt or uncle, reserving that only for the boss, 'Aunt' Elspeth.

John was third in charge at Fernlea, which meant I had Aunt Elspeth as first in charge and an ally in John as third in charge. Lillian, Aunt Elspeth's nemesis, was second in charge.

The other members of the residential social work team were Mary, who was a devout Baptist Christian; Patricia, who fancied Phil and who was Catholic; and Nan, who lived round the corner and reminded me of Aunt Ina from Braeview – stereotypically motherly looking. Sarah was a good-looking married woman with obvious pride in herself; I liked her blonde hair and make-up. Lizzie was older, slim and very quick. She came to work as a member of staff and quickly realised it was not for her. I don't know why. Lizzie was the salt-of-the-earth type with a passion for bingo. This led to her being nicknamed 'Legs Eleven Lizzie'. She exchanged her job to be the home's cleaner. Perhaps the staff politics weren't to her liking or perhaps she'd felt out of her depth, having to deal with troubled kids. As a cleaner, though, Lizzie was well liked; she had a sharp sense of humour and her local dialect always made her jokes funnier. Except when she would batter the Hoover off my bed to get me up. I hated the invasion of my room but never disliked her personally for it.

On a one-to-one basis, I could get on with most of the staff superficially well but I always felt that I was being scrutinised and that, for the most part, their agenda was to carry out a fact-finding mission about me, to be discussed when I was not present. It was the same for the other children and it led to me being very careful. I questioned everything they asked me and monitored my answers. Hamish had a discussion with the staff about *them* being more open with me. He wrote in his social work log about the discussions the staff had concerning me but would never actually speak to me about them. Hamish was too professional and sensitive to my situation to gossip about the staff personalities; however, he always gave me a positive summary of where he thought I needed some guidance and he subtly tried to give me a flavour of their perception of me.

Though I sometimes felt it, I wasn't the only one who had run-ins with the staff. My room was next door to Diana and her wee sister Debbie. One day I heard the sound of crying and went through to see what was wrong. Diana didn't cry for nothing and now she was lying on her bed sobbing hard, so I rushed over to her.

'What's wrong?' I asked, repeating it when she struggled to answer.

At first I could get no words from her but eventually she looked up at me from her pillow. Her eyes were red from crying. 'Phil hit me,' she said. Her voice lurched between the sob spasms. 'I want my daddy.'

I tried to calm her down, stroking her hair, and sat down on the quilt beside her. 'Have you asked if you can phone?' I said. Instinct told me she wouldn't be allowed to.

'They won't let me. I'm not allowed,' she said. 'I asked them and they wouldn't let me.'

I thought of my own wee sister being lashed with Jock Sutherland's dog's chain when we were at Clydeview and how I'd felt then. Diana was just a year or so older than Cathleen. I felt angry and sad at the same time. How dare Phil hit her? What right did he have? She'd obviously been sent to her room out of the way. What could I do?

She broke down into sobs again, repeating, 'I want my daddy,' over and over.

Incensed, I promised to get her daddy. 'Where does he live?' I asked.

Her eyes brightened.

I had a plan. With Diana as my lookout, I sneaked along to one of the staff sleepover bedrooms. Taking a penny from my pocket, I inserted it into the lock on the door and turned it. I nodded to Diana, silently reminding her that she was to look out while I went in. I opened the door. And I was in.

The austerity of the room surprised me. I sat on the staff bed and lifted the phone to dial, my heart pounding in case they caught me. I dialled Directory Enquiries and gave them the town, name and address that Diana had told me. I dialled the number they gave me and waited for it to ring. All was silent in the corridor.

Diana's father answered the phone. Quickly relaying what Diana had told me about being assaulted, I blurted out that I was sorry, worried my actions were causing him trouble.

'Don't worry, hen,' he said, his voice stern. 'It's not you I'm angry at but he's in for a hammering.' There was a pause before he asked, 'Where's Diana now?'

'Wait and I'll get her,' I said.

I put the receiver on the bed and went to the door. I stuck my head out and looked down the length of the corridor. Mirroring mine, Diana's head was sticking out of her room door. I beckoned her to come quickly.

She flew up the corridor and into the room.

'Your dad's on the phone,' I said as she passed me. I waited in the corridor, wishing I had the kind of dad who'd rush to avenge me.

Diana came out of the room after speaking to her father and I put my arm round her shoulder. We walked back to her bedroom. I was frightened by my actions but I couldn't have stopped myself. I had to do it. As I sat upstairs when Diana's father appeared that afternoon, listening to angry voices, I wondered what the payback would be. It wouldn't be long till I found out.

My own father still visited on the odd occasion but his visits led to further uncertainty on my part and confused my feelings towards the staff even further. On one hand, they totally opposed alcohol and wouldn't tolerate any disturbing behaviour connected with it from the children but, on the other, whenever my father appeared his drunkenness was overlooked and I was forced to constantly endure it, alone with him in the visitors' room. As the eldest daughter, I was expected to show respect: after all, I was told by the staff, your father is your father. I was too ashamed to reveal my true feelings, to tell them I was afraid of him and disgusted by him. What kind of daughter would that make me? Yet, at the same time, I was still intensely worried about him. The situation caused turmoil within me, as I couldn't understand that such strong feelings could co-exist.

Even my sanctuary at school was to prove fragile. While sketching a still life in my art class, someone knocked at the door and I looked up. The teacher answered and stood there in discussion for several minutes before turning back to the class and calling me from my seat. Fearful that something bad had happened, I searched his eyes for answers. 'Mr Chambers wants to see you in his office,' he said. Mr Chambers was the head teacher.

As I went into the office, I realised that John from Fernlea was already there. What now? My body just wanted to run but the situation dictated that I should do as I was told. I sat down.

'Eileen. Do you have any idea where Lillian's watch is?' Mr Chambers asked me.

What? Oh, shit, it looked as if they suspected me of stealing it. In a second, I went from thinking something bad had happened to someone I loved, to realising someone had stolen Lillian's watch, to understanding that I was the one who was under suspicion.

'No! No! No!' I repeated, defensive and suddenly intimidated. What was Lillian trying to do to me? 'I don't know anything about her watch.'

Mr Chambers suggested I go home. I felt he didn't want a thief in the school. On my return to Fernlea, Lillian was upstairs. Almost as soon as I arrived, she found the stolen watch in the bottom of Diana's drawer. I went upstairs. Seeing Diana's wardrobe drawer removed and lying open on the floor, I looked Lillian straight in the eye, feeling angry and hurt. To me, this had been personal. The police were called off. When Diana came home from school that afternoon, she denied taking the watch, in tears. Was that the payback I feared? If it was, it had backfired.

The Diana situation and Diana herself reminded me of my wee sister Cathleen, whom I was worried about, mostly because I feared for her safety and felt I was not being a responsible big sister. Failing to fulfil my role added to my feelings of confusion. Not being able to understand or vocalise these thoughts with staff or others added to my isolation and loneliness.

15

The Order of Chaos

As always in my life, cogs were turning in the background, whirring away without my explicit knowledge. I did have an implicit knowledge, though. I was always aware at some level that many people made decisions and judgements about my situation that I had no input into or control over. Most of these people I would never meet but I always knew that social work conferences were held regularly to discuss my situation and ongoing placement. Decisions could be taken at these conferences that would have a major effect on my life and I believed there was nothing I could do to influence them.

My placement in care was legally bound by Section 15 of the Social Work Scotland Act 1968. It was legally seen as voluntary care. This Act meant I was in legal limbo. For me, it wasn't voluntary: I had no choice; I had nowhere else to go. As my father had agreed to the voluntary care, I was caught betwixt and between, without anybody having full responsibility for my interests. I was still legally his daughter, with a foot in the family camp, and legally the social work camp had a duty of care for me. I couldn't be fostered at this point unless it was directed by the Social Work Department, and the ethos at the time was to keep children with their families no matter what. Voluntary care, to me, was just an illusion. My father continued to visit sporadically, often paralytic, and at night my bad dreams continued.

Even when things seemed to be going well, I was too afraid to relax completely. There were reasons for that. My past being one and my constant nightmares another. Add to this the knowledge that when I reached the age of 16 I would be too old to live at Fernlea. I had less than a year to go before I'd be automatically turfed out. Nobody had ever raised this subject with me and I was afraid to bring it up. Small wonder the future loomed heavily in front of me.

Hiding round the back of Fernlea with my cigarette, I thought of how I longed for my own home. A home that would be rightfully and forever mine whenever I needed it. At the moment, only the law directed that I should have a home, not people who shared a bond of love or kinship with me. It was always a legal act that governed my life, allowing this or disallowing that. How I wished that sometimes it was a form of love that influenced the decisions that affected me.

Oh, to look over my shoulder and to feel that something was there, some kind of safety net. That was what I wanted. Instead, all that was behind me if I glanced over my shoulder was emptiness, nightmares and longing. It would have been personal and social suicide to have talked about my past – so how could I look forward?

If, at the age of 15, I'd had the knowledge that adulthood and distance have brought, I could have understood my emptiness and my longings, and I might well have had a better perception of my future. As it was, I was young and stayed confused, and because I was confused I was secretive. Reticent. Guarded. Nothing in, nothing out, remained my watchword. My custom-made self-protection strategy kicked in again. In order not to reveal my vulnerability, everything I felt had to be hidden. And it was as a result of this that shame arrived and fully stuck.

By now, I had begun to get to know a girl who lived round the corner from the home. Her name was Tracey Leggate and she was in some of my classes at school. She was friends with my cousin Lena, too. Tracey had gorgeous long, thick, dark hair. John, the staff member, took a particular interest in her and eventually asked me to ask her out for him. Initially, I didn't do it but I did let her know of his interest. Anything further just didn't seem right to me, though I was confused about why.

Being young, I didn't realise it would be completely against the rules but I did have an in-built sense that it wasn't ethical.

I was learning by way of the males in Fernlea that I could be a good friend and it was fun as well as safe to have male friends: it took me back to my days of playing football and climbing. However, I had also begun to be more aware that I was attracting attention from the opposite sex. Boys! My cousin Lena was winching – going out with – a boy and it transpired that a neighbour of hers was interested in me. As she put it, he wanted 'to get me' for a date. Excited, I arranged to meet him 'to get him' but at the last minute I panicked, feigned illness and didn't turn up.

The truth was I was terrified, and it wasn't just normal teenage nerves. I thought it was bad for boys to look at me that way. Sex was bad, I had learnt. Hadn't my mother told me? I was bad – a bad girl. Urquhart had also made it ugly and dangerous. Now this boy would find out. Just by kissing me, he could reveal my sordid status. They – everyone, any boy – would be able to tell. I was sure of it. Even though I'd had that first kiss from the twin in Braeview, I feared this. Was it because this boy was closer to home and because I was afraid my family might find out? I think so. It never occurred to me that because Lena was kissing boys it was all right for me to do so, too, that it was a natural stage of adolescence. No, in my frightened mind I decided that Lena would be able to justify it to herself and her family because she was good, whereas it was obvious to me – and I believed to others – that I was bad. So I would be condemned for it.

At the same time, I was becoming increasingly aware that I was attracted to boys. I wanted to be held and kissed in that way. My feelings frightened me. In my fragile state, this further convinced me that I was bad. My mother's words were never far from my memory. I was a whore, hadn't she told me? I used this memory to deny myself. It became the way I kept myself in check; it was my control mechanism, my method of self-regulation.

However, this self-regulation was under constant threat by my own natural curiosity and my teenage hormones, the effect of which I just didn't understand. I truly had no idea what was happening to me. Moving around schools and homes had denied me a formal sex education. Would it have helped? Emotionally, I don't know. All I did know was that it was my duty to self-regulate by suppression.

While being tortured by these confused feelings, I met a boy in my art class. Dougie also enjoyed punk music. He spoke little to me but as the teacher taught and other pupils chatted I'd catch him staring at me; this was uncomfortable as well as fascinating to me. The strange thing was that he was rude to me when he did speak. I couldn't understand the undercurrent here. Why was I attracted to him and why was he rude to me? I didn't understand the other reasons why boys pulled pigtails or flicked dish towels. My own hormones were a mystery to me, never mind theirs. I was ashamed that I partly liked this attraction. It was so strong! Even I couldn't deny it in private to myself and it must have been obvious to others in the class, as eventually we were teased that we 'fancied each other'. In true 15-year-old form, we denied it vehemently. In fact, it was me that was most vehement; he mostly smiled at the taunts and stared at me sneakily through his spiky fringe and long eyelashes.

Eventually, and almost unwittingly, as these things seem to happen when you're young, a date was set up through classmates. I met him at the swing park and the first thing I told him was that I was in a children's home. This was always a huge issue for me. As always, the way I tackled the revelation was to be upfront and first in with it. Others took this to mean that I wasn't ashamed. It might even have seemed like a challenge to the person I was telling. Social workers love to use that expression, 'She was a challenge.' The fact was it was a truth to be told immediately in order that rejection, if it came, would come sooner rather than later.

Dougie came back and spent some time with me in the home before we walked to my aunt's house. I didn't know what to do on such a public date and it seemed that neither did he. We sat for a while in my aunt's living room. I was nervous, glancing back over my shoulder in case one of my cousins was spying on us through the ferns etched on the glass door. It's as if I took him there to show him I did have a family in some way, in the hope that this compensated for my shame at losing one and ending up in a children's home.

After half an hour or so of sitting nervously, trying to make conversation and resisting the urge to bite my nails, my cousin Lena came in and we all went up to her room. We talked about music, trying to impress one another with our knowledge and, we thought, individuality. The atmosphere definitely lightened. Then Lena left us alone and we kissed.

Although the kiss I'd had from the twin at Braeview was special because it was my first, and although I was caught up in relief to get this first kiss with Dougie out of the road, this one was lovely in a stranger way: it was lovely because I had longed for it from him. I had even allowed myself to daydream about it, and him. His brown spiky hair and deep eyes were so entrancing to me, as was his silence. His dress code of subtle anarchy appealed to the punk in me. The area where we lived was not a forerunner in the punk code, therefore spiky hair, drainpipes and sunglasses were all that was needed to define you as a punk. No ripped clothes or safety pins were required.

We left my aunt's, me living out the cliché of walking on air. He walked me home without speaking and we kissed again, longer this time. I liked the silence between us; I didn't understand that I needed to let him know I liked him. I thought that being there with him was enough. I said nothing about my feelings, played no games of teasing him and waited for him to ask if he could see me again. He left without asking but he was smiling. Enigmatic. I didn't know what to do but I went straight upstairs to my bedroom, climbed under the orange duvet and wrapped my arms round myself. I was smiling. Punk sure did have a day-glo about it.

By the time I returned to school on the Monday, I was excited to get to the art class. The lesson went by with sly little glances at each other and half-smiles. Nothing more was said, though, and by the end of the lesson I had stopped smiling at him. It was over. Not interested in playing this cat-and-mouse game, I closed off, refusing to meet his glances. My bubble burst. Returning to Fernlea, I took solace in my poetry.

Friends made in children's homes often disappeared overnight to be swiftly replaced by others but around this time I became close to a boy called Alex, who had moved into Fernlea. He was a year older than me and he and the others would often tease me. I didn't resent this or become surly and precious. It felt like being part of a family, albeit a borrowed one.

I really liked Alex but saw our relationship as a temporary brother–sister arrangement. He was the archetypal cheeky chappy, small with dark thick hair and lovely blue eyes. He was always witty in his cheek so no one could take offence at it. And he was very precise in his clothing: his jeans had an ironed press in them you could slice your finger on. He was, in a word, 'spotless'.

Alex came from a 'broken home'. His mother had left many years ago to go to London. He and his brothers had been in minor trouble with the law, which was one of the reasons he'd ended up in Fernlea. He was joined by another boy called Tim, who was also from the same village. Tim was a big lad with a very bad temper, as fair as Alex was dark and as tall as Alex was small.

Alex and Tim were the first of an influx of boys to Fernlea at this point and a bit of a clique formed amongst those who came from the same hometown. Another boy soon became a fall guy. He was sneered at and teased relentlessly as he had apparently – the others said – been caught 'sheep shagging' and they also said he 'liked children'. That, and the fact that he couldn't look at me – or anybody – straight in the eyes, was enough to make sure I tried to stay away from him.

Another male who joined the home at this time was called 'Smiddy'. He was from a totally different area, and he was a skinhead with plooks, ears too big for his head and a bulbous nose. His teenage years weren't kind to him in terms of appearance and, in the testosterone-filled atmosphere of the home, this led to him becoming an easy target. Smiddy took some of the heat from the 'sheep shagger' and was ridiculed as the outsider, simply because he was from another area.

The home was now mainly populated by boys but the relationships I had with them were completely unlike the one I'd had with Dougie. In Dougie's presence, I'd watched secretly for his reaction, spying on him through my own messy fringe. I'd wanted to gauge how he felt about me. My feelings for the boys in the home were platonic and I could more than hold my own at the teasing. I always rose to the challenge, not allowing them to get the better of me. Mostly this was fun. My saving grace, or so I thought, was that I was female. My self-delusion and naivety made me think I could be a match for the boys but I was to be proved wrong.

Back at school, I was now dreading the art classes. Dougie's secret smiles had become sneers. I was so confused. And now another lad was giving me attention. His name was Mark. One weekend when I was sitting in the office at Fernlea, I looked out of the window and there stood Dougie and Mark together. It turned out they were friends. I was embarrassed and ignored them, even when they devised antics to catch my attention.

Of course, I sneaked little glances to see what they were doing. Dougie lay down in the middle of the road at one point but I still refused to go out. It was a fairly quiet road then but buses and cars did go along it.

By now I was getting scared. I didn't know what was expected of me. Should I go out to speak to them? What did they want? Eventually, when I didn't respond, they gave up and left. The whole event left me very confused. However, rather than appear so, I pretended I knew exactly what was going on and it must have looked as if I was playing it cool. Far from it.

16

0791 Trahuqru

Hamish, meanwhile, continued to visit once a month and I continued to pretend that all was well. Pretence it might have been but I didn't know I was pretending. I needed to believe myself in order to convince others.

At this time, I began to keep a secret diary, which I wrote in code. At the back, I made a list of boys I liked and gave them stars according to looks, personality and how much I liked them. I suppose, for a teenage girl, this was normal enough behaviour.

I also began writing down memories of things that had occurred in my past and would not leave my mind. This I did this by writing disciplined one-line sentences. I didn't know why I was doing it but these sentences were my attempts at record-keeping – a way of preserving evidence. For example, I'd write down Urquhart's name and address by writing a number as his first name, usually the year he visited me back to front, followed by his second name back to front:

0791 Trahuqru

Only the address would read normally. Was this not only a way of making sure a record was kept but also the start of the painful process of acknowledging what had happened to me? Who knows? All I did know was that I was tormented trying to make sense of it all. I was trying to keep some kind of concrete hold of the past that now existed only abstractly in my head. And I couldn't separate the repercussions of what had happened from what was now going on in the present. My body was changing and I couldn't reconcile my emotions about the past with the way I had started to feel about boys now.

Sometimes, and in particular after a heavy night of nightmares, I felt so distant, like a whisper, a whisper that I could barely hear myself. I would find contentment and sanctuary in reading and attending school lessons but the other side of the see-saw was always threatening to fling me into the air. Constantly performing an internal balancing act, I was at emotional war with myself. Who was I? Who had I been? I was also reading philosophy books, living adrift emotionally: an existential life.

I was plagued by playing catch-up; I needed answers to fix this teenage problem. After all, I thought, didn't everyone else know the answers? If I revealed I didn't know them, people would guess my secrets, my flaws. They'd guess that there was something wrong with me. So I had to find the answers myself. I had to fix myself if I wanted to fit in. That, too, was my responsibility.

This fear of being found out was terrifying. I wrote in my diary:

FACT?
When is When?
Who is who?
Where is Where?
How did you.
Become you.?
Instead of me
Or her
And not
He?

ANON
Null
Veto.
Motionless.

Destructed.

Nothingness.

Empty.

Black.

Cavernous.

Demolished.

Forget.

Dismal.

Numb.

Dead.

Torpid.

Vacuum.

Obliterate.

Absorbed.

If I feel no emotion, then why is the pain of it hurting me?

It scared me writing these things: surely it was proof that I was crazy? I feared it was criminal evidence that could be analysed and used against me, such was my fear of being locked up. However, just as I read to get a fix, to fulfil a need, so the act of writing allowed me to express my feelings and realised a hunger in me. I wrote for relief. It was another way of getting an instant fix. The fix of release.

I had no understanding of the things – the big philosophical and moral questions – I was writing about, and there was nobody I trusted to discuss them with. I didn't know I was questioning the accident of birth and the social and genetic factors that play a part in who we all are. I didn't know that, apart from the mechanical functioning of a human being, emotion was hugely important.

Due to my circumstances, I felt that people had a lot of preconceived notions about who I was, and the only way I could influence their opinion was through the way I presented myself to the world. So, each day, I would rise from my bed and apply my make-up, make sure all my clothes were clean and ironed, raise my head up, thrust back my shoulders and enter the world with a smile. Whether I was going to school, the shops or the cinema, I went suitably armoured by make-up, clothes and the ability to articulate the right noises.

And so my life continued, battling against my nightmares, keeping the façade as perfect as I could make it. Afraid of this new interest from boys yet painfully fascinated by it. Feeling somehow a fraud by privately basking in the few snatched moments of normality in my favourite classes or while I was alone reading in my room, always terrified it would change at any minute. This fear showed in a complete lack of trust. I couldn't relax my guard at any time. For me it was like my father's game of 'smell the cheese'; it was like the way I'd immediately distrusted the girl at school who'd told me she'd seen me skipping. I didn't trust anybody, including myself.

I was never one to take up the option of school dinners. Instead, the Fernlea staff made up packed lunches at night for us to collect the next day on our way out. Every morning, after going through my usual routine of make-up and uniform, I would whisk my packed lunch off the kitchen counter and into my bag before rushing out the door for school but one morning I discovered, during the modern studies class, that all was not as it seemed.

I liked Mr Dow, my modern studies teacher. I enjoyed the discussions we had in his class – about social structure, care of the elderly, politics – and this particular day he was waxing on about the political system in some other country.

I sneaked my hand down into my school bag. I was constantly hungry and could never wait till lunchtime to eat my sandwiches. It was an art to be able to open this red transparent package without rustling and being discovered, never mind eat the sandwiches contained within. I did it by keeping my face up and maintaining the opportunity for eye contact with him, feigning interest. It was always a lively class anyway and I could judge when I could get away with it.

As I tilted to one side, my hand disappeared into the wrapper. The first sandwich should be just within my reach. Yet my fingers didn't find the usual soft bread, moist butter and filling. All I could find was slice after slice of ordinary, dry white bread. Panic set in, I was so hungry. What was I going to eat?

After the lesson, I was able to get a proper look. In my bag was half a loaf, still in its wrapper. Who did that? All I could think was, 'Who tricked me?' My mind tracked back to the morning and I remembered. My aunt Elspeth had been shouting at me that I was going to be late because I was too busy applying my make-up. I couldn't – wouldn't – let myself leave Fernlea till it was perfect.

The other children were lining up to eat their lunch by now, so I had no option but to leave the school premises to tramp back up the hill to Fernlea, convinced she had done it on purpose to teach me a lesson. I fumed all the way home, in no doubt they'd all be having a good laugh at me.

Arriving at Fernlea, I took the package from my bag as I entered the office. Aunt Elspeth stared at me as I dumped the half-loaf on her desk. She looked down at the contents and burst out laughing. There was something in the tone that surprised me. The laugh was infectious. I had to stifle the urge to laugh myself, refusing to let the giggle bubble out of me. Instead, I looked on in mock indignation, waiting for an explanation.

'Oh, it was you,' she laughed. 'Go and look in the kitchen.'

I stomped my way into the kitchen, with her following me. There on the kitchen bunker sat one lone packed lunch.

'We wondered who had left theirs,' she said.

I burst out laughing, as did she again. It was so good to get it wrong, such a relief. I was teased but I enjoyed both that and my packed lunch, eaten with Elspeth and other staff members at the kitchen table. Being wrong and being teased about it made me feel like I might actually belong; it seemed a normal family thing to do. This incident would keep the staff and me amused for days.

17

A Bastard Abroad

My school was organising a school trip to Germany and Switzerland, to take place from 4 to 12 July 1978. On one of his visits to see me, Hamish asked if I would like to go. I was stunned. Me, go to Switzerland? Me, the kid from the children's home?

To this day, my face still lights up from my heart at a surprise. However, the thought that I might be entitled to the trip soon gave way to the dread that I might be disappointed.

Resolute, Hamish's ideology was always, 'Why shouldn't you be allowed to go, just because you're in a home?'

I couldn't believe it. Where did this man get his ideas from? How could someone see things like this, so differently from all the others? I was discovering that there was an ideology of egalitarianism at this time in Scotland.

As I rushed along the road to school the next morning, part of me was afraid it was a joke: was I smelling the cheese again? How my father had loved to tease me in that way. He had loved to see my eyes light up, then how he'd laughed at the realisation in my face as the joke was discovered. Absentmindedly, I pulled leaves from the privet hedges that bordered the pavement on the way to school, tore them up and scattered them. Surely he wouldn't? Not Hamish. Not about something as big as this. In my eyes, Hamish was everything. I wished he was my father, or my brother, or even just an uncle. Maybe Hamish would adopt me. I had passed the test that day at his house; just maybe he would adopt me.

Alive with excitement, I got the permission forms for the trip from school and filled them in with Hamish's help. I could detect a mixed reaction from staff members. I wasn't worried about the positive reaction from John and Aunt Elspeth. I knew I would have to keep an eye out for the others, though. Whenever I walked into the office, discussion would stop. When they openly asked me about my trip, my reply would always be met with their eyes darting to each other. Who did I think I was, indeed. That was the silent transference they communicated. I never thought that adults could be jealous; indeed, I had never acknowledged the emotion myself. I just thought fearfully that they might be right, that I was not deserving of this. Who did I think I was?

Hamish, however, had managed not only to secure the funding for me to go on the school holiday but had also arranged for a small amount of money to be made available for me to buy some clothes from any shop I wanted. This was fantastic news for a clothes-mad punk follower.

However, it was put to me that I was representing Fernlea and I should dress and behave accordingly. Some of my shopping for the trip was done at the shops with which Fernlea held accounts, such as Marks and Spencer and British Home Stores. At this time, the clothes in these shops might have been of good quality but to me they were anything but fashionable, and they were also very expensive in my eyes. I was horrified at the price of a pair of trousers. I could get several pairs somewhere else for the price of one from there.

I did manage to find a beautiful pair of distressed tan t-bar pointed shoes, which, unlike my punk gear, made me look quite the young lady. I also got a khaki skirt and several shirts to match. These items hung in my wardrobe, possessions adored in the way of the broken pieces of coloured glass from my father's job at the bottle works. They hung in my wardrobe like hope. Waiting to be worn.

Aunt Elspeth designated Phil to take me into Glasgow for the day to spend the rest of the money Hamish had obtained for me on fashionable clothing. I felt slightly nervous at this; Phil, however, seemed fine. So excited was I, and having no choice anyway, I had to forget about everything that had gone before, when Phil had assaulted Diana, and I just looked forward to the day. I pacified myself by saying that at least Phil would enjoy a day out from Fernlea.

I had never gone shopping with friends for an event, so this was my closest experience. We chatted away, me the child, him the carer only a few years older than me. We had lunch in Glasgow. I got a few pairs of skin-tight drainpipe jeans and then, with a strange feeling of being spoilt, I spotted a dress. I tried it on in the dressing-room; it was a baby-blue gypsy-style dress, with a frilly underskirt that hung down, as was the fashion. It exuded femininity and beauty. Delirious because of this day out, and in retrospect due to the attention I was receiving from Phil as I tried clothes on, I birled out of the dressing-room and stood in front of him, wearing this dress. When he smiled and told me I looked great, that was the icing on the cake for me. I felt special. All the way home on the train, I must have been radiant. As the train went through the tunnel, my eyes smiled back at me from my reflection in the window. It was a reflection of a young woman without fear.

Back at Fernlea, mutters were being made about how unfair all this was on the other children. Then, Aunt Elspeth said so as well. In public, she supported the trip; however, when we were on our own, she told me on several occasions, 'I couldn't afford to send my children, you know.' She was prone to doing strange things like this: first, building me up by saying how lucky I was, then following up with a sting in the tail in order to bring me down. The sting always came in private, when I least expected it, and she always stared long into my eyes. What was she waiting for, and why? I usually deflected this by ignoring it or being overly cheerful in my reply.

Linked to this was the way she wheedled out of me information about the behaviour of the other staff. She would carefully question me as to what was done or said. When I thought I had found a way round answering, she wouldn't let it go and would repeat her question. It was very confusing and uncomfortable. Other than Hamish, I believed she was the only person I could rely on for protection from the others. Yet sometimes I just didn't know where I stood with her.

I discovered that Laura, the daughter of a neighbour of my aunt, was going on the school holiday, too, which delighted me. Looking for someone to share my happiness with, I sauntered up to my aunt's house and popped in to see Laura. We chatted about the trip and I told her all about my day out in Glasgow. I was pleased she was going: we would be good company for each other, as we had known each other for quite some time. I considered her a friend. As I blathered away, I thought I detected a slight tension in the air and a distance coming into her eyes. This was always a warning to me. Then Laura's mother spurted out, 'We've had to work and save hard to be able to afford to send Laura on this trip, never mind buy her clothes.' Her eyes were full of resentment. Emotionally slapped, I left, feeling guilty and ashamed.

A staff member, Mary, told me her sister Gillian was going on the trip, too. I had mixed feelings about this. It was good that someone else I had a loose connection with would be there but my worry was about what would be reported back, and anyway I hardly knew Gillian, so I worried even more that she would put a nasty slant on her report.

However, when the day came and all fretting was fruitless, I arrived, driven by Aunt Elspeth, at the school, ready to be picked up by the coach. It was 4 July and a certain type of freedom was to be mine. The school playground was busy with buses, cases and parents. It was only eight o'clock in the morning but already the sun was high. I was dressed as others had never seen me before. As we stood around saying final goodbyes, Aunt Elspeth whispered in my ear that someone had said to her, 'Is that one of the Fernlea children?'

I had made her proud.

Laura and I found seats on the coach and waved frantically as we left the school grounds. Gillian, Mary's sister, had acknowledged me. I discovered Dougie, the boy I had taken to my aunt Helen's house, was also on the trip. A further two girls from my year and some of my classmates were seated near the back.

As we hurled down the M74 towards the M6, songs were sung and food parcels opened and eaten. Busy chats electrified the bus. We arrived at Hull in the late afternoon, ready to board the six o'clock ferry to Rotterdam. The boat was fantastic. It had a casino, bars and a deck that we all ran around on. I felt slightly seasick once we were under way;

Gillian gave me something to help. I retreated to my cabin and slept well. Unable to eat breakfast, I pressed against the cool windows of the passenger lounge as we passed the Hook of Holland. At moments like this, I enjoyed being alone.

After a long coach drive, our first tired evening was spent in the Goldene Rose Hotel in Heidelberg before we set off the next day for our main destination of Interlaken. As the scenery changed and more landscapes with cuckoo-clock chalets appeared, I began to relax. By early evening, we had arrived at the Park Hotel, just in time to see the stunning backdrop of hills before the light disappeared.

One of the lovely memories I have of this time was being on a lake called Blausee in Switzerland, on a small boat. The crispness and cleanness as well as the open expansiveness of the area were stunning. The water shimmered like coloured mercury.

Another memory involves going up Interlaken's 'own mountain' in a funicular railway. Supper was to be at the restaurant Harder Kulm, which was at the summit. The journey was terrifying, as the train headed straight up the side of the mountain. I remember feeling I couldn't stand up and I was sure it was going to fall off. After all, the track didn't have Velcro qualities. How could it possibly stay on? My anxiety seemed to gather speed with the train hurtling in an upright position.

Once we arrived at the top, we had to wear sunglasses. It was so glamorous I felt as if I'd walked into a Bond movie. I stepped onto the blazing whiteness of snow, and fell. Everyone laughed – even me – because it was funny. I lost my sunglasses in the snow, as well as my hidden cigarettes. As I laughed and struggled to get back on my feet, I began to find it difficult to breathe. I was filling my lungs as full as I could but it didn't seem to have any effect.

'Are you all right?' Laura asked me, brushing the snow from my jacket as I stood, hunched, with my hands on my thighs.

I looked up. The snow was sparkling. 'Yes,' I said, in a half-laugh, half-husky whisper. Still I couldn't catch my breath. By now, the party was making ready to walk away towards the restaurant and I was becoming light-headed. Despite this weird feeling, I could take in that all around me was beautiful; it really did feel like being on top of the world. There was such a sense of space. It was white and airy and light with a spectacular view of the Bernese Alps and the Eiger so close by. Funny how beauty makes you want to cry.

The next thing I knew, the teacher was standing with me and there was another kind of hasty case conference. It was said I was having an asthma attack and I had to be promptly escorted back down on the train again. This was even more terrifying, as the funicular was otherwise empty. I am not sure if it was asthma, or a panic attack, or an altitude issue. All I did know was that I was disappointed and terrified, and I was on my way back down the mountain just as soon as I had arrived. I had images of the track realising – uh oh! – its lack of Velcro and me ending up face down at the bottom in a concertinaed train. At least I did have that brief glimpse of the beauty of the world up there to remember. Whatever it was that had happened to me, it did leave me breathless.

The hotel was mostly wooden; it was everything I had imagined from postcards and there were cuckoo clocks everywhere, too. I was having a wonderful time, another world away. Laura and I shared a room with the other two girls from our year. We washed our underwear in the bedroom sink and sat them on the window ledge to dry. One of the nights, as we were in the bedroom getting ready, I hung out of the window, having a fly puff. Our window was almost directly above the entrance and I could see several people standing below us. Sliding my body over the ledge to see more, I heard a shout. I leaned out further. Directly under my window was a male with a pair of knickers in his hand, with his other hand on his head. He had been crowned by a pair of our wet knickers! We girls howled with squeals of laughter and half expected a knock at the door. I was secretly worried: after all, I had been smoking.

After this, I started putting my cigarettes out down the plughole so no evidence could be detected. But on my return from a trip one day, the girls in the room told me that the sink had become blocked. Apparently, a teacher was en route to check it out. It took a while for me to realise it was a joke. After the relief, I found this funny, being included in the fun. However, from then on I would sneak down to the entrance and have a cigarette there. And it was there that I met up with Dougie and Malcolm having a cigarette. We talked about nothing; Dougie gave me the same moody mean stare through his hair. Just as I was starting to feel awkward, a teacher appeared round the corner. We all ran, breaking into laughter once we had escaped capture.

Somewhere along the line we met up with another school party there. Laura and I met two Irish boys and arranged to meet them later that night. Walking along the dark road from the hotel and chatting away, romance touched me. The sky was dark, with twinkling stars, and the moon was bright. There were just us four. Tall pine trees, barely green in the dark, surrounded us. I felt so free, so relaxed. The stars in my eyes must have been shining as brightly as the ones in the sky. We stopped at a small opening by the trees next to the road, then Laura walked on for a few minutes with her acquired boy. Funny how it's decided so easily who is with whom, without a word being spoken. Just a slight movement of the head and maybe an eyelid raised to each other is enough. My tall Irish boy called Sean bent down and kissed me. For me, it lasted a teenage for ever. I almost heard the bells.

All was wonderful till I felt something on my leg and my romantic bubble was disturbed by a strange noise. In the dark, I could see something jumping around. I lost my cool and squealed. It was a frog. Laura came rushing back and we all laughed. Such innocent fun.

The moment had passed and we decided to return to the hotel. However, as we got closer we could see that there were teachers standing at the entrance, smoking. Not wanting to be caught, we had to think quickly about how to get back into the hotel without being seen.

Fields surrounded the hotel, edged with small fences. We jumped over the fence, deciding to sneak along the field and then in through the back entrance. Suddenly, one of the boys shouted, 'Down!', then, 'Lie down!' We did so, straight into the dirt in the field. He blabbered, 'This field has lasers shooting across it for protection.' He had us laughing as we crawled all the way back to the hotel. Laura and I got to our rooms, exasperated and exhilarated. My clothes and hands were filthy.

Not perturbed by our experience, or perhaps spurred on by it, we decided we should have a ride in one of the ornate horse-drawn carriages we'd seen in the streets of Interlaken. People sat in these, looking very sophisticated and glamorous, with rugs over their laps. The schools had arranged, however, to have a bowling competition. Again, the romance won out. Laura and I disappeared, even taking the boys Dougie and Malcolm with us, and rode around the city in one of these decorated carriages drawn by a horse with a jingling harness. It felt so cultured and grown up. I was deliriously happy, trying to put out of my mind what the consequences of our actions might be. On reflection, I was in love. In love with this experience.

The lights sparkled from the quaint shops; horses clopped everywhere, pulling carriages with a master at the helm; people waved to one another from the carriages. I was in a postcard scene right enough. Free from harm and ugliness, just on a journey.

And I was in good company. We became hysterical with laughter when Dougie tried to get Malcolm to go into a 'shop', which he later claimed was a gay bar. Malcolm played the fool the entire trip. All too soon it was over: we were back at the hotel and consequences loomed. A lecture awaited us. I was threatened with being sent home and was told the home had been contacted. I don't know if the others were given the same threat. I do know that I felt it was all my fault. As always. I was the 'homie' – the one who lived in a children's home. As I went back to my room, I was consumed by the horrible feeling that I'd let people down, Hamish in particular, and it hung heavily on me. Did I deserve the holiday? Maybe Laura's mum and the staff at Fernlea had been right all along. Guilt-racked, I behaved for the rest of the holiday but those lovely scenes I had witnessed didn't leave my head.

Before we left Switzerland, Laura and I exchanged home phone numbers with our Irish boys. Unusually, I didn't tell Sean I was living in a children's home. I was too ashamed. I wanted this experience to be untainted by my past. It was that precious to me. That wonderful kiss, free from ugliness or explanations. That's how I imagined other people lived their lives.

To break the journey home, our coach party stopped overnight at Remagen in Germany. This, too, was a new experience for me. At liberty for the afternoon, we strolled about beside the river. The Rhine flowed by my eyes: grey but hugely powerful. Something that fascinated me was the number of bikes beside the Rhine – row after row of motorbikes; I had never seen so many. A community of bikes. All these jeans and leathers, badges and long hair, mingling everywhere. I was truly entranced by the people. Everyone to me looked like they had a reason, a purpose.

I didn't want to go home; I didn't want this visual and emotional experience to end. I would have stood there for hours just watching, if I had been allowed. Although it was alien to me, I was feeling alive.

Laura and I shared a small mouldy room high up in a hotel. We got to dance that night. We even got to buy a beer in the pub in which we were dancing. I spotted the teachers up at the back of the pub but they kept their distance. (Would it happen nowadays?) I had to wear my baby-blue dress that night. I am not sure how suitable this was, as the place was awash with jeans. We four girls laughed about a man in the pub who watched me the whole night. It wasn't frightening like when I was on holiday in Ireland, though. Here, I was with friends and the teachers weren't far. Here, I was alive and happy.

I sent the staff back home a postcard. For most of my life when I heard my peers or my family chatting about having been on holiday in the sun, I adapted by referring to people I knew who'd been to the same places. Holiday by proxy. I always asked people to send me a postcard. Postcards, to me, were the equivalent of holidays to others.

Journeying home on the ferry, rumours started that there would be trouble. We were all rounded up and given a lecture on switchblades and other gang weapons. I was fearful, thinking I would be blamed automatically for any brewing trouble because of my 'homie' label and my previous behaviour. Everyone else had families to go back to who would defend them. Anyway, a ceremony took place on deck during which all the blades were thrown overboard. I wasn't to know that a similar ceremony took place on many school trips.

Sadness was overwhelming me as we returned home on 12 July. I knew my father would be wearing his sash and drunkenly parading either at home or in Ireland. As the Irish Troubles peaked in the '70s, so did mine. Even seeing Malcolm falling asleep on the bus and the others rubbing Dairylea cheese into his overgrown eyebrows barely lifted my spirits. The bus wheels might be moving underneath us on the long stretch of conveyor belt taking us home but I wasn't seeing fields of artichokes or left-hand drivers or villages of houses. I was kissing Sean in the moonlight, surrounded by pine trees, or I was riding with Laura in a horse-drawn carriage, the sparkling lights from the shop-lined streets blinking the ugliness away.

18

Message in a Bottle

One Saturday morning, there was a knock at my bedroom door. I was reading a book, lying face down on my bed.

'What is it?' I yelled.

Alex had been sent as the messenger. He pushed the door open with his finger. 'Phone call for you,' he said, leaning on the bedroom frame.

My school trip was becoming a distant memory. 'Who is it?' I asked him.

He shrugged and tossed his long fringe out of his eyes. 'I think they said it sounded like he was from Ireland.'

My heart flipped. Sean was from Ireland. I slipped past Alex and ran downstairs. I went into the office but the duty staff wouldn't give me privacy to speak to Sean on my own, so I cut the call short. There were no cordless phones in those days. No mobiles. The sadness of being 'home' at Fernlea was accentuated by this phone call and later when I received a letter from him. I decided not to have any contact with him because of the shame I felt about the reality of my home situation. Regretfully, I hadn't told him. This had allowed me to be someone else on holiday.

Before the summer, I had done well in my third-year exams in English, despite having had a strange experience while sitting the exam.

Sitting at the back of the class at my wooden desk, paper in front of me and pencil in hand, I was writing my response to the question when blind terror struck me. I wanted to run out of the class but was rooted to the school chair. My heart rate was rising, my eyes darted about the classroom and my pencil hung in my left hand. I had forgotten how to spell the word 'the'. Fighting frustration and panic, I knew that it was a basic word; I could even visualise it like a photograph in my head. I just could not get it down on paper. I began sweating and my breathing became shallower. My voice raced through my head, saying this is crazy. What's wrong? What is wrong?

It seemed like an eternity passed. The three symbols that made up the word 'the' were imprinted on the screen inside my forehead but I couldn't make the sounds *tee aitch ee* come. I tried to find another word to use but couldn't get out of my panic. The three symbols floated about, like an air bubble in a garden hose, unable to go back or forward, temporarily disabling the functioning of my brain and stopping me from continuing with the exam.

Eventually, to my relief, the silent sound impediment in my brain ended; I heard the sounds of the three letters and wrote the word. Despite this episode, on my return to school in August 1978, my marks had earned me a place in one of the top English classes. Of course, I was extremely pleased at this result, and this longer period of stability at a school was showing me that I might not be stupid. The downside of this success, however, was that I lost an excellent teacher in Mr Lamont.

Excited at being in a new class, I soon found there was a different teaching style: my new English teacher was more regimented in his teaching. He would read us the poems and other texts himself, then set us homework. There was very little interaction with the class and very little opportunity for me or any other pupils to ask questions and discuss the class work. I found myself becoming quite restless in this situation, with a million questions running through my head as he read.

However, he did introduce me to some of the best work of the war poets. The sensory perception and descriptions used by these war poets

– Siegfried Sassoon, Wilfred Owen – I fell in astonished love with. I felt as though I had found something that I was relating to, which I did not fully understand. I identified with what these young men were going through, even though their experiences were so different from mine. As I recognised some of the emotions they were describing, I felt that maybe I was not alone in the turmoil I was feeling. Maybe other people felt the way I did. I got into trouble for talking on several occasions in this class. I often wished I was back in Mr Lamont's class, where I had been respected and where I also respected the opinions of the other pupils and revelled in the discussions and vibrant atmosphere.

My modern studies class continued with Mr Dow, as far as I remember. This remained a wonderfully animated class with different opinions being valued and encouraged. Mr Dow was a fantastic teacher. I also found out he had a wife involved in social work and this might explain the extra respect I felt he showed me and my opinions, which I became more and more confident in formulating and expressing in his class. Mr Dow – looking like a man who taught politics to pupils, in his cord jacket, his beard and limp – never patronised me in any way. He never mentioned Fernlea and no social work jargon such as 'further rejection' ever entered the classroom. I was an equal purely due to my academic ability and my conduct in class.

These subjects and my time in those classes always stay with me with a mixture of appreciation and sadness. I wish I could have had more of that and I wish that I hadn't been so wrapped up in my shame, worrying that they might know all about my past as well as about me and my behaviour. I was never sure what other people knew about me. My behaviour out of school wasn't worse than that of any of my peers but whatever they got up to was private, not subject to institutional authority. If they misbehaved, they had to face the consequences from their parents rather than the school finding out. Their home life mostly remained so – at home. The family unit afforded protection and respect, plus privacy. If I ever tried to explain how I felt about my lack of family support, people would say to me, 'You never miss what you never had.' They couldn't have been more wrong.

✳ ✳ ✳

Two things happened that term, which were to send me into a spin. Dougie's friend Mark asked me out on a date, which I refused. Then Dougie asked me out and I said yes. Still fascinated by him, though not knowing why, I dressed and put on my best punk make-up: pale face, dark eyes and outlined lips coloured in with red. Ready for our date. Before I left, I checked my look in the mirror and hung my head upside down to apply another half ton of hairspray. It was a late summer evening, warm enough to go without my jacket.

When I got there, both Dougie and Mark were there to meet me. My excitement vanished and my feet slowed down as I walked towards them. I hadn't expected this. I felt confused, and this feeling intensified when Dougie walked away, leaving me with this boy I'd already turned down. Here I was, left sitting on a wall in the area where they both lived. I don't know why I didn't just leave.

Mark sat beside me and we chatted, though he was the one that did most of the talking. Told me I looked not bad. Said he'd always fancied me. Then he put his arm round me. I concentrated on the red crumbling bricks that made up the wall. I felt afraid – betrayed – and I could feel myself freezing. Quickly, he was upon me. I thought if I was nice to him he would stop, so I smiled and pushed him away, ludicrously trying to extricate myself through my usual eloquence – this time trying any inane chit-chat. But my heart was thumping. There was nobody else around. Although it was still light, the houses behind me looked unlived-in. As usual when I felt frightened, my throat clamped, so my screams were silenced. Anyway, I didn't want to draw attention to myself. I thought I would pee myself, yet I was determined not to show fear. I didn't know then that you can smell fear.

Mark was smiling; I was thinking how I could get home. That fixed smile on my face gave me no protection. With his lips kissing me roughly, I tried to speak in order to stall him but his hands were quickly up my skirt. He forced his fingers into my pants and shoved them inside me. I was thinking, this is not happening, this is definitely not happening. I can't remember what I was saying in my distress but eventually I freed myself. It was still light. I began to walk away, still gibbering; he smiled and asked if I was OK. I said yes and returned home on my own. I went straight to my bedroom. I couldn't tell anyone. What would they take me for? I was such a bad girl and I was angry with myself for walking into it.

The following night, I went round to Tracey's house, the girl who lived round the corner from Fernlea and who John, the staff member, had fancied. Her parents were away for the weekend and a bottle of vodka sat in the cupboard. Like a girl on a mission, I was to drink most of it. Bored in the house, we took it with us and wandered about the local area, giggling and laughing, eventually reaching the park at my school. Too drunk to drink any more, or perhaps because my friend was frightened of my state, we hid what was left of the carry-out behind the school, tucked behind a bush against a wall so we could find it again.

I was so drunk I almost fell in front of the local bus while trying to find my way home. I fell into hedges and knew somehow I couldn't go back to Fernlea in this state, so got myself to my aunt's house. Fortunately, my aunt Helen was out at work. My cousin Annette and her baby had been housed, so Lena put me in the spare room, after I was sick. In the morning, I woke to the realisation of what I had done: worse, to the realisation that I'd wet myself. I crept into Lena's room and she gave me some clothes, then I returned to Fernlea to face the music, all before my aunt woke up.

The smell of ham and eggs cooking for breakfast met me at the door as I entered Fernlea. It was awful. I went straight to my room, feeling sorry for myself. I knew the staff at Fernlea would have 'missed' me overnight. The knives would be out for me. I had really blown it.

John was the only one who appeared to give me sympathy. I didn't know he had been sent in order to get information from me to be added to the list of complaints to be relayed back to Hamish. I could offer no explanation as to my behaviour; indeed, I didn't know why I'd behaved in such a way. At that moment, I believed I truly was the girl they thought I was. My cover was blown. My aunt knew, the staff knew and soon Hamish knew. Hamish was told again that I had no morals. I had given the staff what they wanted. I felt stupid and thought they must have been right about me all along.

To add to my problems, for weeks now the local bus driver had kept stopping to offer me a lift even where there were no bus stops. I couldn't figure it out at first. Why should he be doing that? Initially, I complied, grateful for the lift and feeling broken and beaten into the person my mother had said I was – the 'little whore' she'd called me when she caught the stinking Urquhart in my bed when I was seven.

As he dropped me off at school one time, the bus driver gave me his phone number. I realised he was the driver of the bus I'd almost fallen in front of when I'd been so drunk. From then on, I tried to avoid him and his bus. Even he could smell my past on me. He would stop his bus full of passengers just to speak to me. It even happened in my aunt's street. I stopped getting the bus from her house to Fernlea and began walking everywhere. I felt trapped but couldn't understand why; after all, I wasn't locked up.

Things didn't end there. The night I got drunk and stayed without permission at my aunt's house had also seen a burglary at the home of a couple who were regular visitors to Fernlea.

The first I knew of it was when I was summoned to the office. I opened the door and saw two CID detectives waiting to question me. Also there was a man from the Social Work Department's Supportive Services section. He was called Douglas Law.

Following a suggestion by my aunt Elspeth, I went to the kitchen and made tea for the visitors, bringing it through on a tray with a plate of biscuits and with the cups chinking. The atmosphere in the office was awkward as I passed round the cups, trying not to let them see my bitten nails.

My aunt Elspeth looked up to Douglas Law. He was affable and assured, with the easy confidence of middle-class authority, and she admired him for this and wanted to impress him. As he took a sip of tea, we could see his hesitation. My earnest attempts at waitressing led to him erupting into laughter. I'd left the teabag in his cup, as he discovered when he drank it.

His laughter was such a relief to me; it changed Aunt Elspeth's mood completely. I had turned a potentially bad situation of letting her down into an icebreaker. Had he not responded in the way he did, it would have been very different for me.

The CID men had massive ties on: strange thing to remember but I focused on these ties once the questions started, as I hung my head in shame. Again, my heart was thumping as if I was guilty just because they suspected me. Aunt Elspeth sat behind her desk without speaking.

The two men fired questions at me, putting names to me, including one name I recognised because it was a boy who'd recently asked me out. My hearing was fading in and out. I protested my innocence, horrified that I would be considered so bad, so opportunist, as to do that to good God-fearing people who were always so kind to the children in Fernlea. The earlier goodwill of the meeting had disappeared. Incensed with anger and shame, I realised I really had given Lillian and co. what they wanted. I could feel the sneers and later I overheard some talk about me. I was on fire with shame and self-hatred.

Aunt Elspeth never told me that the CID men were convinced I had nothing to do with the burglary. I only found out when, as an adult, I obtained my case files through the Freedom of Information legislation. Why were they interviewing me, then? Who had put them onto me? Hamish wrote in my case files that the staff members still had their suspicions about me. Why did Aunt Elspeth never set the record straight?

It must have been obvious to Hamish how low I was feeling. For some reason, he arranged to meet me at Glasgow Zoo, as it took me out of the home and was neutral territory for us both. I enjoyed this day and was aware that Hamish was concerned about the attitude of the staff towards me. He was also aware I was angry. I tried to hide it but when he spoke to me about it I acknowledged I could do more to keep the staff on side. They'd claimed I'd been very cheeky since the Germany trip. I'd also stayed out overnight. No wonder I was angry and giving them cheek. I should say, here, that I never told Hamish about the incidents that happened in Fernlea. The only way he heard anything was from the staff when they were complaining. I know he was upset over the way they judged us children. I dared not tell him that I'd witnessed other things, such as what had happened to Diana.

I wouldn't tell my aunt Helen what was going on either, always afraid that it would come back to haunt me in some shape or form. I never had the confidence that I would get support. My experience in life was that if I spoke up, a payback would come in some form or another. I had no control; they had all the cards. At case conferences, they'd make their report about me, or about their perception of me, and this – at a meeting where I had no input to defend myself – was the way my card was marked. I was deemed to be the troublemaker, having never been violent. I was aware that no matter what legal power or support was seen to be put in place to protect me, it would always come back to the staff's word against mine. I more or less promised Hamish I would play the game.

After this, things quietened down on the surface. A new staff member arranged to meet me in the park. Sandra was only a few years older than me. It was good to get away from the constant distrust and I wandered about, happily chatting to her. She didn't want the other staff member to know we were friendly. She warned me about the staff members I had to be afraid of. I took this very seriously, as she was present at the staff meetings and privy to certain gossip between the staff. The whole thing scared me. I had hoped somewhere in my heart that maybe I was wrong about them: that maybe, as in fairy tales, everything would work out right.

Always living with fear, anchored to the subtext of my world, was exhausting. However, continuously living under such stress made it normal: you know nothing else. Yet adrenalin is always running through your body and no respite comes even in sleep.

No sooner had she come but Sandra left Fernlea. Perhaps the internal politics were too much for her. I had also built up a friendship with another female member of staff called Barbara. Barbara was young, slim and seemed so unperturbed by the staff politics at Fernlea. She had that air of having come from the middle class rather than aspiring to it: a confidence in herself. At the same time, another young girl joined the Fernlea children. Her name was Cathy. I hadn't had female company of a similar age in this home before and it was a pleasant change from just having the boys and younger children to chat with. Cathy was local and had plenty of family ties.

Soon I was delivered another blow. It concerned the unwritten practice between Phil, John and me, that we could borrow cigarettes from one another when we had run out. As I'd done in the past, I took a cigarette from Phil's packet. This time, though, he reported it. He said I had stolen cigarettes from him.

Again, my heart began its claustrophobic thumping when I was called into the office. I felt as if some kind of net was closing in on me. The accusation was made and how could I defend the practice? I was on my own again – my word against his – and as a result my pocket money was stopped. I was very close to tears because of this and – tough cookie – I never cried in public if I could help it. But this was so unfair! Phil knew the arrangement we had: it had gone on for months. The complete confusion and rage I felt! And yet I still didn't reveal the practice. After all, the unwritten rule was that you didn't grass. Why I couldn't speak up for myself about this practice, I don't know. It must have been a strange kind of loyalty. I can only assume my fear crippled me in a way that made me sit tight, hoping trouble would go away, even though I knew from past experience that I would end up being the one who was blamed. I loathed the deviousness and duplicity that the staff were accusing me of. I felt I had no comeback either. I was reeling, reeling totally stitched up, with no anaesthetic for their needles.

The shit was piling up fast and furious against me. As I returned to school on the Monday, I was called in to the headmaster's office, again from my art class. Again, my panic set in. Who had died? What had I done wrong? Mr Chambers' secretary indicated that I was to sit in the waiting room till I was called. This I did, feeling smaller and smaller, shrinking with panic.

'Come in, Eileen,' called the voice.

That dreadful moment when you want to run, the second before you step through the door to face the music whose tune you don't know, always has to be met with resilience. Shoulders back and chin up. Nothing in, nothing out.

Standing bolt upright, Mr Chambers asked me how I was.

Detecting that I might be about to fall into a trap, I replied sharply, 'Fine.'

He stepped over towards his desk and asked how my weekend had been.

'Fine,' I said again.

He looked at me. 'What did you get up to?'

My heart beat faster. I thought I knew where he was going with this, but wasn't 100 per cent sure.

Then, from under his desk, he pulled out an almost empty bottle of vodka and two cans of Carlsberg. He told me John had phoned him to tell him where the carry-out was hidden.

I was near to tears because of John's betrayal and because of the shame I felt, standing in this office, imagining the images of me, drunk, that must be going through Mr Chambers' mind. What must he think of me? Was there nowhere where I could be free of the shame I constantly felt? Was there no privacy?

I thought back to John coming up to my room to see me that morning after I'd been drunk. How he'd shown me sympathy, asking me in confidence what had happened. Asking me about Tracey, the girl he fancied, which was something I wouldn't tell him. I imagined Aunt Elspeth's voice egging John on to winkle out the information and divulge it, then make the phone call to the school. My insides curdled with rage. I had no one I could trust, only people who had a use for me.

Heavily, I made my way home to Fernlea. John could hardly look at me; Phil was around somewhere, out of sight. Barbara, the new staff member, came into my room. I could barely tell her what happened. I didn't tell her about John, because I was ashamed to reveal what he had done. I was afraid to acknowledge that I meant nothing to anyone.

Almost immediately, in September 1978, John went on holiday for the weekend with a few of the kids. They went to Fernlea's caravan, which had been gifted to us by the very couple that had suffered the burglary.

So there I was, pocket money stopped, tired and left on my own to deal with Lillian and Phil while Aunt Elspeth, too, was off on holiday. To keep out of their way, I retreated into my room, pretending I was going to study but in reality my books lay unopened. I had recently been allowed to put up posters on my bedroom wall. As I sat, morose, on the edge of the bed I reread one of them. It said: 'If it feels good do it'.

Just then, Cathy came into the room. She was grumpy because she had her period and she had cramps, and also because of an incident that she told me about but which I don't recall. Cathy was one of these girls who could walk about swearing in front of the staff, never seeming to flinch or be afraid.

Somehow, after a joint wallow, we decided we should run away. Packing sanitary towels and a few other bits and pieces in a bag, we made up our minds that we'd run away to – of all places – Ayr, to the caravan park where John was staying with the children. Here I was, running away again, but to what?

Darkness was our cover as we snuck out through the heavy fire doors. Jubilantly free of Fernlea, we wandered down towards the town centre, then carried on until we reached the motorway, where we started hitching a lift. Almost immediately, a vehicle slowed down for us. A police vehicle. I found out later it was the staff at Fernlea who'd asked them to pick us up.

Seeing the bright lights pull over on to the hard shoulder, Cathy and I had started to run towards it but we'd stopped abruptly when we realised it was a paddy wagon. Two young policemen got out and headed towards us. The traffic hurtled past, noisy. Before we could run away, they grabbed us by the shoulders and shouted that we were to get in the van. The back doors of the van were open and I suddenly became terrified. As one of them tried to shove me inside, I resisted with all my body strength. I'd heard violent stories and I'd often seen people being huckled away in the back of them when I was a child. This included my father. I didn't want to go into the back of the van to find out if the stories were true.

Packing us up like that was crazy. I wanted to run or even just to talk to the police. I wanted a chance to explain myself. I asked them, 'Will you get your paws off me?'

They perceived it as insolence and I was hurled into the van. Cathy climbed in after me. Our belongings followed. I was sure something terrible was going to happen to us. One of the police officers shouted and bawled at us. He finished up with, 'It's only animals that have paws.'

'My point exactly,' I replied.

Why oh why, in my terror, was I being so provocative?

They turned the car at the next junction and took us back into town. When we arrived at the police station – only a five-minute drive away – Cathy and I were placed in separate cells. Even before that, I'd realised that Cathy had changed from the confident, loud, brash, swearing female I'd known into a sobbing wreck. Now I could hear her crying in the cell next door to me. This made me more afraid, which in turn ensured there'd be no tears from my eyes. Tears never have come easily; my body doesn't work that way.

As I sat in the cell feeling all was out of control, I looked around at the shabbiness and the graffiti on the walls. One of the police officers stood outside the cell and taunted me through a panel on the door; he had a sanitary towel in his hand. Disgust overwhelmed me at being powerless and female. When they'd searched me, they'd missed the eyeliner pencil and mascara I had in my back pocket. I stared at the door from behind which he was taunting me. I stared at the graffiti. I could hear Cathy crying next door and sensed that she was free from being taunted.

I wanted to be disappeared. I started to scribble 'All police are bastards' with my eyeliner. Doing this kept me focused. I matter, I was saying. I count. Hamish had told me so. Surely the police wouldn't notice this amongst all the rest of the graffiti? The door burst open. Did they see me through the slot in the door when they were coming back to taunt me again or check on me? I don't know.

I had no warning. Two police officers were upon me. I barely had time to retreat to the back of the cell and slip my eyeliner into the back of my jeans pocket. Almost instantly, my arms were up my back and a smack to my face numbed my reactions. They were shouting at me, 'Where is it? Where is it?'

I knew they meant the pen or whatever I had used to write with. Before I had time to tell them, my face was smacked again, this time knocking me onto the floor. Then a foot met my ribs, then again my face was struck. I honestly don't know if, in my defiance, I would ever have told them. Maybe I was hoping they would make me disappear.

After retrieving the pencil from my back pocket, they left me on my own with their verbal onslaught still hanging in the cell. I could hear

Cathy crying louder next door. Cathy had heard it all. I lay there. The door opened again but I didn't react. A bucket of water and a cloth were set down beside me. I turned my head to look at the bucket. Reacting in the same way as I did when my mother broke the brush over my back, I rose from the floor in slow motion, feeling huge. I stood up and tipped the bucket of water onto the floor. That's where I ended up again after it, back on the floor with a few more footprints on my body. My nose was numb but I could feel the warmth of the blood.

Aunt Nan, a member of the staff, was sent to take us home to Fernlea, or so I thought when I saw her. She stood at the cell door, emotionless. The same police officers who lifted us and gave me the beating spoke calmly to her and escorted me out of the cell. I whispered to her, 'They did this.'

Sharply, under her breath, she said, 'Be quiet.'

I knew, truly I knew then, that I was beaten.

I was escorted out towards the reception desk and the front door. Absurdly, as I passed the reception desk, I stopped and in my most articulate speech and manner, I addressed the officer on duty there.

'May I have my make-up back, please?'

The officer looked at me from behind the desk, a mixture of astonishment and disgust in the folds and creases of his face. He passed me a bag with my make-up in it. I could feel the officer who had beaten me standing close, tense now he couldn't impose on me.

Repeatedly, I asked Aunt Nan if I was going to Fernlea. 'Just get out to the car,' she kept saying.

We went out to the waiting car, leaving the large-windowed, heavily lit police station behind. Quiet, I stared down to where I thought I had been held in the cells. It soon became clear that, as I feared, I wasn't going back to Fernlea. As we drove on through the streets to yet another home where no one would care for me, the voice in my head tortured and tormented me. Why could I not cry?

19

Nil Carborundum Illegitimi

We drove through the dark. That's what I remember. No other details are clear to me other than that I suddenly found myself in the local assessment centre.

The legal situation was that if a 21-day assessment order were placed on a child, usually as a result of a criminal or out-of-control charge being brought against them, they were brought to the assessment centre to remain under close supervision during that time.

Cathy, left behind crying, was in my mind. At this stage, I didn't know what would happen to her and I wondered if she would follow me here. I later found out she was taken back to Fernlea. She wasn't the one who'd caused the affray.

I wasn't allowed off the premises, so it was a form of prison. In fact, it was an assessment centre for a List D school – the Scottish term for a borstal. So now I'd reached the place I was always told I would end up in: a bad place for bad children.

My clothes were taken away and I was given a set of 'prison' clothes, which included Crimplene trousers and plastic sandals. 'Bobby washables' this rig-out was called. The building in which I now found myself was large windowed, made of concrete and set back off a twisty-turny, cottage-lined road.

When I arrived, a figure stood in the shadows of the curtains. No doubt it was a lookout who would pass on details of what was walking through their doors. My bruised face would have told them a story. I was subjected to the usual inquisitive looks from the other children and given no chance to ask a question or reply to their 'What you here for?' I was sent straight to bed, once again being expected to settle to sleep in another room full of strangers.

I felt nothing much but fear, my old companion. The memories I have of the three weeks I spent there are fragmentary. I had no friends, no family. I wasn't even allowed to go to my own school, thereby missing not only the companionship of the pupils and teachers I had got to know there but also missing another three weeks of my education.

I was called to be interviewed in an office by someone whose face and body language I will add to the list of those I don't remember. He told me to read a passage from a book, which I did. After I had finished, he told me I would not be going to the school within the assessment centre. On a visit to the toilet, I pulled the door open to discover a boy and girl about my age, in an embrace. They pulled apart and chatted to me. I don't remember their names. They were in different classes from each other and always arranged to leave for a toilet visit at the same time, so they could be together. I promised not to say a word. Shortly after that, I was taken with a member of staff to tour the classrooms. I was shocked to see that Janet and John books – which I had read in early primary school – were being used here as standard.

A day out was organised to go swimming. Embarrassed by my regulation outfit, I didn't want to go, horrified at the idea of being seen. Clothes, make-up and outward appearance had become crucially important to me: they were my way of facing the world. They were usually something I could control. However, I'd lost control of even this aspect of my life at the assessment centre. About the swimming, too, I was given no choice, so under duress I went and spent the entire day feeling ashamed.

That night in bed, I stared across the room as the other girls slept in their beds. What was wrong with me? What was going to become of me? The questions marched round my head. In the morning, we had to get up, make our beds properly, tucking sheets in envelope-style for inspection, and stand at the bottom of them. Someone was trying to drill discipline into me.

During a recreation period, a boy of my age approached me and started chatting to me. He is someone I do remember. His name was Derek. He was a big lad, with large hands and dark hair, and he, too, had come from Glasgow. I tried to appear friendly enough, frightened to rock any boats, and he asked if he could meet me in the toilets at a certain time next day. I agreed to this. Part of me agreed because I was afraid for my personal safety if I said no, but another part of me, the part deep inside of me, was desperate to run away from it. That part won out. The excuse I gave him for not turning up to the clandestine meeting was that I was called to the office, which I was, but not at the time arranged.

Hamish had made arrangements to see me; I was to meet him in a café in Blantyre. So wound up with fear was I in this place that I suspected this arrangement was a test. I fretted about it on the way to meet him. If they let me out, would I run away? Well, would I?

I was so glad to see him. My bruises fading, I could feign normality but I was so afraid of the situation I'd found myself in. Eating lunch with Hamish, I could barely hear, never mind listen to what he was saying to me. I just kept repeating over and over in my head: don't run. Don't run. Go back. Prove to them.

Unbeknown to me, Aunt Elspeth and the staff had had a meeting and told Hamish they weren't willing to have me back. Elspeth had supported the decision made at the time by her staff. I'm glad he didn't tell me. I only found out as an adult when I read what he'd written in my files. Hamish expressed his 'total unhappiness at the way the matter had been handled' but my aunt Elspeth stuck by her decision not to have me back. My cheekiness, my nights 'AWOL' and the unfounded rumours that I'd been involved in the burglary were all too much for her.

I didn't know any of this, of course. And I was also unaware that my treatment by Fernlea was the cause of a serious spat between two divisions of the local authority. Hamish McColl, my social worker, was still employed by the Glasgow authorities but Fernlea was in another district and Hamish recorded the blunt statement: 'On Thursday I called at the assessment centre with the intention of removing Eileen, as [the regional authority] seemed to be refusing any responsibility for her future.' Incredibly, the manager of the assessment centre also expressed his unhappiness at Fernlea's decision. He had initially not wanted to keep me for anything other than an overnight, saying this centre was not the place for me.

The head of the assessment centre was able to call in the district manager, Douglas Law, from Social Work's Supportive Services. He had been present on the occasion when CID had questioned me about the burglary and was the one who'd laughed when I'd left the teabag in his cup. Like Hamish, Douglas Law was middle class and had a quiet, imposing presence. It worked in my favour – though I didn't know it then – that he was very much respected by my aunt Elspeth. These three men were able to insist that Fernlea overturn their decision not to take me back.

One morning, I was told to go to the door of the assessment centre as someone was coming to see me. I was almost overcome when I saw Aunt Elspeth walking towards me. Running to her, I actually put my arms out and wrapped them around her, hugging her in the driveway.

'Do you want to come home?' she asked me.

Gratitude and relief radiated from me. I didn't know the truth. I thought she genuinely wanted me.

'Yes,' I said.

As we walked back into the building, she told me, 'Lillian and the others didn't want me to take you back but I stuck up for you.' It was a lie. Not realising this, it compounded my feelings for Lillian, which suited Aunt Elspeth. Allowing me to believe that she had accepted me back against the wishes of the others drew me even further into her debt. Being forced by her superior to overturn her decision following pressure brought by my social worker and the head of the assessment centre gave her other reasons for wanting payback.

So I was free to leave the assessment centre, in theory. A little later, Hamish arrived and took me to my aunt Helen's house for a few days till a case conference could be held. When I was at my aunt Helen's,

I was where I had always wanted to be but I knew they were fed up with me. I had let everyone down again. I still wanted to be there but I accepted that the only option open to me was Fernlea. Eventually, I was allowed back.

On my return to Fernlea, I ran upstairs to my bedroom to discover I'd been moved from my old room next door to Diana and her wee sister Debbie. I was now in a room at the end of the corridor next to the staff. Discovering this almost made me cry. Worse, some of my belongings were missing. Writing books and make-up had disappeared. It was as if the staff had already moved me out for good then had to take me back. But I had to remain cheerful and accept it. Later, I was to suspect it was my aunt Elspeth who had taken my things. I felt even more isolated when I discovered that, in my absence, my friend Cathy had gone home to her family.

Whichever part of Fernlea I went into now, whether it was entering the kitchen first thing in the morning to eat breakfast or walking upstairs to my room after school, I detected an atmosphere. I felt wary, ill at ease and confused. Of the staff, I remember only John asking me if I was all right. My nightmares continued, too: bloody, gory, oppressive nightmares, leaving me exhausted in the morning.

These nightmares had become so normal for me that I assumed all people must have them. Once I made a rather sly enquiry, while some of us children sat around the office chatting to staff about dreams we had. I was unsettled to hear that most people claimed not to remember any and I made a mental note not to ever reveal mine. I felt it wouldn't be safe for me to do so. Nothing in, nothing out, once again.

When I returned from school one day, Aunt Elspeth was sitting in the office with Penny Wheeler from Supportive Services. On entering the office, I was asked to do the teas. This time I made sure the teabag was removed from the cup. While I set the tray on the office desk, there was a lull in the conversation and I could feel Penny and Aunt Elspeth watching me.

Penny began to enquire as to how I was and how I was getting on at school. In my most articulate way, unwilling to let my aunt Elspeth down, I responded with all the correct, rehearsed answers.

Penny listened and sipped her tea. She always liked to drink from a china cup and I'd remembered that. That's the way I'd served it to her. Her long enamelled fingers looked perfect, immaculate, holding the cup, and her speech and dress were impeccable.

After she'd drunk her tea, her hand went into her bag and she brought out an expensive lipstick. An aficionado of make-up, this one fascinated me. I watched her twist the bottom of the tube to wind the lipstick up. Looking in her compact, she applied the colour to her lips, aware of me watching. 'Do you like it?' she asked me as she wound it down.

I nodded. It was lovely. The casing in itself was expensive and luxurious looking.

'Have it,' she said, and presented it to me.

I accepted with restraint and perfect decorum, thanking her with the right amount of gratefulness; I knew Aunt Elspeth was out to impress. In fact, out of the side of my eye I could see Aunt Elspeth smiling.

That evening, Aunt Elspeth and I chatted in the office while she was tidying up some paperwork. She told me what Penny had said as the two women had watched me walking towards Fernlea and up the outdoor stairs earlier in the afternoon. 'That girl's carriage is beautiful,' she'd said. 'She holds herself well.'

I could see that this had pleased my aunt but to me, although it was good to receive a compliment, it didn't seem so very important. I didn't have the wherewithal to understand why something that I felt was superficial should be so highly valued. I always went out fully made up but my make-up was a mask for me to hide behind. Maybe her attitude was a gender thing, like the difference in the standards of behaviour they would accept from Tim and the boys and what they expected from me.

There were other confidences shared that night. Aunt Elspeth confided in me about Lillian. According to Elspeth, the matron or first-in-charge who'd run the home immediately prior to her getting the post was a woman who had left under a cloud. Lillian, however, had apparently been friends with her. Aunt Elspeth told me that Lillian had expected to be promoted to first-in-charge herself, or so she'd heard.

Over more tea made by me, Elspeth elaborated on her gossiping, turning her vitriol to Lillian's personal life. She said she'd had suspicions about Lillian's choice of partner. 'She's not as pure as she makes out,' she said, grinning smugly. Privately, I wondered what business it was of mine. Elspeth then spoke about the staff member John and his troubled relationship with his mother. I'd guessed that something was going on there, as often the door to the office was closed when there was only John and Aunt Elspeth present. And John would often appear afterwards, visibly upset. Evelynn, another staff member, was also discussed, specifically that she was always 'putting it on a plate for Phil'. I don't think there was much that wasn't discussed that night about how Aunt Elspeth felt towards people. She talked about her own marriage, which was perfection, she said. She further stunned me by telling me she'd had a call from a 'lovely young man named Derek' – the boy I'd met at the assessment centre. He'd told her he wanted to come and see me, and this she was allowing.

Through these conversations, I knew I was being drawn deeper and deeper into her thrall. By favouring me as her confidante, she had left me unable to do anything to set myself free. She had saved me from the assessment centre. Now I was tightly bound in her web. She owned me, as she subtly reminded me by saying, 'It was lovely to get a cuddle from you.' She owned me, which meant few of the other home staff would want anything to do with me. In return for all her favours, I had to watch the staff and report back on anything that might be useful to her.

I found myself agreeing with everything she said, with her every opinion, but I went to my bed that evening feeling confused. She had uttered the words 'further rejection'. I vaguely remembered Hamish saying this, or somehow tied it into his ideology, and realised they must have spoken. She'd also waxed lyrical about Douglas Law and Penny Wheeler. She liked to impress these people and was impressed by them. I was just a means for her to gain approval. Not only did she choose to manipulate me to her own ends as a way of spying on her staff but she also saw that by mentoring me she could win approval from the people she admired most.

Before I went to bed, I watched her silver Charles Rennie Mackintosh pen scribble something on a piece of paper.

'Here. Take this,' she said. On the paper was a phone number. 'This is my home phone number. Use it next time something goes wrong here at Fernlea.'

My hand curled the phone number up and quickly hid it in my pocket.

'Contact me first,' she said without smiling.

I knew this meant any situations could be kept in-house. I also wanted to believe it meant that, if I was in trouble, she cared about me.

So, while I was useful to her, she would be good to me. How many facets were there to this relationship?

Upstairs that night, I lay on top of my covers and thought about my drunken mother singing her dreams and hopes to me, laying her disappointment at my feet. Why did this keep happening to me? I'd always been privy to the confidences of adults: from my mother to Aunt Helen, to staff members in the various homes I'd passed through, people poured out their feelings about their families, and their regard – or disregard – for their fellow workers, along with their views on all the tittle-tattle of work politics. Insignificant me, it seemed, was a fine person on whom to dump their misery. Misery knows misery, and I was in no position to challenge anyone. It must have felt safe to dump it on me. Who would believe the word of a rootless 15 year old that nobody cared for?

As I heard the children and then the staff move through the corridor making their preparations to go to bed, flushing toilets and switching off lights, I thought of how Aunt Elspeth had re-emphasised something she had said several times to me before. 'Never worry what people think of you; always have them worry about what you think of them,' she'd say, reinforcing her ethos by repeating what she'd led me to believe was a legitimate Latin phrase: *Nil Carborundum Illegitimi*. It was a fine phrase on which to strengthen a Spartan spine. I surely wouldn't let the bastards grind me down, though I think she'd made me even more confused that night about who 'they' were.

20

Using Your Loaf

So now I was in this precarious situation of being Aunt Elspeth's favourite. That was fine when she was there but whenever she was on holiday or off duty I was even more isolated from the rest of the staff. I felt that some more than others seemed to have scores they wanted to settle with me. In order to avoid them, I spent the time in my room. My sense of isolation increased as we rarely had access to television or to newspapers in the home, something I had had when I lived with my parents. I had always known what was going on in the news but now I felt completely cut off from the outside world. Phone calls at Fernlea were always supervised, too, and therefore calls were only allowed at a time that suited the staff.

Around this time, one of the boys in the home, Alex, began to take more of an interest in me. When I returned to Fernlea, he came to see how I was and over the next few weeks our friendship grew.

One evening, he came to my bedroom for a light. I was already in bed. I moved over and he sat on my bed, laughing, and then he put his arms around me and kissed me.

Next to me, Alex was Aunt Elspeth's favourite. Did this make me feel safer? Did the fact that I knew him, and him me, make it feel all right to grow so physically close? I have no idea, other than at the time it felt safer. Time spent with him was my refuge. I agreed to keep it secret, though.

I think it was Alex who suggested I go to his room, as mine was too close to the staff bedrooms and they would find us out. We would talk late into the night, murmuring so as not to disturb the children in the rooms on either side. At the weekends, he'd often go home. I had no idea what his life there was like. I just knew that at certain times, someone would be here to hold me. Someone wanted me. I missed that at weekends.

I think it was during the short time I'd been in the assessment centre that I met a girl called Alison. I'd known her at a distance, as she was a year below me at school. Alison was aggressive in her manner yet I liked her. She began to visit Fernlea around this time and I knew straight away that she was troubled. Anyone who finds a children's home more comforting than their own surely is.

She appeared at the front door and asked to speak to me one night when Lillian was on duty. I had already had a spat with Lillian that night, being told to wait till the boys returned from their home visits before she would open the food cupboard for supper, so I was sitting upstairs in my room, hungry but reading. I overheard the swing doors opening and then shutting again, so I peeked out of the window to see who was trying to visit and saw Alison leaving.

The fire stairs were just to the left of my bedroom door. I sneaked down them, my feet making no noise on the black rubber-tipped covering. I opened the fire door and whispered, 'Alison! Alison!'

She eventually heard me and followed me in, sneaking through the door. She quickly told me she'd been sent away. That irritated me. Why was Lillian like this towards me? I felt confused by the way she treated me, angry and hurt. It felt deliberate. Then there was the whole thing about being denied my supper till the boys came home. It pissed me off. To avoid confrontation, I'd slunk back to my room, knowing she was boss tonight and it was her rules. Now, however, I took Alison back upstairs to keep me company.

Suddenly, Lillian appeared at the door. From her pursed lips and her look of disgust, I knew I would once again lose the little pocket money I got. Upset that I had been stupid enough to play into her hands, I ran as soon as her back was turned, my heart too closed for tears. My reaction was immediate and as I ran down the street Alison followed me. Aunt Elspeth's phone number was going round and round in my head, so I ran in the direction of the nearest phone box and dialled it but the line rang and rang with no answer.

I didn't know what to do. I hung about the red phone box and tried again five minutes later. Peter, her husband, answered. Throat tight from swallowing my tears, I asked to speak to Aunt Elspeth.

'She's not here,' he replied.

I didn't know what to say. I wanted calming down. 'Can you tell her Eileen phoned?' I asked, with a false cheerfulness. It was dark and damp outside. With phone in hand, I watched Alison standing outside the phone box, smoking. Where was I going to go?

Alison told me she was babysitting that night and suggested I could go with her, to which I agreed. Not that I saw the children she was babysitting for. I waited outside, hidden, until the parents left, then Alison let me in. By then, the children were already settled in their beds.

Sitting in the flat, Alison began to tell me all about her family situation – the beatings, the alcohol. Alison's father had become known as 'Mickey the Knife'. Just that evening, she had had her head smashed by him. As with many other similar story swappings, I listened but didn't reveal too much about myself. I felt moved for other people and had empathy for them while I had none for myself. After all, I was bad and what had happened with Urquhart and my mother were my own fault. How could I reveal that?

Once again, reality dawned on me: I had nowhere to go, felt trapped in the place I had run to and didn't know what to do about it. Why had I not just slunk back up the stairs to my bedroom?

A knock came at the door. Alison answered and two boys entered the living room. She introduced them to me as Joe and Sam. It was clear she had been expecting them. They asked all about me, Joe chatting mainly about music and bands. Then, after a while, they left in Sam's Ford Escort car. Alison talked more about her life, as the children slept next door.

Time passed and I was becoming agitated about what I was going to do. I knew I was in big trouble now. Then there was another knock at the door. A quick look out of the window and we spied a police car. Based on my previous experience, this was real cause to panic. What to do now?

'Go in the kitchen,' whispered Alison, like an expert. 'Hide.'

I backed into a cupboard in the kitchen, lowering my head under the shelf and closing the door behind me. I could only hear muffled movement from inside the cupboard until a noise came closer. Someone had opened the kitchen door. Startled, I jerked back against the cupboard wall, banged my head on the shelf and a loaf fell on me.

The cupboard door opened. There in front of me stood a policeman and I had nowhere to run.

'Out you come,' was all he said.

Cagey, I moved from the cupboard into the kitchen and then into the living room of this small flat, trying to keep facing towards him so he couldn't grab me without warning. In the living room, the other officer was chatting with Alison. She looked relaxed and seemed to know them.

'OK, Eileen. Let's get you home,' one of them said. Very different from the other two officers who had taken me to the cells.

I looked at Alison, hoping my look would tell her I was afraid, and, yes, I could see from her eyes, she understood.

'She's not bad,' she told the officers. 'She just had a fall-out with the boss at the children's home.'

I found myself being escorted out of the flat, alone, and downstairs to the waiting police car. They held the door open for me. Resigned to whatever might happen, I slid into the back seat. The whole thing was my fault; I would get what was coming to me. There was no way of escaping it. Not two against one.

The officers got into the front.

The journey back home, for me, was strange. They were very nice to me, not asking probing questions, merely asking if I was OK. I was surprised as much as I was relieved to find the car pulling up outside Fernlea. I was so sure they were going to take me elsewhere. I hadn't even questioned where I was going, just accepting whatever would happen to me because I had no control over it.

The officer in the passenger seat got out and opened the car door for me. I was even suspicious of that, thinking it would get slammed on me as I attempted to put my foot out. But no. He indicated with a flick of his hand that I should walk on in front and lead the way. I waited to be struck from behind as I walked up the few stairs to the swing doors. The office light was on and I knew Lillian would be sitting with the china cups and the watercress sandwiches.

Still nothing untoward happened to me. I found myself standing at the door of the office as the thin Lillian came fuming out. Her eyes were blazing, her lips tightly pursed and I felt she was about to launch her usual at me, about how I was an 'immoral girl'. Here's where it'll all fall apart, I thought.

I was amazed when the police officer's voice behind me came over my shoulder saying, 'I think you should let her go to her bed.'

The expression on Lillian's face! I looked at her, then turned and stared straight at the policeman.

'On you go,' he said.

My eyes switched back to Lillian. She just looked at me. Confused, I bolted up the stairs. As I lay in bed, I tried to work out what had happened. Why did the officers behave the way they did? Was Alison going to be all right, or would she get another smashing? And Lillian, how was she going to react to all this tomorrow? Round and round it went.

I'd been right about the cups and sandwiches, too. I had spotted them through the door of the office. I was still hungry and I never got my supper that night. I stayed in my room till two the following afternoon, waiting for the staff changeover as I often did on a weekend or holiday. Lillian stayed away from me, too.

21

It's an Own Goal

The boys were all Glasgow Rangers football supporters. Whenever a big match was on television, they would gather in Alex's room, where there was a television that he was allowed to borrow from a staff bedroom. Though they were underage, they were even allowed a carry-out, so long as it was well hidden. Well, that's what I was led to believe. Smoking in Alex's room was also permitted for the length of the football match. It was as if the ethos amongst the staff was one of 'boys will be boys'. I and the other girls had to live by different rules. I was allowed in the kitchen as long as the cook wasn't there, to make food for the boys. That was definitely seen as a girl's role. My carriage, speech and conduct were all important, too.

One day, I decided to join the boys watching football; after all, I had been to many matches in my life with my dad and probably knew all the players and chants better than some of the boys. Earlier that year, my father had even taken me on a rare trip to go to the John Greig testimonial match in which Rangers played against the Scotland Select at Hampden. I vividly remember seeing John Greig riding round the park in a horse-drawn chariot after the match. The atmosphere in the stadium was celebratory, unlike the time I'd had to comfort my mother all night while she was drunk as we waited for news of my father after the Ibrox disaster. Sixty-six fans – men, one woman and children – had died on Stairway Thirteen when some of the crowd rushed back in to see a late goal. Hours later, after pub closing time, my father came home drunk and more concerned about losing the match than about our worry. He'd left the match early to avoid the crowds, as he felt the game was over.

Football had held an ambiguous place in my heart since the early days but I loved the atmosphere and wanted to be with the boys in Alex's room so I could once again feel part of that crowd during a good match. There was no girls' company for me in Fernlea, anyway. It was seen as me rebelling again but by being there with them to watch the football I got to be part of something that seemed valuable. It was in moments like these, lost in time and caught up in the moment, that I had a sense of belonging. Alex kissed me again, after the match and a few beers. It felt safe. It was Alex, it was in Fernlea and there were other people around.

Other good times when I felt I had a place were when I was allowed to have a voice, such as when I was with Hamish or when I was in the modern studies and English classes. Although I was growing ever more uncomfortable at school, I still felt that in these classes I could express my opinions on exploitation and prejudice, national and international. My nascent understanding of the world and the people in it was encouraged in these circumstances. It was perfectly valid for me to hold an opinion and my views were accepted for discussion.

My art classes also offered me a place where I felt valued. I enjoyed them and the teacher was very open to allowing me to explore different media. One afternoon, he asked me to do a piece of writing in poster form. In the time the lesson lasted, I wrote words in bright yellow colours entwined in flowers on a black background:

> One little child; One little hurt
> One little heart asking
> One little hope; one little love
> Not a little heart to be broken.

I wonder what my teacher felt, reading that. Sentimental teenage angst or genuine despair? I know how I would feel if I read this from a child. It saddens me now to remember this scene. My overwhelming feeling at the time was that the light in the tunnel was behind me rather than in front.

Aileen, an art classmate, asked me if I would like to go out dancing. Dancing! I was delighted and we chatted about it as we sat side by side in the classroom. She told me about a disco in Bellshill called the Charleston. It sounded great and I had images in my head of a building in dramatic 1920s decor.

You had to be 18 to get in, she said, but she had been before. Her parents had allowed her to go. I was amazed at this. It all sounded so normal and relaxed. I knew the staff at Fernlea would never let me go. Some of them might let their own children go but I was not one of their own. I had to be seen to be cared for following the letter of the law rather than parental discretion. However, the date was set, so I had to work out a way of obtaining permission.

Somehow I managed to convince the staff that I was going to an under-18s disco not far from Fernlea. It helped that John, the staff member, knew Aileen, who lived only a few houses away from him. She was from a good family, so I was allowed to go out with her. I wore my baby-blue dress and matching baby-blue metallic sandals, and left, teetering down Fernlea's front steps before floating into a waiting taxi, feeling excited and sophisticated.

Aileen and I and two others arrived at the Charleston in Bellshill. In my amazement at all the lights, and at the very fact of getting in past the scrutiny of the bouncers, the reality didn't register with me that instead of Art Deco sophistication the Charleston was housed in a concrete building with a garish neon sign and that it was packed with a clientele of underage girls. In search of elusive glamour, we ordered cocktails. I had only enough money for two but I could dance. Soon I was dancing away, when I was approached by an older boy named Rab, who made such a fuss of me that I danced with him all night. He bought me another drink, then another. Across the circling lights and sparkle of the dance floor, through the hubbub of the crowd and the music, I could see Aileen and the others dancing and mingling as the songs melded into one another: 'Do Ya Think I'm Sexy?', 'Take a Chance On Me' and even 'Three Times a Lady'.

As the night passed, I found myself outside, shocked by the chill after the heat of the dance hall. Rab lit my cigarette. We kissed, blathered and smoked some more. Then back in for another dance. When I decided I'd had enough and went to search out Aileen, she had gone.

I searched everywhere, pushing through people on the dance floor and peering into the groups of twos and threes in the seating area. I knew her father was coming to get us; surely she wouldn't go away without me? Frantic, I ran outside to see if she was outside waiting for me but I couldn't find her or her dad's car anywhere.

By now, the lights were coming on in the dance hall and the music had ended. In the harsh white glare, I searched again among the strained, painted faces. The lipstick and eye shadow were gaudy. The nightclub clothes were tacky in the stark overhead light. My ears rang after the amputation of the music.

Rab told me not to worry; he said he'd phone a taxi from his house and give me the taxi money. I didn't even have the money left to make a phone call. How could I afford a taxi any other way?

He assured me all would be well. He seemed capable and in control. He promised me he would give me the money, that he had it at home and I could catch a taxi from there.

He hailed us a taxi to take us to the village where he lived. I got in and began to retreat into myself. I watched all the streets we drove through – I'd never been in this part of Lanarkshire before. All I knew was that we were travelling in the opposite direction from the home. He folded his arm round my shoulder and pulled me in to his chest. In my mind, I told myself I'd just use the toilet then wait for the taxi at his house.

When we arrived, his 'house' turned out be a sparsely furnished flat, which he lived in by himself. As soon as his front door closed behind me, I visited the toilet. I sat on the toilet long after I used it and weighed up my situation, chewing on a fingernail. Aileen would be home, Fernlea would have been informed and the bad girl had fucked up again.

When I eventually came out of the toilet, Rab told me he couldn't get hold of a taxi. He said he'd get me one in the morning. Afraid, I just murmured, 'OK.' Again, I resigned myself to the situation, afraid to say how I felt, afraid of unspoken violence. Not a single person knew where I was. Play pleasant to stay alive, I told myself, *and get yourself out of this in the morning.*

I told him how tired I was, hopelessly hoping for understanding.

I didn't get it.

The inevitable happened. Rab showed me to the bedroom and left me to get into bed. The flat was cold. I shivered convulsively as I kicked off my shoes and climbed under the covers. Then he joined me. No amount of pretending I was asleep kept him from me. He had sex with me. It hurt. I dug my fingers in and I felt nothing but ugliness.

'You're a goer,' he told me. 'You love this.'

It was the first time I'd had sex since I was seven years old. Lying there as he slept, still in full clothing, baby-blue dress up around my waist, I stared at the ceiling. I'd got what I deserved. I was careless. A voice resonated in my head. 'That will teach you,' it kept saying.

Morning came. I hadn't slept. Rab woke up and could barely look at me, nor I at him. He went out to order me a taxi from a phone box; he'd even lied to me about having a phone. Incredibly, he asked me for my phone number. Incredibly, I gave him Fernlea's. I had no idea why, other than that he said that way I could return the taxi money to him. He didn't know that I lived in a children's home or that I was only 15. I left in the taxi.

I had no choice but to lift my chin, push my shoulders back, take a deep breath and walk through Fernlea's door. I stood at the entrance to the office, staring in at my aunt Elspeth, who had come on duty. The police had been called and Hamish had been informed but this time she had asked him not to come out.

I stared at Elspeth with emptiness flowing from me. Black holes I had for eyes. Had she spoken to me, I think I'd have burst into tears. Instead, she stared back into my eyes and held the contact. Could she read my desperation? Or did she not want to acknowledge or deal with the event? Eventually, she simply said to me to go to my bed. I did so. Lying there, not a tear was shed. I never wore that blue dress again. It seemed like a symbol of my folly, just like the second-hand blue dress I wore at my only birthday party. Who the hell did I think I was?

Two days later, the phone rang and Phil answered. He shouted on me to take the call, sneering as he handed the phone over. I heard Rab's voice on the other end and turned my back to Phil. Rab was inviting me over to his house.

I hung up without speaking and walked out of the door, avoiding Phil's gaze. It burnt my back as I left the office to run upstairs to my room.

I hardly left my room for a week. Very rarely did I miss school, which was a refuge for me, but I did that week. I told the staff I was ill. In the mornings, I could only just get out of bed to go to the toilet and then crawl back again. I couldn't bear to face people. My aunt Helen was out of bounds to me. I knew she'd be angry with me because I'd caused trouble again. Aileen wouldn't want me as a friend and her parents would certainly not want someone like me around.

What I didn't know at this time was that the staff at Fernlea were being criticised at review meetings about their behaviour, and in particular about the way their social and religious prejudices were being brought out in full view of others. Hamish, the city social worker whose yellow Citroën Diane I called the 'HamishMcCollmobile', instigated the review. Though of course it was valid and the right thing to do, I wonder now how their biases being aired and their privacy being breached affected them, and in turn how their resentment might have affected me.

Reflectively, as I saw my life careering out of control, I knew that I had no religion, when seemingly all around me did; they were certainly not flawless, yet were in positions where they could remain largely unscathed. Power and position, in the past and in the present. Pebbles and ripples. The cauldron of unconscious calamity boils.

Running low on sanitary towels one morning, I walked to the other side of the building to the toiletries cupboard on the off chance it had been left open for a delivery. I hated having to ask staff for toiletries such as towels, soap and toothpaste – especially the male staff. I found it embarrassing, especially if any of the boys were around.

The cupboard was locked and as I came, unusually, down the left-hand stairs, Aunt Elspeth appeared. I was startled, as I had almost been caught. From behind her back, she pulled my diary. I was right:

she had taken it. She went straight to the back page, where I had given innocent stars to boys I liked.

'What's this then?' she said, then with a knowing smirk, having clearly come to her own mistaken conclusions, she handed it back to me and walked away.

When things occurred like this in private, in secret, I would later find myself querying if they even happened. I had this hurdle to get over before I could even begin to question what they meant. Especially when I felt I had no one to tell about it. Even if I did confide in someone, I knew there would be a price to pay further down the line, so it seemed easier just to assume it was all my own fault. This was always the simplest solution and that confused mountain of self-loathing just piled up and weighed me down. I spent so much time trying to behave in different roles according to who was around, while living above myself like a disembodied me with a mind that remote-controlled and analysed the movements of my body. From this distance, I watched my back, I read signs, I anticipated the next move, so that when it came I'd know and I'd be ready. Yet ready to do what? Exhaustion and powerlessness dictated that I should run even though I knew it would cause me even more trouble in the long run. The alternative was that I accepted everything that was happening, diminishing my idea of my own self-worth as well as my place in the pecking order.

Later that afternoon, still in my room suffering from an unnamed sickness, I heard my aunt Elspeth coming up the stairs when all the children but me were out at school. I lay listening, stiff under the quilt, hoping she would bypass my room. She did. I heard her going from room to room. My curiosity got the better of me; I feigned a visit to the toilet. Once in the toilet, I timed my exit to coincide with one of the room doors opening. Aunt Elspeth was standing in the corridor holding a handful of porn magazines. She'd been raiding the boys' rooms while they were at school. We looked at each other, her small but bright rounded eyes challenging me from a head that tipped to the side. Say something, those eyes said. What are you going to do about it?

I said nothing and returned to my room. At the two o'clock staff changeover, I watched silently from my upstairs window as she got into her car, carrying a bag full of magazines. Years later, after she died, her son told me bitterly how she'd taken them home and thrown them at him as he lay in bed.

When I did go back to school, I was astonished to find that Aileen sat beside me in class and chatted away as if the whole Charleston event had been exciting. No explanation was given as to why she'd gone away without me, and I never asked. She further astounded me by telling me she had met a guy there whom she'd agreed to meet later to pose for photographs. It was clear they'd be nudes.

'Are they going to be published?' I asked, oblivious to the teacher at the front of the class and the whole class scribbling.

'Och, aye,' she said, 'but they're only for a magazine. They're just for the wee post-stamp pic on the corner.'

'What about your mum and dad?' I said.

She shrugged as if she thought they wouldn't mind.

Bewildered by her blasé attitude, I sat in that class asking myself repeatedly what was wrong with me. Everyone seemed to be able to do and say things without any consequences. She even came to see me again in Fernlea. John was on duty and he and Aileen chatted away. There was such an air of normality: they chatted about their parents, school, music and people they knew. Later, at my suggestion, he allowed us to bake in the kitchen. Affable John. 'Lock the doors and have fun,' he said.

That we did. Aprons on, we started off making flour mix. Aileen was fascinated by the large machine that sat on the kitchen counter. She'd never seen an automatic potato peeler before. John had opened the food cupboard so I could have access to anything we needed. Soon the metal baking trays were full. The ovens were on and natural chat came from our flour-covered faces. I couldn't have cared what we were making: the warmth and cosiness of what we were doing raised me up.

When we realised we had a large amount of surplus dough left over, one look at each other saw us erupting into a dough fight. It clung to doors and walls and fell to the floor. We laughed so loudly that eventually John knocked on the kitchen door. Aileen opened it for him; I stood in this demented, dough-strewn kitchen, my hands caked in dough, thinking, 'Oh-oh.'

He looked around, straight-faced at first then his eyes crinkled. He laughed out loud. 'Just remember to clean it up,' he said. He shook his head, still smiling, then left, closing the door behind him.

I had expected it to be so different. I had expected to be given a lecture about waste. As the door closed, John didn't need to give me that lecture; internally, I was giving it to myself. The magic had gone. I'd taken stock of what we'd blundered into and all the chaos around me was shouting 'wastage'.

I was growing up.

In late October, a holiday was arranged at the caravan in Ayr. John was taking some other children away and the house was riotous as the young ones who'd been chosen to go ran about asking what they'd need to take. In the office, after yet another anxious request from Harry about whether he'd need his fishing net or his plastic snorkelling tube or something, Aunt Elspeth suggested I should go, too.

Me? Getting away? I was excited by this. Didn't think I deserved it, especially as I'd had the school trip only months ago, during the summer. But Fernlea was short-staffed at the time and I would be a good assistant to John. As we left Fernlea, John and I in the front of his green Allegro and three kids in the back, the boot full of shopping, we waved frantically at the rest of Fernlea's motley crew and I felt like part of a real family.

John was a member of the Royal Society for the Protection of Birds. He chatted about it on the journey to the coast and all five of us sang. Arriving at Ayr, we all piled in to explore the caravan. It was beautiful – a big, clean, modern caravan – and we raced in and out of the rooms and toilets, high as kites. John and I sorted out all the shopping into cupboards and made up beds. The kids – Hugh and Harry, who were brothers, and another little boy – went off exploring. It felt like normality, domestic bliss. It was living. Happiness. No scrutiny, no files, no staff changes, no judgements, no faces of disgust or disappointment. Only my secrets to keep in check as always.

After we had unpacked and settled in, John and I cooked, cleaned up and wandered down to the caravan park's reception area with the kids. Attached to the reception desk there was a bar with a dance floor. We found a table and sat down. There were soft drinks for the kids but John bought me a beer. I was so pleased at this. The mood was light and we were all happy. I knew it might look like I was John's girlfriend and I enjoyed the fantasy of being part of a loving family unit. It was a safe fantasy, as the boyfriend–girlfriend relationship existed only in the minds of other people. I trusted John and felt there was no risk of a repeat of what had happened with Rab. There was no need for me to fulfil any other role, no expectation.

We decided a day out at the nearby swimming pool and ice rink in Irvine would be great. I had only ever been ice skating a few times and certainly wasn't adept at it. When our turn came in the queue to exchange our shoes for skates, they didn't have any left in John's size, so he had to sit it out and watch us from the spectators' gallery in the hope that a pair his size would be returned. As we sat putting on our skates, I noticed that Harry had disappeared. I laced up my skates quickly and clumped over to the ice to look for him. I couldn't believe my eyes. Harry had obviously never been skating. The sight before me was astonishing. There on the busy ice was Harry, jerking all over the place, National Health glasses perched on the tip of his nose, his adolescent buck teeth hanging onto his bottom lip and the laces from his skates trailing behind him like party streamers. I looked up, still agog, to John in the gallery. He was red-faced and doubled-up in hysterics at the sight below him. Many of the other people on the rink had joined in with John and were holding on to the side of the rink howling with hysterics and unable to skate.

Kids and teenagers were swishing round the ice between Harry and where I stood at the changing area. He couldn't hear me hollering at him, as the latest pop tunes were blaring out. There was no way I could push onto the ice, holding on to the other two, to catch up with Harry. Struggling to contain my laughter, I shouted and bawled at him till I got his attention then hauled him off the rink. Trying to ignore the sniggering all around, I pointed out to Harry that he hadn't done up his laces and that he had to or he might have an accident. He pushed his glasses up his nose and watched for an opportunity to dash back on the ice.

'Harry!' I said and pushed him onto the seat so we could do his laces up. I showed him how and he started to do one up. I did the other, my head down and body racked with suppressed hilarity. We were soon back on the ice. The rest of the session was spent, for me, belly laughing out loud till the tears came. Every time I looked up at John, he was howling with thigh-slapping laughter.

Harry's look was intent and he remained unconscious of the hullabaloo around him, his heart and soul put into staying upright and getting round the ice. On the way home, John and I tried not to look at each other for fear we might laugh again in front of him. We drove back to the caravan park, the journey punctuated with random outbursts of projectile laughter. Harry sat in the back with very little to say and my memory of him is of him pushing his glasses up his nose and having one of the gawkiest, most appealing grins. We had another day of swimming and it was set in stone on holiday that to look at Harry was to laugh.

On our last night at the caravan park, we all set off for the bar and entertainment centre. John and I positioned ourselves on the couch area against the wall, looking out across the dance floor. How different this was from the Charleston. The kids sat around on chairs or came and went from the games room to check in with us and slurp from their soft drinks. John and I chatted, winding down and taking stock of the week. Harry sat opposite us, swinging on his chair, grinning behind his glass and straw when we asked if he'd enjoyed himself.

Suddenly, his chair tipped over backwards and he went skating across the dance floor, the four legs of the upturned chair and Harry's two legs coming to a stop in the middle. His drink had been thrown over the table and all around us people were in hysterics. He had done it again. With John doubled-up, I got up to see that Harry was all right. I couldn't find the words for laughing. Harry was a bumbler – appealing, but a bumbler nonetheless – and his unconscious comedy act was one of many happy memories I have of that short holiday.

22

Insanity Intact

Our holiday over, we made our return to Fernlea. The break had done me good, storing up enough good times to keep me chirpy for several days. Principally, this was on the back of the Harry tales being recounted, which united everyone in laughter. Apart from that, life continued adrift at Fernlea. Daily staff changeovers and personal politics, holidays and illnesses all combined to keep me feeling unanchored.

Aunt Elspeth had her own story to tell. On her leg, she wore a bandage, girdled round her calf. She had apparently challenged the sheep shagger over something he had said. Aunt Elspeth just couldn't hide her dislike of this boy and it was clear to the staff and to the other kids. I wondered what had happened and she soon told me. In retaliation for her challenging him, a lamp had been 'thrown' from the hall table and it had caught Aunt Elspeth on the leg. In general, this boy was very moody and the way his eyes were always downcast only provoked more negative attention in this mainly male peer environment. For Aunt Elspeth, the icing on the cake of this confrontation came when Tim had said he was going to 'hammer him'. She basked in this perceived gallantry. The story was told many times, embellished in the repetitions until she was triumphantly able to add that even his social worker had threatened him.

According to the 'sheep shagger', the lamp had simply fallen from the table as he'd tried to get away from the nagging Aunt Elspeth. The patsy didn't stand a chance. The message from this episode was loud and clear to me: when you don't own an organ of your own, you have to be a good monkey to the organ grinder or there will be a price to pay. It was increasingly obvious to me how powerless I was in my life.

This was reinforced by the situation with my sister, about whom I constantly worried but whom I was powerless to protect. While I was at Fernlea, Cathleen continued to visit my aunt Helen's, which I was glad about. I wanted this for her: this level of security and family solidarity. I was always afraid an Urquhart would gain access to her and I felt this was one way to keep her safe. I loved her protectively and dearly but the rare opportunities we got to see each other weren't enough to alleviate my anxiety about her safety.

My feelings towards my aunt Helen remained confused. I loved her but Aunt Elspeth was the central female power in my life now. All my relationships seemed to operate separately from one other. I could never tell one camp what was happening in another. To me, this would have been carrying tales and would cause trouble. Also, I had learnt that other people tend to downplay any incidents you tell them about, too busy with their own lives. If you describe an incident when something bad happened to you, they tend to say, 'Oh, it can't have been that bad. You must be exaggerating.' Or even worse, 'Hell mend you. You must have deserved it.' It's always easier to blame a victim.

I didn't want to burden people with what was happening in my life and expect them to deal with it for me. Although Aunt Helen was aware of certain 'bad' things I had done, such as running away or staying out all night, it was generally other people who had told her. I tried for the most part to stay positive and happy in her presence, always listening to her and not reacting when she was angry. I was also afraid of revealing how I really felt about my life and experiences. Not that I was entirely sure of how I felt sometimes, as I'd kept my mouth shut for so long. Being so guarded and constantly playing a part means you are no longer able to give a natural response. You lose part of what you feel and of what you are.

I was also afraid that if I opened up my heart to my aunt Helen, spilling out all the filth that was rotting inside me, she would turn away from me, unable to cope or in disbelief, and this would lose Cathleen a relationship, too. I desperately wanted Cathleen to be safe, and even hoped that my aunt Helen would foster her, feeling it was too late for me. I can philosophise about it now but at the time this wasn't something I thought of calculatingly. I wanted a 'good family' for Cathleen, even though I knew I had ruined the chances for myself. Wanting this for my wee sister seemed the most natural, least devious thing for me to do.

When Aunt Elspeth asked if I had ever wanted to be fostered, I replied with a forced resounding no. I wouldn't admit to her or anyone else how much I wanted a family. She also started to take an interest in my past – the one before my recorded past. My genetic beginnings intrigued her. And I suppose, partly through talks with Hamish, she may have been attempting to help me 'come to terms' with who I was. However, she didn't know that the issues I had about my social and genetic background were only part of my present personality make-up. The 'social issues' that had affected me – from the lack of care from my adoptive parents, to the sexual and emotional predators who'd moved into the space my parents had vacated – were not something I discussed with anyone. These were my secrets and I thought I was protecting myself by keeping them hidden. Elspeth was scratching a surface that would, in the current environment, expose me to a salty wind.

My old friend Alison came back to see me. Her father had indeed given her a hammering that night she had been babysitting, not for anything she had done but merely because the police had been at the door. The main thing was not to get caught.

Alison was awkward in her gait and had a slight turn in her eye. Solid in stature – 'well at herself' – she was never afraid to confront anyone, male or female. By the end of October, she was talking about running away to London. I remember one evening on the cusp of darkness when we walked up one of the streets to the top and looked down at all the lights coming on over Lanarkshire. Beyond the valley with all its lights, the sky was blue-black; behind us, the blue of day had turned almost white. She asked if I wanted to go, too.

I was astounded. For me, even then, London was not a desirable destination: someone had done a good PR job on me about its evils. I knew the streets weren't paved with gold and that there weren't wonderful opportunities there. For me, all the difficulties I was experiencing in maintaining an ordinary, everyday life would only be magnified in London. I didn't know how to tell her that. I looked above me. In the sky directly overhead were waves of thin cloud on inky blue. Haphazardly scattered beneath them were puffs of glowing orange and red. I brought my eyes down to street level again. Where I was, things were shit but it was familiar shit.

'No,' I told her simply. 'No. There's no way I'm going to London.'

On one of the last evenings I saw her, she appeared outside the front door of the home in the car with Sam and Joe. I joined them and we drove round the back country roads, heading to East Kilbride. My mind was full of high hedges still bright with their late autumn hawthorn berries and rose hips, breaking into distant views and landscapes – escaping back to the bubble I lived in as a child in my back garden. We came to a stop beside a power sub-station built on the big plateau at the top of the hill between Hamilton and Limekilnburn and got out for a look. Even the half-human, tubular-style pylons that stalked through the fields fascinated me: large, grey, futuristic statues towering over the distant town of Hamilton. In my head, they were apocalyptic, androgynous guardians protecting the power supply.

My curiosity and imagination certainly made me drop my guard. Alison hadn't told me she was going to disappear with Joe; she just did. I didn't know what to do. I certainly wasn't going to walk about up there in the middle of nowhere by myself, especially with the sun beginning to go down, so I got into the car and sat in the back seat to wait for them, having a cigarette. Sam had gone over to the hedges to relieve himself and when he came back he slid in beside me. I didn't want him there. I wanted to wander about and chat. However, the script that was unfolding was by now becoming familiar to me. I could have kicked myself. I wasn't even attracted to Sam or impressed by his car. I thought it was easier to be friends with boys; I thought that they would know you weren't interested just by the fact you did not show any interest.

Had I been interested in either of them, it would certainly not have been Sam. It would have been Joe.

Again, I found a male upon me, kissing me and asking me to let him have sex with me. He asked in a way I found scary in its desperation. This time, I shouted, I wriggled and squirmed, I pushed away. He fumbled with his trousers then climaxed on my clothes. That was it, over. I wiped away the stain on a tissue found on the seat and threw it out of the window, hoping the staff at Fernlea wouldn't notice the smell off my clothes and the stain when I got home. I smoked another cigarette and stared out of the car window. Then we chatted like nothing had happened.

I was still alive. The power station no longer fascinated me: it was a dead monument of steel, colourless and cold, no longer possessing androgynous Amazonian qualities but a male witness to my shame. Joe and Alison reappeared and we drove back to Joe's house; it was an 'empty' – his parents weren't home.

Alison disappeared upstairs with Sam. Chatting with Joe, I felt agitated. I knew I'd have liked him. I didn't know that boys teamed up in order to split up. I didn't know about premeditation. Did Joe know about Sam? I hoped not. How naive I was. I made my excuses and left.

I walked home alone, grateful for once for my loneliness. And I was lonely. I had seen Hamish on only three occasions in five months. I never knew in advance if my father was going to come to see me and had to wait for his rare visits. Curled up on the floor of my bedroom on the hard-wearing industrial carpet that night, with the duvet wrapped round me, my pillow against the warm radiator, I began to read and recite *Othello*.

Aunt Nan passed by my room. I heard her stop outside my door. I paused in my recitation, holding my breath, and stared at the dark wooden door. She moved on. Later, having fulfilled a need and replaced an emotional memory with a disassociated event in my reading, I went downstairs. John asked me if I was OK. Aunt Nan had told him I was talking to myself. I explained that I'd just been reading out loud but then we were interrupted by Mary shouting. A beeping noise could be heard. My pillow had gone on fire. John and the other staff ran about in a frenzy to put the fire out. They accused me of smoking in my room.

After the fuss had died down, I returned to my room and lay on the bed. The window had been opened and the radiator was now discoloured with black streaks. The smell of smouldering foam still hung in the air. Aunt Elspeth had removed all the posters from my walls as a punishment. They had come free with the horror comics I collected and had been reminders of my collection of comics from home, which was now lost to me. I couldn't complain: I was accused of nearly burning the place down.

That night, Alex came to my room. In the silence, the kissing progressed. I gave in to it. We had sex. It was our first time.

The sex, for me, wasn't enjoyable – shame saw to that – but being held was. I needed to be held. The trade-off for a feeling of sanctuary was sex. I accepted this. Why did I feel I had no choice? With the usual teenage embarrassment and awkwardness, Alex and I carried on the next day as if nothing had happened.

Meanwhile, there were other pressures on me at Fernlea.

It was around this time that unknown people in a social work conference decided that my sister Cathleen should be moved to the home I was living in at Fernlea. It was thought that it would be of benefit to both her and me if we were able to restore our close family ties. Hamish phoned me to tell me she was to be transferred.

I was looking forward to her arrival, as I thought it would mean a respite from my anxiety over her welfare. I was always deeply afraid that I wouldn't be there to protect her from the evil people – the fabled bogeymen I knew from my own experience really existed. She was my responsibility, my sister. I hadn't managed to keep my mother alive. In my eyes, I had sat and allowed my mother to die in front of me. No amount of cooking, cleaning or sorting out the violence between my parents had fixed that. She had died as I watched her. If only I had been more responsive, she might still be alive. Now all that anxiety to protect was focused on my sister.

Cathleen arrived at Fernlea on 8 December 1978, just in time for Christmas. I thought that being able to watch her and have her close, as well as having my aunt and cousins around to visit, could only be a good thing. I rushed home from school to see her.

I ran into Fernlea. 'Where is she?' I asked the staff on duty, dropping my bag at the office door.

I dashed off to look for her. Excited, I beamed a smile at her. Not much had changed in her. She was still the same wee Cathleen. However, I detected coldness from her, a disconnection. Was she still angry with me for leaving her, for not being there? I didn't know but I felt guilty, as if I had let her down.

Not long after she arrived, Cathleen picked a fight with Tim – big blond Tim with the bad temper. Cathleen was always prone to picking fights. Even in primary school, when my mother was alive, she'd pick fights and come running to me to sort it out. Usually, I could resolve any of her disputes through the power of words. More than once, I'd refused to grass on my sister to my mother and had taken a beating for her, like the time when Cathleen had bought sweets with the money she'd been given to buy milk. Now she was living at Fernlea, she still expected me to sort out her fights. I'd been sitting in the spacious lounge, typing away on an old typewriter John had given me, when she ran in.

'Eileen,' she shouted. She was the closest to crying I'd seen her in her time there.

'What is it?'

'Tim's going to get me.'

I had to step in. I stood up and went through to see him, still holding the heavy typewriter. Cathleen, who was only eight or nine, ran away as soon as I went to confront him.

Up until that point, Tim and I had always got on well, so I tried to reason with him but he wasn't having it. I don't know what she'd done but she'd really riled him. Words quickly turned into an argument. I could see the rage colouring his face as his features became more and more twisted. I argued back. My sister might have done wrong but she was just a little girl.

Tim was a boy and he was much bigger. By now, his shouting was even louder. His voice blasted into me and I couldn't walk away from it.

I was stuck there, frozen like a deer caught in full-beam headlights. His rage was something he was beyond controlling.

I watched him surge forward towards me. In fear, at the last moment, I threw the typewriter at him. It hit him and then he hit me. His large fist smacked me right in the face. My nose went numb and down I went, only to rise immediately to another punch and more verbal rage.

By now, Phil had arrived and pulled Tim from me, his arms still rigid. The typewriter was upside down on the floor, with all its keys jangled. I caught my breath. The other kids were crowding the door or standing back against the wall, their faces registering the shock. 'Get up to your room!' Phil said to me.

The incident was put down as my fault initially, only to be sorted out later by Hamish. The staff reassessed the situation only to conclude that Cathleen was made from the same mould as me: manipulative and needing a 'good thrashing', as I later discovered during a covert reading of my files.

This 'same mould' and 'good thrashing' notion came, strangely, from my aunt Elspeth and I found it bizarre she would say that behind my back. I was only defending my sister.

Tim was never apportioned any of the blame. Again, in my innocence, I didn't understand the testosterone world. I didn't know that possibly the staff, and in particular Phil, were afraid of Tim. It never occurred to me that staff could be afraid of children. To me, I was powerless, insignificant, a project for them to use their training on. They held all the cards and could choose how to present a situation. They were the only ones whose word and prejudices could have any consequences. Any delusion I had been carrying about a thin veil of protection for me in Fernlea was shattered. I was still a young female vulnerable to violence and with no means of redress.

The incident with Cathleen and Tim had a ripple effect and the pebble that was dropped by the confrontation resulted in Cathleen packing a suitcase and fighting to get out through the front swing doors. As she was leaving, her case burst open and her teddy fell out. I rushed to the doors and picked up all that was left: the teddy.

I turned to see Aunt Elspeth sitting in the office, smiling. 'Let her go,' she said. 'See how far she gets.'

I was furious. Concerned, too. Hadn't I run away myself before? Look at what had happened to me, sleeping in toilets or under park bushes. And I'd been older than she was now.

Not heeding Aunt Elspeth, I dashed to the end of the road, looking for Cathleen. It was dark and the main road was long, like a tunnel with lights. She was nowhere to be seen.

Perhaps realising I wouldn't – couldn't – just let Cathleen go, Aunt Elspeth called the police but they weren't needed after all. Cathleen only made it yards down the road to a local shop in which Mrs Torrance, a neighbour of my aunt Helen, worked. Cathleen had gone into the shop, struggling with her bursting suitcase.

Eventually, she was persuaded to come home as quickly as she had left but she refused to speak to me, presumably because I'd inflamed the situation rather than resolving it. Once again, I was left feeling the failing had been mine: it was me who had let her down. This was always the case.

The other ripple from this incident occurred days later as I quietly wandered up the stairs to the bedrooms, reading from a book I was holding up. As I opened the top door to walk into the bedroom corridor, I sensed a tension. Then I heard a bang. I lowered the book, catching the door before it closed to prevent any sound, and listened. I could hear Tim shouting, 'I'm going to kill you.'

I rushed to his bedroom. Phil was holding Tim by the throat up against the wall.

'Go on – hit me,' Tim was saying.

Phil was red with rage and had his fist in the air. He saw me and dropped it.

I ran downstairs, thinking all the time, what do I do, grass? I'd grassed on him the time he'd hit Diana. The repercussions for me and for Diana had been serious: I'd come under suspicion for having stolen Lillian's watch and it was discovered in poor Diana's wardrobe. He shouldn't have hit her but when I told on him I'd suffered and felt guilty about it. Either way, I couldn't win.

Now, I feared Phil more. I waited for a payback that I knew would come. Yet for a while nothing more was said or brought to my attention. Tim and I spoke and he acted as if he'd forgotten all about the incident between him and me, as well as the one with Phil. But I was even more wary.

Despite this friction, my relationship with third-in-charge, John, remained intact. When he was on a sleepover, he slept in the next room to me. Sometimes I would sit at the bottom of his bed and chat. I thought we got on well together and had shared happy times on holiday at the caravan, too. One day, he asked me if I wanted to go and see The Stranglers in concert in Glasgow and I jumped up and down on his bed as he lay there. The time came and we went. Once again I was a normal teenage girl enjoying normal teenage pursuits. As far as the crowd around me were concerned, I could have been anyone, had any background of my choosing.

I thoroughly enjoyed the concert. I think the white-clad Devo supported them. Either that or some boy in a white straitjacket fuelled by an adrenalin rush fell over the balcony at the wrong concert. I was mesmerised by the whole event, sitting up on the balcony, looking around at the crowd almost as much as at the bands. Miraculously, the boy in the straitjacket gave a wave and appeared to be all right. A big cheer went up when everyone realised he wasn't harmed.

I became entranced by Jean-Jacques Burnel in his shiny PVCs and Doc Martens. My dress code by now had regressed and there was no place for a dress of baby-blue. Androgynous and aggressive was the image I thought would protect me and help me express myself.

23

Lessons Lost

Hogmanay and Christmases couldn't pass fast enough since my mother died. These anniversaries were always a reminder of what had been. For a present in the home that year, I got to choose something from a selection that the local Celtic supporters' club had donated. I chose a toiletries set. My father, being a Rangers man, certainly would not have been pleased but I don't remember seeing him over Christmas.

Even if I didn't really want the chestnuts-round-the-fire scenario I daydreamed about, a home, instead of constant uncertainty, was something I did want. Like Mother's Day and birthdays, Christmas was a topic of conversation I could never become involved in with classmates, friends, staff or even my family. I couldn't get into the spirit of things either. On the fringes, always listening in, all I could do was accept my situation, knowing my stories were hardly full of festive cheer and nothing could change that. My classmates at school and the staff in the home were all buzzing about what they had bought for their families and what their own children had asked for, what they were doing for Christmas, what parties they were going to. The only place at which I felt part of the festivities for a short while was my aunt Helen's. It embarrassed me, though, that I had no money to buy the family gifts and I felt that badly. Cathleen was too young to understand this. Anyway, for her I was cheery and she appeared to enjoy her time there,

at the heart of all the excitement. I felt grateful there was a wee plac
for us.

New Year came and the nation seemed to be celebrating somethin
joyful and good. For me, New Year was a dead mother in a chair tha
nobody remembered and not having a place where I belonged. I di
enjoy the singing and the build-up of expectation. I was desperate t
believe in the redemptive power of the New Year but I wasn't naïv
enough to trust that 'ringing out the old and bringing in the new
would somehow change the way I felt about myself and my life. Th
thin light of the early January days proved it never did. The few week
after Christmas and New Year were always difficult, having to avoi
conversations about what I got for Christmas and where I went to se
the Bells in. I don't ever remember feeling jealous of what the other kid
at school got from their parents; I just felt shame, somehow, and sadnes
that always pained me physically.

This year, however, I wouldn't have to face that problem. Why
chose to leave school at Christmas of 1978 is still a mystery to m
With nothing written about it in my social work case files, and with n
family around who could tell me, I never will have an answer to tha
Why would I leave when it was a haven, an escape, somewhere I coul
lose myself in the lessons? I don't even know if it was me who made th
choice independently. All I remember is that I was ashamed that th
school knew about some of the events that had happened over the las
few months. My depression (though I didn't recognise it as such) wa
getting worse, too, and I could barely concentrate in class. I left schoo
at Christmas and didn't go back. Now I was at Fernlea every minute o
the day.

The internal politics at the home persisted and my nightmares, fea
and depression continued. In my mind, I was walking around witl
a huge stamp on me that was becoming more and more visible. Th
secrets I was keeping felt like they couldn't be contained. I was th
whore my mother said I was. My secret night-time liaisons with Ale
were proof of that and although I felt that way about them, I could no
resist the comfort they brought me. I knew I was going behind the staff
back. And some of the staff thought badly of me, too, remembering th

overnight I'd had after the Charleston disco. They didn't know the half of it. Why could I not stop?

My future looked and actually was uncertain. In February I'd be 16, and at 16 I was of an age where I'd have to leave Fernlea. The care the staff were obliged to give me there was officially approaching an end.

By now I was of the mindset that wherever I went, I would be the same person – not good and not worthy. My anxiety was increasing. I hid my hands when I met anyone to prevent them from seeing my nails, which were bitten to the quick. I painted them with special lacquer then scraped it off so I could bite them again. Home had been bad, with my mother and father, and the children's-home situations I'd been in had been bad, too, but I knew the outside world had unrestrained people like Urquhart and without the precarious protection of Fernlea I feared being exposed to and becoming the prey of other dubious people. I was convinced I would be killed.

I woke to nightmares three and four times a week. I'd lie on my back in bed with a poetry book or try to hum myself to sleep, remembering all the other rooms I'd slept in and the particular pattern of shadows cast over their walls. I'd listen to the staff members settling to sleep, and the creaks and snores of the night, and drift off eventually into the elusive comfort of sleep only to wake abruptly with the tension still in my body from a nightmare.

I couldn't stop bathing every night. A comforting hot bath and scrub with soap always felt cleansing, although, with a quick succession of children waiting to use the bathroom, it was hardly relaxing. After this, Alex and I snuggled up in his room on an increasingly regular basis. He would never come to mine. He would tell me of his family, his brothers and sister, but I never gave my secrets away, preferring to listen. Hearing him talk made me feel the same way I felt when I obsessively looked through other people's photo albums, as if I could own part of a life just by seeing and hearing about it. I was trying to steal memories. Connections. I was people-watching not just to pass the time but looking for someone who had my eyes, my nose: anything to signify that I wasn't alone.

Another strange, and in retrospect sad, behaviour that I was

compelled to engage in for most of my young adult life, was to as
more intently than you normally would who people were, where the
came from, where they had lived – always trying to find some commo
ground, as we all do, particularly as youngsters. However, rather tha
being nosy, I was really looking for a connection to my past. Someon
might know something from my past, someone good, or I'd be tryin
to detect if they were in Urquhart's bracket. Maybe they might kno
someone I remembered. It was my attempt at keeping my past alive
less transient, something solid that would anchor me. Another thing
would do was read the local paper – the deaths, births and marriage
page – looking for more than an emotion, looking for how, maybe
my mother's intimation would have read. Craving for the event I ha
missed out on, looking for evidence as to how it might have been, I wa
always struck by how unemotional I would feel, only now and the
shedding a few tears as I wallowed through the sad verses. I was lookin
for my own hidden, lost grief. Hoping for comfort that would explai
how and why I felt the way I did.

It was Friday, 23 February 1979, the night before my 16th birthday. I'
had a bath and got into my nightdress, ready for bed. It was getting late
Phil and Patricia were the staff on duty, with John due to come in at 1
p.m. for a sleepover shift. Patricia, long-haired and large, sat downstair
in the office on her own and must have agreed that Phil could slip awa
to the nearby pub.

With all the children asleep, silence filled the hallway upstairs. A
I left the bathroom, Alex gave me the nod through from his bedroom
door. We'd both overheard Phil sneaking through the swing doors. W
took our chance. Absorbed in each other and unconscious of the time
we didn't hear Alex's bedroom door open. Something made me look
up from the side of the bed. There stood Phil. Time literally froze an
framed the look of horror on his face. I looked back, helpless, waitin
for what was going to happen next. Anything Phil would decide to d
was beyond my power. So I continued looking at him, wide-eyed an
pleading, unable to break my gaze.

When he got over the shock, he ran along the corridor and downstairs shouting 'Oh, my God!' over and over again. Alex and I were left looking at each other, not knowing how to deal with the situation. Two skinny adolescents, we pulled away from each other in the shock. I tugged my nightie down and sensed Alex becoming remote. I knew I was on my own and it was every man for himself. Through the fearful silence of the room, we could hear a human buzz downstairs, a buzz almost of excitement.

My memory is a blank as to how the subsequent events unfolded. The next thing I remember is sitting in the local police station, fully clothed, with my nightdress in a plastic bag clutched on my lap. I was on a chair that was pushed tight against a wall, in a small room with Patricia, who didn't speak to me. Her long blonde hair hung over her shoulders, her large thighs spread out over the space of her chair, and she was wearing those Hush Puppy shoes only certain types of people wore. I could sense a certain suppressed excitement in her, almost like triumph. It was the drama she was enjoying.

She didn't speak to me but she engaged happily enough with any officers who popped in and out. Nobody spoke to me. Above her head on the wall was a large round clock with black numbers and hands. By now it was almost midnight. I watched those hands ticking the time down. At midnight, I would be sweet 16.

The door opened again and a police officer told me to follow him. He showed me into a second room. This one was clinical. Inside was a high bench-bed. A female officer spoke to me then, though I can't remember what she said.

Soon, a police doctor arrived in the room. He told me to lie on the bed and remove my clothes. There was no curtain. The doctor didn't turn his back as I undressed. Compliant, I did so without a word. The doctor stood beside me, told me to bend my knees and let them fall outwards. Now would be a good time to disappear, I was thinking. Wishing. Again, a part of me surrendered. I slowed my breathing down and fixated on the ceiling as he proceeded to examine me. If my eyes had had lasers, they'd have bored holes into those tiles on the ceiling. I had no magic flower on my tummy to rub to disappear, no shoes to click three times. I lay there, half-naked, open-legged in the company of strangers. Once again, I was powerless. My body was entered clinically and coldly. Shame burnt at the very epicentre of me. Stoic in disgrace, my humiliation was complete. My body was available and legally accessible to all. And nobody cared or loved me enough to protect me.

My mind played silent stills of my aunt, my father, Urquhart, my aunt Elspeth, Hamish and the other staff at Fernlea. I would rather have received a beating, kicked and battered against the cold wet slabs of the police cell floor. At least I would have felt that.

The police took my nightclothes away in the plastic bags. Evidence of my humiliation and disgrace, they'd be tested for semen stains. I heard Patricia being told this. In the silent darkness of the wee small hours, I returned home to Fernlea, broken and empty. I was glad no one spoke to me, for I could barely contain the tears I always needed to keep imprisoned. I couldn't break down, couldn't allow myself. With all I had left, I had to force myself to stay strong. *Nil carborundum illegitimi.* This time I was surely beaten and ground down. I couldn't bear to phone Aunt Elspeth. With that great nothingness in my heart, I walked up the stairs, exhausted, and into my bedroom, pulled back the covers and got into bed. I left the curtains open. What was the point of shutting them? I had nothing left to conceal. No ability to care any more.

My bedroom door pushed open. It was morning.

Hidden under the quilt, I waited, pretending I was asleep though my eyes had sprung open. My fingernails were bleeding and throbbing from having bitten them but I lay still, staring into the underside of my quilt and playing dead, waiting to see what I was going to have to face, my breathing almost non-existent.

A voice whispered my name.

'Eileen.'

It was John.

I felt him kneel down beside my bed, near my head.

His voice was intimate, gentle and wavering.

I couldn't come from out of the covers, afraid of his emotion. I would break my resolve.

Again, he whispered, 'Eileen.'

I felt his hand on my head with the quilt cover between us. Slowly the quilt peeled back to reveal my face. Our eyes locked: there's no place for hooded looks when you're stripped of your dignity.

The pain in John's eyes was too much for me to bear. He whispered, 'Happy birthday, Eileen,' and handed me a wrapped box.

I took the box in my hand and slid it under the pillow. Tears surged into my eyes, so I turned and buried my face in the pillow, too. The pain hurt my throat, my stomach, my chest and my head. All that pain caused by training myself to keep everything held tightly inside, never allowing any tears to escape.

John's arms went round me. I reached my arm up behind me with my face still in the pillow and put it round John's neck. Somehow I knew that he needed comfort, too. As third-in-charge, he had not taken control of the situation, either morally or professionally. He must have felt he'd let me down. No words were exchanged between us about what had happened. Just the unspoken acknowledgement of awfulness hung between us. He left me with my 16th birthday present still wrapped up under the pillow. I don't even remember what it was.

In contrast to John's response, the silence I was met with from the other members of staff over the next few days forced me to confine myself to my room.

Hamish had obviously been informed and soon came to see me. We sat in the visitors' room; I waited, stoically faced, for the event to be mentioned. Gently, he said to me, 'Eileen, there are many ways you can lose your virginity. Horse riding, for example.'

I stared down at a fixed point on the carpet in front of me. I knew, then, he was giving me a get-out-of-jail-free card but what he didn't know was that I had not been a virgin since I was seven. Like John, he felt for me and was trying to give me some dignity back. I wanted to cry again but swallowed back the tears. I had invented a private name for their kind of kindness and I used it in a poem I wrote. 'Kalashnikov Kindness,' I called it. An angry punch to the jaw I could bear but a gentle word or hand on my shoulder was dangerous. That might break my glassy resolve of 'nothing in and nothing out'. *Virgo intacta*? Certainly not. But everyone's insanity remained intact.

24

Lack of Hunger

Just as I'd defended my father when the police found the knife after my mother died, so now I found myself defending Alex. The virginity test came back proving that I was no virgin. Enduring that and the sham statutory rape inquiry that was inflicted on us both brought enough shame. As a child, I had played and explored with my peers: typical, innocent games of 'doctors and nurses' and 'wee houses'. Wrapped in the comfort of my quilt in my room at Fernlea, the past came back to me in random scenes. I recalled the games I'd played with May's son Allen. Memories filtered through my thoughts and I allowed myself to smell the grass, imagining the whistles and cricks of starlings beyond the blanket-tent flap. Looking in my eyes in the mirror, I'd wondered back then if 'shagging' would make me a woman. How I wished for that innocence. I remembered my mother's castigation of me over Urquhart, and thought of the way he and Rab had claimed I had 'wanted it'. Now where was I? Fully contaminated.

I knew that in the eyes of some of the staff I was seen as the Lolita character, liable to ruin a man's reputation for life. I could contaminate others. Interestingly, it was mostly the women that saw me this way. Yet to me, I was the exact opposite: all I'd wanted was to feel safe and to know the comfort of being held. Sex with Alex had been the trade-off I'd accepted in order to obtain that. It had been only hours before my 16th birthday yet I'd been vilified for it. My need to be held had resulted in the instigation of a police investigation because Alex had had sex with an underage girl – contaminated jailbait. I couldn't possibly endure a court case, so I did what I could to avoid it for both of us. Yet it would not be long before the events of that night would have an even bigger impact on my life.

Soon enough, Alex had to face a court case of his own. His weekend activities had caught up with him and he was placed on remand in a Young Offenders Institution. I accompanied Aunt Elspeth to visit him at her request. As I thought I was in love with him, it was a chance I jumped at.

A grey steel fence topped with barbed wire surrounded the remand unit, calling to mind a metal moat round a fortress. My hand clutched my stomach as we passed through the security gate, and I was frightened of a body search. As Aunt Elspeth and I sat across the divided table from Alex, my hand rose to my stomach again. This place was awful. Crowded by the people at the tables round about me, I felt awful. My tension was, I imagined, replicated at the other tables. We couldn't say what we wanted to. As Aunt Elspeth and I left, I gave a backward glance towards him. We couldn't speak of our secret, as we had done in snatched conversations back at the home before his imprisonment. What needed to be discussed remained unsaid because of the lack of privacy.

Aunt Elspeth didn't have too much to say to me about all these recent events, other than to tell me there was a certain amount of gleefulness, as I suspected, among certain members of staff. They had been proved right about me. However, as we sat in a heavy awkwardness in the office, she expanded on this by saying that when Lillian had been gloating, Aunt Elspeth had taken her aside, closed the office door and chastised her for judging a child. As she told me this, I listened straight-faced. I wanted to hear this but I knew I was being drawn further into my aunt Elspeth's web. As I looked at her stiff curls, her cream silk blouse yoked with tiny perfect pearls and her impenetrable front, I reflected on my own privacy, which felt violated. Sad, I wished I still possessed at least the public façade that I'd previously been able to hide behind.

She followed up with her *pièce de résistance*.

'What kind of example,' she told me she'd asked Lillian, 'do you believe you set the girl yourself?'

In my mind's eye, I can still see her at her matronly best, delivering this in triumph. How long she must have waited to shoot this ball from her cannon. Now I understood why she had always been gunning for Lillian. 'Don't think I don't know how you allowed your fiancé to arrive at Fernlea – don't deny it – on two occasions, late at night and the worse for drink!'

The prim, pristine persona of a pinched Lillian was visibly shaken, or so Aunt Elspeth told me. For Lillian and Aunt Elspeth, this kind of behaviour was not the done thing. A whiff of scandal about their virtue amounted to social suicide. Churches would need to be avoided, lunches, women's guild groups cast aside.

Aunt Elspeth had obviously been biding her time to bestow this acquired knowledge on Lillian. She relished being able to stick some dirt on her and it must have been particularly good that she had my misfortune to use as a platform to strike from. The delicious double whammy of the poor misfortunate child from the impoverished background set against the hypocrisy of the pious. I thought then that the acquired knowledge might have been extracted from John.

In my imagination, I could visualise Aunt Elspeth, tall and solid in stature, gloating over Lillian, whose small lips would have been tight and pursed as her own cause for shame was exposed.

But where did that leave me? This was not the kind of information you thank someone for, and I was exposed as the platform from which the opportunity to deliver it had arisen. However, it did, if only temporarily, make me feel better. Even my misery was used.

As I was leaving to go back to my room Aunt Elspeth told me a story that revealed something of her own pathos. She had been out on a date with Peter before he became her husband. She was a young woman in the '50s and the date took place when her parents were away on holiday, so her brother was supposed to accompany her home. However, when her brother failed to turn up as arranged, Peter had taken her home in his car. Though she'd sat in the back of the car on her own while Peter drove, her brother had informed her parents that she had been alone with Peter in the car.

I could see the cold anger as she told me. It was slight but the tremor in her voice was unmistakable. This, she was telling me, was her shaming, by way of her virtue being brought into question. She never spoke to her brother again. This story is one she told me many times, including one occasion shortly before her death, many years later. It had stayed with her. Though I didn't grasp this situation fully as an adolescent, I recognised that she had transferred some of her anger and shame onto Lillian. It was only later on in life that I understood: the virtuous woman needs the demonised bad girl so she can maintain her moral high ground.

Though Hamish had been gentle and pragmatic with me, I learnt later that he went into full swing, all guns blazing, at the staffing response and their behaviour in the aftermath of Phil catching Alex and me in bed together. All actions and agendas were questioned again. Phil was hauled over the coals for being unprofessional in leaving his job to go to the pub and in the level of his response to the situation. While it may have been the right thing for a social worker to do to protect a child whose well-being he was responsible for, his actions worried me all the more. Hamish didn't have to live with these people. The only possible outcome for me was being on the receiving end of even more resentment.

By now, all pretence of communication between certain staff members and myself was gone. I began to sleep even more and stay in my room. Nausea and exhaustion would often overcome me. My books allowed me some escape. Other than that, I was trapped.

Receiving a deferred sentence, Alex left the Young Offenders Institution after about three months and started working. He was back living at Fernlea and changes were being made in his life. He hadn't seen his mother for years but now she was in touch and he was planning a visit down to London to see her. Though he tried to reassure me that he wasn't going to abandon me, I suspected that something more permanent was on the cards and so I started to prepare myself for the possibility that I might end up on my own again. Aunt Elspeth commented on this renewed contact by saying that his mother only wanted him now he could earn money.

The Fernlea staff never spoke openly about that night but it was surely good meat for a gossip sandwich. As for Alex and me, within the confines of Fernlea our physical relationship was over. However, we did still talk in confidence and he continued to make promises to me about the future. As for Tim, his reaction to the event on my birthday was strange: he asked me if I was all right but seemed angry at Alex. I found that curious, considering that on the surface they were comrades.

So my loneliness engulfed me and I didn't seem to have the power to do anything about it. I resigned myself to it. At breakfast or meal times, when I was obliged to leave my room, any communication I had with staff I carried out just going through the motions till I could go back to my room.

One evening, John attempted to instigate something with the children in the home, maybe partly to revive something that had been lost or to alleviate some guilt in him as well as me. A midnight drive was suggested for us older ones. Off we all went in his green Allegro car to the Fenwick moors. Alex, Tim, Stephen and I all piled into the car and for the duration all was well. We drove through the darkness, excited; the expanse and wilderness of the moors was welcoming. Through the little village of Jackton we went, stomachs left behind over the hillocks. Fully laden, the car struggled up Eaglesham's quaint main street, the dark branches of tall trees on the common green meshing with the black clouds. Gaining the top of the road, the car followed the sharp bend to the left and the moor dipped and stretched, featureless in front of us. John pulled up on the verge, judging by full-beam headlights the distance between roadside and ditch.

All out, we wandered about the moors, free and laughing in the moonlight, the boys all competing to be the funniest. Loving male company in this environment where I could be accepted as one of the gang, with no sexual threat, for a while I was happy. I even raised a laugh by having to disappear to go for a pee, only to catch my trousers on barbed wire and nearly fall on my face, toppling over the fence. There was no one to hound me here, no one to spy on me and take back tales. The only other creatures who were privy to our liberty that night were the sheep, whose distant baaing couldn't threaten us.

As we began our return to Fernlea, the invigorating sense of freedom started to evaporate. After eating a late supper, I returned to bed. As the bedroom door shut behind me, that ever-lurking feeling of depression – the sense that I was trapped in something I could not get out of, something I didn't understand – settled back onto me. Never having been diagnosed with depression, I didn't know what it looked like, far less how it felt. My problem, I believed, was that I was valueless, like something people scraped off their shoe.

As arranged, Alex went for a trial visit down to his mother's. I felt fear and sadness as he left but accepted it and said nothing.

As ever, plans were being made for me and discussed without my consultation or knowledge. I felt vulnerable. Where would I go now I was 16? I asked Hamish if I could stay at Fernlea, near Cathleen. He couldn't make any promises but he said he would see what he could do. I didn't have the emotional energy to move somewhere else. I had secrets to keep. Even more now. I spoke to Hamish, John and Aunt Elspeth about going to college. I wanted to do art and English. An appointment was made for me to go along to Motherwell College and a few job interviews were suggested to me. I agreed to all of this but in my heart I was again just going through the motions, buying time and stalling.

Out of the blue, John asked me if I wanted to go to the Apollo – the legendary venue in Glasgow where bands would kick-start their national and international tours. He'd bought me a ticket to see the punk group The Jam. John's friend and his girlfriend were going and John was his usual hyper-excited self about it. I sparked up a bit at the thought of it; I knew I would enjoy this.

'Yes,' I said and we grinned in complicity with each other.

The day of the gig arrived. It was teatime and thoughts on what to wear, plus what make-up to brighten myself up with, rattled about my head. I had to make a good impression – had to fit in with the crowd in terms of style but show myself off to best advantage, too. I hadn't thought that way for ages and I was happy for my mind to be occupied this way. I'd been spending more and more of my time in nightclothes, eating and not wearing make-up. I remember struggling to get into my jeans.

Teatime arrived and I was prompt so I would be ready to leave on time. I sat down to eat but, being excited, I could hardly swallow my food. John arrived, bouncing through the swing doors, and popped into the office for a quick chat with the staff. The food was being passed from the kitchen through the hatch into the dining room. As I sat next to the head of the long dining table, I went about the usual business of passing the plates down to the younger children first. The older boys were out with, apparently, no questions asked and no member of staff was at the table. I could hear John buzzing about outside the dining room. His enthusiasm rubbed off on me and got me even more excited about the night. I was simply and deliciously happy. After all the cleared dinner plates were passed back up the table in reverse, I handed all the pudding plates for the next course down to the children but I really didn't want any for myself. I dished tapioca into all the children's bowls then stated that I was ready to go and didn't want any pudding. What I heard next pulled the plug abruptly from my heart and all my happiness drained away.

'You're going nowhere till you finish that pudding,' the cook said.

I felt disbelief. This had never happened before. I looked at her, with her head stuck through the serving hatch, her cheeks flushed from the heat of cooking.

'What?' I said, aware that the children beside me had stopped talking.

'I said, "You're not going anywhere till you've finished that pudding."'

Initially, I thought she was teasing me. I kept expecting her to burst into laughter but she was deadly serious. I glanced down at some of the other children, who looked as stunned at the sudden inflexibility as me. Then I understood: this cook was on very friendly terms with Lillian and Phil.

John stood at the dining-room door, hidden from the cook, looking at me and then pleading with me to eat my pudding.

'Here,' the cook said and held out a bowl of gloopy white stuff.

I didn't take it.

The tapioca was placed in front of me by one of the younger children. My eyes went from the bowl in front of me, to the cook, then to John. Surely, I thought, John as third-in-charge will step in and overrule the cook? Surely he knew what this was all about?

He didn't. Hands together behind the door, he begged me to comply.

Whereas before, in other children's homes, I had hidden food up my sleeves if I couldn't eat it, here I had no hiding place. All the young children were watching, as was the cook. Anyway, tapioca wasn't like liver: you could hardly keep it hidden up a sleeve. For me, it was now no longer the fact that I couldn't stand the slimy feel and taste of the tapioca that bothered me. Instead, it was the fact that, even though she wasn't a member of the child-care team, this particular cook had the power, coupled with a malicious agenda, to decide whether I deserved to go out or not and her decision was overruling any that could have been made by John. Lillian, meanwhile, sat in the office and said nothing. This was another message to me. My life didn't belong to me, just as I felt my body didn't. There was no respect for me left. Had there ever been any?

I pushed the bowl away, all happiness gone; I'd been bullied into a corner. I stood up, pushed my chair away, walked past John without looking at him, shoulders back, and returned to my bedroom. There was no rising of emotion from within, as I had felt when my mother broke more than the sweeping brush over my back; no desire to challenge another, as I'd felt when Cathleen was being attacked. That surge didn't come. Instead, taking off my clothes and getting back into my nightwear, I felt almost nothing. All I wanted was to go to sleep.

John came to my room. He asked me to change my mind and I said I couldn't. It never crossed my mind to say to him that, as he was third-in-charge, he could have overruled the cook. This wasn't a typical thing. This was new territory: an unprecedented attack. Anyway, I suspect I felt too embarrassed for him and I was afraid that if I'd pointed it out to him it might anger him or damage our relationship further. One thing's for certain. That evening, my appetite for everything was gone.

25

Another One Bites the Dust

Perhaps as a result of Hamish's chastisement of the staff at Fernlea for their treatment of me after Alex and I were caught, and in a move to give me greater understanding of what had led to my life being the way it was, Aunt Elspeth made an appointment for me to investigate my genetic past. After all, I had turned 16 and she must have thought it would be a good time for me to see my adoption papers and original birth certificate.

I was curious. The secret dreams of a magical life that I'd harboured as a child were stirred up again, not in such a fantastical fashion this time but nonetheless I did want to know. Elspeth looked into it and discovered that my papers were kept at Glasgow Sheriff Court. She decided that she herself would take me, her curiosity obviously aroused.

I agreed initially and then changed my mind. It was too scary for me – the prospect of finding my roots and possibly a family. It was what I longed for most but what family would want what I was and what I was hiding?

Mulling over the circumstances of my birth and adoption added to the turmoil I was already feeling, instead of relieving it. So the subject was dropped and I returned to business as usual: lying in my bed all morning and hardly coming downstairs so I could avoid the Fernlea staff wherever possible. Cathleen was the only one I kept close to, feeling the bond with her every bit as strong as before.

As my undiagnosed depression continued, my life, my will and my self-respect diminished. I suppose I can understand to a certain degree the dynamics that were causing the staff to feel such frustration towards me. As always, though, this frustration was never discussed with me; it was revealed by their assessment that I was lazy, surly and uncooperative.

It was being made clear to me at this time that I had to start making some plans for my future, though this was something I found very difficult to face. I'd thought about starting work in a bakery but the job fell through. I'd thought about going to college to study for my O Grades, as I'd dropped out of school without them, but then I thought I'd be better off studying something more vocational. As a result, I did nothing. All the dreams I'd had about having a career as a writer or an artist left me.

Aunt Elspeth called me to the office one day. 'Eileen, you've an interview at the flower shop up the road,' she said. The decision appeared to have been taken out of my hands but on the morning of the interview I refused to get out of bed. The staff were dismayed and I knew I should get up and get on with it, but I couldn't.

In truth, it's a job I would have loved to have taken. I loved flowers: how pretty they looked, the colours, the arranging. Yet my heart sank at the thought of it. Soon Hamish came to see me, no doubt at the behest of the staff, who wanted him to talk me into it. While I was at Fernlea, though, Hamish's position on relationships was less about blaming the child and more about looking at how staff members could help to facilitate solutions to the issues that children in care understandably have.

I had so many issues. I saw myself as a burden and a failure. It felt as though it was my fault that my mother had died and that the family had been split up. I had too many secrets now, secrets that I couldn't share with anyone, and my sense of isolation increased.

One night in bed, not long after this, I found that I couldn't stop scratching myself. I clawed and clawed at myself. My legs were bleeding in places with the friction burns I'd inflicted on myself, as my fingernails were so short. The ends of my fingers throbbed with the pain of gnawing at them. I tried not to chew them or scratch my legs when I was awake but I couldn't stop myself doing it while I was sleeping.

I awoke the next morning to find myself covered in a rash, mostly across my stomach; I had been feeling more unwell than usual. Scared, I hinted about it to Aunt Elspeth, afraid at the same time of being accused of making a fuss. She looked at my stomach and told me to go back to bed. Days passed, with only my hunger driving me to emerge to eat. I dragged myself to the dining table for food. As I attempted to eat, a comment came from the kitchen about how lazy I was. I returned to my room. Tears fell; I could no longer hold them back but at least they were shed in private. No one came to check on me; the staff changeover happened and I watched from the window as Lillian left her car and entered the building. I heard the swing doors wafting away and the chat as the previous staff headed off to their own lives and homes.

Soon I was to receive another blow. In April 1979, one of the two people who supported me and sustained me decided to leave. It felt like another abandonment. For a year and a half, Hamish had fought battles for me. Whenever I'd pushed the boundaries too far, running away, getting into trouble with the police, staying out till 2 a.m. without permission, he'd listened to me, calmly talked it over with me, helped me see the other side of the story. When Braeview, Kidron House and then Fernlea had had enough of me and had refused to take me back, he'd negotiated for me, even to the point of castigating the care staff for their prejudices. Way back in January 1978, only a few months after I'd met him, he'd written in my notes how important it was for us to have close contact. He believed that I was very sensitive to any kind of rejection, as it was something that I had suffered almost constantly since birth. I needed people that I could rely on and confide in, and to Hamish's mind at the time, he and my aunt Helen were the only two people who could perform this role.

I could barely rise to acknowledge that he was leaving; it was just too awful. I was devastated but showed no outward emotion at the news. He'd got a new post as a medical social worker and assured me he'd keep in touch. This I did not believe. I promised myself I would not get close to anyone again. Though most people might have thought that I hadn't trusted Hamish because I hadn't told him my secrets, I had needed him. I'd liked him very much and relied on him to keep the wolves of ignorance and prejudice from my door. Now I was at the mercy of new secrets on top of the old ones and I didn't have the comfort of seeing Hamish's quirky yellow Citroën Diane pulling into the street like a drifting anchor in my life. How many times had I fantasised about him adopting me? Now Hamish McColl was moving on. Who would I talk to now? I lost all hope.

My new social worker was a woman called Yvette Harrington. She came to visit Cathleen and me at Fernlea for her first solo visit after the handover from Hamish in April 1979, by which time I was unemployed, uncommunicative and often hiding under my quilt. Yvette, though, seemed to have read the same textbooks as Hamish. From her notes at the time, it's clear she was forming her own opinions about me and about the people around me. My aunt Helen, she said, was 'a very pleasant woman' whose family home was described as 'clean and nicely furnished'. The strange relationship between residential social workers and field social workers, however, was a dynamic in itself. John was on duty when she arrived to see me and she wrote about a conversation she'd witnessed between John and me in the office. Perhaps John thought that his handling of me was cognitively good and straight from the Aunt Elspeth school of psychology. Yvette, however, noticed that while John seemed to have a lot of concern for the children in his care, he was too quick to make judgements and this had led him to ignore some valid reasons that I had had for refusing to take the job that had been arranged for me in the flower shop. Reasons such as my asthma and hayfever. Instead of enabling me to discuss my fears, John had just come to the conclusion that I was lazy and didn't want to work.

I didn't want to have to leave Fernlea. I didn't have the self-confidence to be able to look after myself and I didn't have the confidence in the staff at Fernlea to share these feelings with them. Unfortunately, that's not how the staff there saw it. Even John thought I was surly and too lazy to look for work, and he was one I had a good relationship with! Such is the difference between truth and perception, especially perception that's based on tittle-tattle and preconceived ideas. And this is a minor example that explains how afraid I was of these people, who on the surface were my carers but who were in reality scrutinising my every movement and interpreting it according to their own limited knowledge of who I was.

Seeing me so withdrawn after Hamish left opened the gateway to new discussions about my behaviour. One wrong move and I could be sent away, my life made worse, and I knew it. I remembered stories from my past about women and girls being incarcerated in institutions for stealing bread or even for being pregnant outwith marriage. They were considered mentally ill. Literature, too, introduced me to these Dickensian stories. It sure did feed my fear that I could be locked away or even be diagnosed with a concocted illness invented courtesy of their limited training and shaky egos. I am not sure how often I pointed out this discrepancy between what they thought and how I felt, but I know I did. It must have made them embarrassed to have their inadequateness pointed out and it had always made Hamish sad.

Where did this leave me? I was all at sea. I didn't trust anyone. I was afraid, as I'd always been, but now I was also afraid of myself, because I didn't understand what was going on in my head. The only measuring ruler I had was what other people said or wrote about me. I'd previously asked Hamish why I couldn't go to the conferences the Social Work Department held about me. It was my life, so why did I not have a say in it? He had agreed with me. Then, just before he left, he asked me if I wanted to go to the next planned conference. I must have astonished and frustrated him by replying, 'No'. I didn't want to go. I couldn't go. I felt by now there was no point. My life was no longer my own, my secrets, both those from the past and those I was harbouring in the present, meant I had no future. I was in limbo. I was just existing.

For most of my life, I'd been waiting for my real life to start. Things will change, something will happen, I used to tell myself. And now something had happened. Now I felt I was waiting for my life to end.

Yvette was just another social worker to pass through my life. Her arrival meant I had to go through the motions of being cautious, polite and learning how this one thought, what she expected of me, and I had to tune in to her prejudices in order to protect myself. She arranged to take me to the National Art Gallery and I knew she was doing it in order to gain my trust. I knew by now that that was how this game worked. So I went to Edinburgh with her. Though I was polite, went through the motions and even enjoyed the gallery, I was being careful not to give anything away. I couldn't wait to get home, to get to bed to isolate myself from the world. Bed, with a few books for company, was where I hid, and as I ate and slept, I gained more weight.

Though I was devastated to lose Hamish, after my first couple of encounters with Yvette I became quietly optimistic and felt a glimmer of security in knowing she was looking out for me. We spent quite a bit of time together, including some private chats in my room away from the Fernlea staff. I'd even shown her some of my poetry. The title of one was particularly apt. By showing her 'Jigsaw Puzzles', I think I was attempting to show her that part of me was in order and could make sense of what I was feeling. I was reaching out to her.

Jigsaw Puzzles
a,b,d-c

Here am I, here are you,
Here are we. No. One and two.
I am an instrument to be played on.

Here is a, here is b. Put us together and we get d.
I am a subject that's far gone.

I am like a coin,
a mirror,
two sides,
Just reactions.
Jigsaw puzzles,
not put together right
hiding in the solitary night.

B can't touch me,
neither can d, because there's something missing which is c.
If c was there without a doubt,
A would be able to carry out.

To my face, Yvette praised me for the poem. When she wrote up the case notes of our meeting, however, she said: 'Eileen showed me a poem which was far too cynical for someone her age.'

Round about this time, I wandered into the office one day. Alex and Phil were there, discussing arrangements for Alex to go to London to live permanently with his mum after his successful trial visit. I feigned a lack of interest, as he had promised me, in secret, that he would arrange for me to move down. Soon Alex went to the kitchen to get us all a drink of coffee. As Phil and I sat in the office, a girl appeared at the front door looking for Alex. Apparently, she thought she was his girlfriend. Here he was in the middle of preparations to leave for London and now I discovered he might have had a girlfriend whom he had never mentioned. I could feel the pain splitting in a line across my chest. I clenched my fists, determined not to show my emotions. I was afraid to challenge him. He was blasé about the girl's appearance, not even wishing to see her. He was laughing about the fact that she'd turned up at the door. This was all too much for me: the secrets that we'd shared, him leaving for good, another person I'd become close to abandoning me. I had given my word to keep our plans and feelings secret. The voice inside my head kept repeating, I can't say it. I can't say anything.

I couldn't hold it in. I found myself screaming at him. I screamed at him, unconscious of time or place or Phil in the room beside us. My outburst lasted for, at most, five minutes. All our clandestine promises and intimacy concealed in the night, all trashed. I'd finally lost it. And I'd lost it with the staff present.

Phil was as astonished at me as I was. Alex watched me, remaining seated on the office radiator, quietly faking ignorance about why I should be so upset. My only saving grace was that I didn't reveal my secret, our big secret. My man-made shame held that one contained.

Phil made the most out of that incident. He said that I was foaming at the mouth – that's how concerned he made himself out to be in the aftermath. The reality was that I had exploded when I'd been drinking a cup of milky coffee. His reaction revealed to me just how dangerous people can be. Later it was queried whether I might be schizophrenic. My wee voice, which was mine and was only one, muttered in my head, Jesus fuck! These people could have me locked away on a wrong diagnosis. More than that, I was terrified that they might be right. Tell someone they are something for long enough and they'll believe you. Stupid, stupid girl, I scolded myself, for playing into their hands. My wee voice railed in my head, saying: fool, giving them the ammunition to shoot you with! The old saying comes to me now about keeping your friends close but your enemies closer. I didn't feel I had any true friends but I had many to fear.

At the beginning of July, Yvette came to see me again. I sat with Cathleen, in the visitors' room, waiting for her. She breezed into the room, seeming so pleased to see us. I detected a forced smile from her and was immediately on guard. She told Cathleen and me that she was leaving. I felt my heart growing heavier and heavier as I pretended to listen to what she was saying. I rejected this further rejection. I had to keep all my feelings in. They were beginning to bubble up in my throat, threatening to burst out of me.

Cathleen seemed unperturbed. She'd developed a reputation as unruly and uncontrollable. Social workers believed this was because of the lack of stability in her childhood and so did I. I knew it. I was the only stable influence she'd ever had, though sometimes I was a shaky one at that. For her sake now, I had to keep cool and show no emotion. I couldn't let her see me break down at this. This social worker had only been with us for three months.

So Yvette went back to her office in Glasgow and signed off with a final chapter saying that as she told me she was handing over the case and leaving: 'Cathleen seemed unmoved and appeared not to care less, while Eileen's shutters went down.' I had played a role in many, many people's lives. Each had experienced a little part of me, interpreted and understood by their own mindset and their own needs. Each time it

k something from me and now nothing much of me was left. I felt
rally fragmented. Bits of me had been lost in the past, present and the
ure, and they were now so distant and dislocated from me I couldn't
ch them. I couldn't gather them in or hold them together. I hated
self for feeling abandoned by Yvette; I hated myself for thinking
t Hamish had cared for me, for my secret wish to live in his home.
pid, stupid, foolish girl – that was how I addressed myself. I had
ver heard of self-annihilation or self-loathing caused by trauma and
mpounded by other people's reactions. I still felt I was something you
ped from your shoe. I was to be downtrodden for many years by the
mory of those shoes; they were almost worn out before they stopped
lking.

Depressed and self-obsessed, I wrote another poem.

A Flower's Death 1979

Flowers swaying in the warmth of the sun,
all flowers closing quietly, because the night had begun.
One flower defiant, wouldn't close tight,
left frightened in the unknown night.
The Horizon appears upon the line,
Blooming smiles, they're feeling fine.
But this one's withered almost dead,
the others shiver and turn a blind head.
Bending slowly, down and down,
behind the brown curled petals, the sad face of a clown.
Goodbye world, so dear and fine,
I'm sinking fast. Now's my time.

The sun brings a new lease of life,
but into me she takes a knife.

ays and nights passed. I kept myself distant from the others, staying
my room. No one came to see why I didn't come down for supper.
l I heard were footsteps passing my door. One night, I was sick and

tried to get it sorted as best as I could with an old T-shirt and Det[...]
disinfectant from the bathroom while the night staff were sleepir[...]
The next morning, Phil entered my room, as usual without knockir[...]
I pretended to be asleep, head hidden by the quilt and a small chest [...]
drawers beside my bed. I heard him cursing at the smell in my roo[...]
I had no doubt in my mind that in the office I'd be the focus of mu[...]
disgust.

Nothing had changed in my life. I sat on the side of my bed a[...]
decided I had to do something.

I had a plan. I washed and dressed and went down for lunch. I hu[...]
around the office and when the time was right I took my opportuni[...]
I stole money from the filing cabinet. A five-pound note. I folded t[...]
money into a small square and quickly pushed it down my bra befo[...]
anyone could see me, tucking it under my right breast. I wandered in[...]
the kitchen, got a drink and then went back to the office. Aunt Elspe[...]
had just come on duty and the moneybox was taken out. When it w[...]
realised that money was missing, she immediately approached m[...]
pulled my T-shirt out and looked down my bra, down the waistba[...]
of my skirt then straight into my eyes. She knew but – 'nothing i[...]
nothing out' – I stared straight back at her and nothing more was sai[...]

Later that day, I headed out into town. The sky was overca[...]
indicating it was the end of summer. I remember shivering when I we[...]
through the swing doors as I went out onto the street, though th[...]
might have been because of my nerves.

I headed to the chemist, where I bought a shaving razor and son[...]
painkillers. I returned to my room, lifted my mattress and made a sm[...]
hole in the underside. I tucked the pills in there, leaving just enough [...]
the packet sticking out so I could retrieve them. I didn't have Hami[...]
but I had them as back-up.

26

Privileged Ticket

While I was spending lots of time in my room during the day, I went out sometimes at night. I'd met a girl who was older than me and who lived along the road. I can't remember how I met her but I do remember that she invited me to her house. Her mother made fabulous soup. This girl also had a brother who decided to hit on me but I wasn't interested. I only went back to her house twice after that and only when he wasn't there. Twice I went out with her, to the pub. On the second time, I bumped into Joe. He hit on me again and she wanted us to go back to his house. I wasn't interested in this either. I left and went home alone, realising that was another friendship at an end.

One day soon after this, John called me to the office. He told me that my new social worker was coming to meet me. I pretended not to be interested and asked only whether it was a man or a woman and where they came from. I wanted to know if I was still under the Glasgow Social Work Department and what the worker's name was. I needed the Glasgow connection. John shrugged. He didn't know any more about her than I did.

Having had a gutful of disappointment due to my expectations of social workers in the past, I envisaged another polite woman, well-meaning but only passing through. She'd probably stay a few weeks, write things about me that mattered but didn't change anything. Yvette had been right: I was cynical.

On the day she arrived, the swing doors revealed Rebecca Mowe To my mind, she was a younger, female version of Hamish and, despit my usual reservations, or perhaps because of them, this gave me som hope. She didn't have a signature car or even an ordinary one. She an her briefcase had had to travel to Fernlea from Glasgow by train. I fe a totally unnecessary guilt at this.

Rebecca had visited my aunt Helen, who was still asking for a be for Cathleen and I to sleep in when we stayed. She had also been kin enough to get Cathleen a riding hat. Cathleen had been going on abou horse riding for ages, so Rebecca was going to enquire about lessons fc her. This was good. Also, she did not want the visits both Cathleen an I made to my aunt to stop. I didn't know it but she was enquiring to se if my aunt had any intention of fostering Cathleen.

I had mentioned this to her and to previous social workers. I wante Cathleen to be fostered by my aunt, knowing that I was a lost cause an it was all too late for me. Anyway, with my own plans formulating i grey at the back of my mind, I wanted Cathleen to be safe.

Soon after meeting Rebecca, I received a letter from London. It wa a short letter. In it, Alex told me he missed me and repeated that h wanted me down there. He also phoned Fernlea and I was allowed t speak to him. He suggested that I should try to get down to visit hin I sensed his anxiety, which was similar to mine. After all, he knew on of my secrets.

As I would probably be staying with his mother, I decided the be: way to approach the subject was to be upfront and ask the staff at Fernle if a visit could be arranged. It was refused. Aunt Elspeth told me, as sh had before, 'Alex's mother only wants him now he's old enough to wor and bring in some money.' She implied his mother wouldn't want to b lumbered with a girlfriend Alex would spend his money on. 'Anyway she said, 'it's just not suitable for you to go down there and expect he to put you up. She hasn't been checked out.'

I didn't care about that. I was angry and desperate. My plans ha been curtailed. Who did they think they were, telling me I couldn't go They consulted with the principal social worker and a few days later was officially deemed unsuitable for me to go.

I sneaked a phone call to Alex to tell him the news, desperate for him to support me and try to help me to work something out.

'Get down however you can,' he said.

Warily, I set out to do so; there was nothing else on offer. In my desperation and panic, as I felt time was running out, the answer came to me. My father. He'd worked for the railway. He used to get free passes for me for the train. I remembered the little cards: they were called PTs, which stood for privileged tickets. It wasn't so much a ticket to freedom, just a ticket for escape. With this card, I could travel anywhere for much less than ordinary fares, plus I could get up to four tickets absolutely free.

Somehow I persuaded my dad to get me another ticket. After that, all I can remember is packing a small bag and heading off to the train station. The alarm bells that had rung in my head when Alison had pleaded with me to run away to London with her the year before remained curiously silent. I wasn't running away; I was running to Alex. And I didn't need anyone's money for my fares. I didn't need anyone's permission. I was 16 and no one could stop me travelling.

I stood, with an unremembered companion to see me off, at the train station ticket office. I approached the teller and asked for a one-way ticket to London and showed him my card. He took it from me to inspect. I could see the teller holding the card up to show another colleague. Discussion took place behind the glass screen but I wasn't a lip-reader and I couldn't hear what was going on. I sensed something was wrong but rather than take heel I stood my ground, so desperate was I. There was shuffling behind me. The teller came back and spoke to me through the holed window. He stared straight into my eyes and said, 'I'm going to have to keep this ticket. You can't travel. I'm sorry.' I knew instantly that Aunt Elspeth had called the station.

Anger swirled in my chest and I clenched my teeth in desperation. I turned and saw that the other passengers in the queue behind me were listening. Trying to not let my desperation show, I turned away and left. With nowhere to go, exhausted and feeling sicker and sicker, I returned to Fernlea.

Aunt Elspeth was waiting for me. I just looked at her as she was getting ready to leave for the shift exchange. 'It is not suitable,' she said.

Rebecca came out to see me a few days later. I agreed with her that my actions had been wrong. I said everything they wanted me to say, almost with gusto. I chatted away with Rebecca almost as though I trusted her. One of my ways of getting to find out who I was in company with was to question them about themselves – it was also a ploy to deflect any questioning directed at me. I asked Rebecca all about her training, education and her job in general, and as we chatted she told me a story that would define how I felt about her and reinforce my thoughts about my own place in the world. As she sat in a chair by my left side in the small visitor's room, I listened to this story with horror tightening my insides.

One of Rebecca's cases was a girl in a wheelchair, she told me, unaware of my growing alarm at the unfolding story. Down's syndrome was the Glasgow girl's handicap. Rebecca was frustrated at having to prepare papers for a court case and a social work review when she didn't believe they were just. The issue that had brought the fuss about was that the girl's brother and uncle had been caught having sex with her.

As Rebecca was telling me this, panic was racing through my brain. I was horrified, sure she was going to find me out.

She continued the story by saying, 'Why the need for a court case? The girl is enjoying the sex, so what's wrong with that?'

I was stunned into silence.

She continued about handicapped people having rights. This girl's pleasure, she said, was hers by right.

I didn't know why or how to reply to this. Inside, as she spoke, I was rapidly repeating to myself, that's wrong. That's so wrong. I looked at her through my suspicious eyes and decided if Rebecca felt that way about this girl who couldn't resist assault by her uncle and brother then it was possible that she could be friends with the likes of Urquhart. Maybe she would feel that he, too, had rights. Maybe she could expose me to people like him, and it would reveal what a bad girl I was, as if it was my crime – that I was in the wrong for thinking he was bad.

She could write that I was wrong and he was right.

I couldn't wait for her to go. I never wanted to see her again. I didn't know how she could think like that. She terrified me. Previously, she had given me the address of a known poet so that I could correspond with him. I sent him some of my poems and in his reply he stated that they expressed sadness and troubled experiences. This shocked me so much that I never wrote to him again; I had, in my naivety, thought he would just comment on the structure and language use. Instead, I had almost given myself away. How closely had he read my poems? Did he detect evidence of Urquhart? I thought about his connection with Rebecca. Was his attitude the same as hers?

This further confirmed that the people who had control over my life certainly could not be trusted. In my terror, I thought they might even lead me to believe that 'the interferer' Urquhart and the like were really the good people in my life. The paradox: feeling it was my fault even though I knew they were bad.

After she left, the cucumber sandwiches sat on a long oblong tray in the kitchen. I picked up a few pieces of the watercress that had been sprinkled over them for presentation. Lillian sat in the office with a teacup and saucer, one in each hand, chatting, I think, to Sarah. As usual, no TV was allowed. I felt even more trapped in this place. I paced up and down the corridors, then slipped outside to have a fly puff, sitting on the cold steps leading upstairs, wrapped in my dressing gown. Everything I stared at, I stared through. I had to do something to change this. It had to stop. Urquhart had promised to kill me. But now I knew for certain there were other Urquharts out there. The revelation shocked me. 'Fuck sake,' I whispered. Somewhere out there were other children like me. It all had to stop.

27

Realism Revealed

My room was yet again where I found myself, having nowhere else to go. I closed my curtains and retrieved the painkillers I'd bought with the stolen money. Then I sat on my bed, in my pyjamas, with the box of pills in my hands. Cars were driving by outside; staff and children were moving about from bedroom to bathroom, getting organised for the younger children's bedtime. The older children were out. As I listened to the routine noises, I popped pill after pill out of the packet and lined them up on the duvet beside me.

A glass of water sat on the floor beside my bed. Do I or don't I? There were 24 pills in the packet.

I lay in my bed with the quilt curled round me. After about the 15th pill, I felt sick. I thought that meant I had done enough. Tucking the packet under the bed, I curled up with my knees under my chin. I was lost, in a nowhere land. I had no tears, a huge nothingness. My life was ending as it should. Years of turmoil were being dealt with in the only way I knew, at last. Just waiting for sleep to come, with no nightmares, to end this. I was connected to nothing and nothing was connected to me. A type of sleepiness was upon me but so was nausea. I endured the nausea; I told myself I deserved it and refused to get up. I stayed as still as possible, breathing as little as I could, waiting and hoping for it all to pass.

I had no idea what time it was.

Whether it was light or dark.

I lay still, almost not breathing.

My bedroom door opened and Lillian was beside my bed. She never came into my room. Thinking about it later, part of me was astonished.

I remember being up on my feet with Lillian supporting me, dragging me up and down the corridor. The sickness was awful. I couldn't react to her arms around me, hauling me from the bed, or answer her questions. The sickness rose to my back teeth. I couldn't communicate. It was all over for me; my secrets would come out now. I let it all wash over me, the emotions becoming stronger than the painkillers. My only focus was on not being sick. How I hated vomiting. I didn't feel hate or fear towards Lillian. She was just there and I was too far away to react to her, though I recognised, on reflection, that the tone in her voice was concern. I blinked. Resurfaced.

I found myself in the back of an ambulance, strapped to a chair; my eyes followed the lights and sky as the vehicle sped to the hospital. I could not, would not, speak. I looked blankly at those around me. My body felt disconnected. I had surrendered all fight. I meekly let all happen round about me. As I was strapped in the ambulance, blankets wrapped round me, with noises, bleeps, questions being asked, I just stared blankly. A gulf, a cleaved chasm, between my reality and the reality surrounding me.

Gentle voices called my name but couldn't engage me in any conversation. Like the ambulance, I felt like a used vehicle. The bustle of the hospital and getting me in a bed to be attended to happened without me. I felt I was arrogant, just as they had described me in the past, but this time I didn't care. Behind curtains, I was compliant in getting my stomach pumped. It didn't take much. Tubing was pushed down my throat and water was poured into it, choking me. It elicited an instant reaction and I was sick.

I didn't want to be nursed. I had brought this on myself. My elective muteness persevered. I heard several medical people around my bed; I concentrated on the details in the curtains pulled around me, on small flecks in the off-white curtains. A man in a white coat stood beside me looked at my eyes for a few moments and then lifted up the covers and my pyjama top; he felt my stomach, his eyes meeting mine.

'How long?' he asked.

'About six months,' I replied instantly and without emotion, breaking my silence.

He pulled my top down and the single sheet back up, then, as if they didn't know what to say to me, he and the others walked away.

I lay there, staring, rubbing my stomach. I could feel my baby's body and limbs moving. For months, I had run my own hands over the little bumps that felt like elbows and heels poking and stretching inside me against my tummy.

There was little talk as I was quietly moved from the casualty area to a bed in a corner of a room. I awaited my fate, not knowing what would become of me. Who would want me back now?

The nurses were kind in their quietness; looks and half-smiles afforded me some sympathy. My own sadness began to well up in me. I was too far gone for them to do anything and now I could only wait to see if my fear of being locked up and having my baby taken away from me would happen. For now, this was real; my baby – my big secret – was real.

My silence continued. Rebecca Mower came to see me. I wanted her to go. My fear of her also remained; however, she sat directly in front of me and I sat in silence. Eventually, she spoke, 'Do you want me to say it, Eileen?'

I nodded, still not able to utter the words.

She nodded and swallowed: 'You're pregnant.'

'Yes,' I said. It was over. It became my reality. It would be on file.

I got dressed in the clothes Lillian had brought for me: a dress I had worn to my cousin Helen's wedding in January. It was a long, tiered black one with paisley print on it and buttons up the front from the waist. The boots I had worn to the wedding gave me height. Looking older than I did, I curled up in my clothes. Seeing the pale and frightened kid from the children's home dressed like that on the hospital bed, the nurse did a double-take.

'I didn't recognise you,' she said.

My aunt had been contacted, as were Alex and my father. Six months of emotions welled up behind my eyes and hurt my throat as I saw my aunt Helen walk down through the ward to collect me. Ashamed, I avoided her eyes. She put her arms round me and remained silent. The silence was broken only when she said, 'You don't have to get married.' Relieved at this and the revelation that she wasn't going to be angry with me, I nodded gratefully. I was taken straight to her house from the hospital. None of them, my aunt and cousins, understood why I hadn't said anything. How confused and frustrated they must have felt. More than ever before, the evidence was undeniable: I was a whore. I sat on my aunt Helen's couch, waiting on a verbal slaughtering, but it didn't come.

Rebecca Mower came back to see me several days later. She had seen my father. His response to her news was that I had brought shame on the family. I knew I would have to put my shoulders back and be brazen against opinions if I was to keep sane, to keep it together. My uncle Charles said nothing. My cousin Helen had married in January in a beautiful white wedding dress with a fur trim. She was lovely. In June she had given birth to a baby boy whom she called Daniel. She passed on to me all her maternity wear. Amongst it was a beautiful green and white dress that I wore for most of the rest of my pregnancy.

My shame at letting everyone down was profound; however, I could not convey this completely to anyone, other than state it once to my aunt. I was afraid of breaking down. But my greatest fear was of the birth. I was terrified about what would happen. Would it hurt? How would it hurt? But I was too afraid to show my fear. So many clichés came to my head to haunt me: you've made your bed, now lie in it; there's no point in crying over spilt milk. I knew I had no choice but to face the consequences. Night after night, alone, I was kept awake with the fear.

28

Explained

Many people had questions to ask me; however, very few did.
  I had known I was pregnant almost from the beginning. My urine had taken on a strange smell, the first indicator that something in me was different. My breasts itched, my periods stopped and, along with the nausea I felt in the first months, my body had told me all I needed to know. Still, as I had never experienced this before, or spoken to anybody close to me who had, I was living in limbo, or in a suspended reality. Alex had finally conceded I was pregnant several months into the pregnancy; he didn't want anyone to know. Maybe he thought it would just go away. He had known about it as he was arranging to go to London. He had known about it when the girl came to the swing doors at Fernlea, looking for him. Did I ask him to come and get me? I don't think so. I think he promised to send for me. That's the way I remember it. I didn't know much about his life outside Fernlea. I was never involved with his friends or family and had never been invited to go with him on any of his weekend visits home.
  I had kept my pregnancy secret from everyone but Alex. I was alone with the decision, if you could call it that, to keep it hidden. Alone in my self-incarceration at Fernlea, hoping something would change. Like Alex, perhaps I too thought it would go away if I kept it a secret. A part of me did. Of course, in reality I knew it would not, but I was not living in reality.

I had hoped Alex could help me in some way. Of course, he did not. As my breasts and stomach began to swell, my aunt Elspeth had queried my past genetics. Was my birth family prone to putting weight on, she wondered. When my pregnancy became public knowledge, she said to Rebecca Mower that she'd suspected I was pregnant. Yet I had requested sanitary towels on a monthly basis, knowing I had to if my secret was to remain so. I had avoided being seen by a doctor if I felt ill. I avoided being seen partly undressed in my room, should Cathleen come in. Only once did I reveal anything of my swelling stomach. My cousin Lena was giving me some of her old clothes, as I was desperate to get into something more comfortable. She later told me she had glanced at my stomach curiously. Interestingly, people were annoyed at themselves, confused as to how it was they hadn't suspected.

I could explain that in the fact I'd removed myself from social encounters and communication in what had seemed like a spiralling descent into a cornerless corner. Added to that was the fact that there was no one with sole, constant responsibility for caring for me in my daily life. I was a shared responsibility: that was Fernlea's jurisdiction over me. And of course I'd gone through three social workers in the six months of my pregnancy up till the point when it was revealed. I wasn't working or at school. I just stayed in my room mostly, under my quilt. And so I'd been able to conceal it just like that.

The conference Hamish had invited to me to, which I had asked him to arrange so that I could have some input into the decisions made in my life, as well as to give me some feeling of control, no longer mattered when I realised I was pregnant. I'd lost any control over my future, or so I felt. Hence my reason for confounding Hamish by telling him I didn't want to go. That, too, was the reason why I arranged to go to see people in connection with work or study but then dropped out. I knew there was no point in making plans: they would all be based on a false assumption and be a terrible waste of people's time.

Also, I didn't know if I could keep up the lies – the guilt and pressure being bad enough as it was. My nights were spent hour after hour constantly feeling my baby growing: from a fear, to sickness, to actual movements and the sense that my stomach was inhabited by another. During the night while the staff and other children slept, I would trace the feet and hands, and, nearing the end, it was either the head or bottom I could feel making more room. This was real and I'd become absorbed in it. In the last few weeks, I was transfixed with a mixture of astonishment, fear and wonder, as I could visibly see the lumps appearing outside my stomach and sliding under the skin from one end of my belly to another. My breasts grew, my nipples spread and my belly looked and felt like it was a container for large jumping beans. Ironically, my hair shone and skin was flawless through this time. What should have been a joy to me, to any female, was not shared. Instead, I spent the months in fear of so many things.

29

Real Reactions

Now I was no longer in the child-care system but remained a case under the Child Care Act, Section 15. Rebecca Mower remained my social worker. I couldn't tell anyone that part of me was afraid of her, fearful of what she might bring back into my life or reveal. If I mentioned my fears to Aunt Elspeth, or Aunt Helen, or one of my cousins, it would give the game away about my other secret. My deep-down secret. I could still feel the dread of standing outside his front door, tucked away in the dark of the tenement close, buses and cars going by outside with their sounds and the voices of passers-by temporarily captive in the gloom of the close with me while I waited. The door still closed in front of me. Hearing the heavy tread of a man's feet on the other side and the jangle of keys. Hoping my father would be in – no matter how drunk – to give me his wages so I could run home safe to my mother, unmolested.

Throughout the year he'd interfered with me, Urquhart had said if I mentioned it to anyone he would kill me. The fear he'd instilled in me as a seven year old still gripped me at sixteen. The years had ground it deeper, reinforcing it. He'd kill me if I told anyone what he'd done.

Coupled with this, I believed it was my fault. Men like him were only attracted to children like me because we were whores. Hadn't my mother told me? So, ten years further on, I still kept my mouth shut. My aunt and cousins certainly didn't need this, nor did I need the terrible reactions that I imagined would ensue. So I kept it secret.

When Cathleen found out that I was pregnant and had gone to live at my aunt Helen's, she wasn't happy. She wanted to live there, too. However, smiles appeared when she understood she would be the baby's auntie. This news sufficed to satisfy my ten-year-old sister.

Now I was wearing maternity wear, it was clear to everyone that I was pregnant and heavily so. On my first anxious outing to the town centre, I was met with a retort from a girl I vaguely knew from school but had never spoken to. Her reaction was to walk straight up to me and say, 'What have we done here, then?'

I smiled, not knowing what else to do or say, and waddled on in my green and white dress. As my pregnancy became public and more pronounced, so too did the waddling and constant peeing. This made my family and the staff even more astonished that they'd missed it. My body no longer held itself in check and was allowing itself to appear pregnant now.

In an effort to 'sort things out' in her role as Officer in Charge of Fernlea, and possibly in the role she perceived for herself as my protector, my aunt Elspeth had contacted Alex to keep him informed and he and I had spoken several times on the phone at my aunt Helen's. These conversations always took place from a phone box at his end, as, so far, he hadn't told his mother. I had no idea how the conversation went between him and my aunt Elspeth but after she spoke to him he promised to come and see me when he got time off work. I had never mentioned to him how distressed I had been feeling and how alone, far less divulged to him my deep buried secrets from the past. In my mind, I had to stay together and strong.

I remembered the jigsaw I'd so loved as a child, with all the Disney story characters running round the circle. Now I saw that all my fragmentary jigsaw pieces had to be pulled into place and had to stay in place. The character and storyline from my past must never be revealed to anyone. If I'd been religious, I would have deemed it my cross to bear. That wasn't me, though. I just saw that revealing it would cause untold trouble.

Gone were the tight drainpipe punk silver trousers and creative make-up; gone was all the music that stirred up a spark in me: Poly Styrene's 'Identity', 'Germ Free Adolescents' and 'Oh Bondage, Up Yours!' There was no longer a place for me in that world. Any enthusiasm for my future was exchanged for living from day to day, fearing the labour and what would come afterwards. My feelings of wanting a career, a normal life, a right to more, changed, to be replaced by a single question as my pregnancy continued. Did this world have a place for me?

The Social Work Department bought me a pram, cot and bedding, with nappies and several baby suits. My cousin also gave me baby things that Daniel, her baby, had grown out of. I think Helen felt for me, as it was now apparent that I'd been pregnant at the same time she was. My experience was very different from hers. How different it would have been for me if I could have shared the experience with her, I don't know. As I sat in my aunt's spare room, which became mine in not quite the way I had envisaged living with her, I stared at the new pram, a beautiful, coach-built high-quality pram, and other things such as the bedding still in its wrappers. I stared at it in private. I remained so unhappy. But I could not reveal this and met everyone with a smile so as not to appear ungrateful after all the fuss I'd caused.

Once, a neighbour of Aunt Helen's made her feelings known to me. It was the same neighbour who had been angry about me being able to go to Switzerland 'so easily' with the school when she'd had to struggle to afford to pay for her daughter to go on the trip. Her thoughts on the situation now were made clear to me when I had to go into hospital for a couple of weeks for a scan and some tests, including an amniocentesis. She visited me, at the same time John did, high up in Bellshill Maternity Hospital, almost at the top floor. As John sat and chatted to me kindly, this neighbour appeared and her words to me were, 'If you were Laura [her daughter], I would have hammered you.' John said nothing. It seems some people get away with saying whatever they like without being challenged. Or is it that someone only challenges when they care or think they have the right to? Sufficiently shamed, the visit went on without reference to anything else.

When she appeared in my room at my aunt Helen's and saw the

new pram and all the other baby stuff in the room, this woman spat out, 'Think yourself lucky. Most people don't get new prams.'

I felt so guilty. I would have gladly swapped all my new stuff for second-hand if I could have had a mother and father by my side and been able to get rid of all my unhappiness and fear. But I did not; I had only that blank expression I gave out, which people interpreted at their whim. I was the child. People could do or say anything to me that they wanted. It always came down to that.

Nearing the end of my pregnancy, my cousin Helen, perhaps aware of my tiredness – and loneliness – asked me if I wanted to go to the pictures with her. I was eager to go. This would be some fun, some light relief – something to take my mind off the nightmare I was living.

Off we went to see *Halloween*, the new horror movie. Helen joked that I'd better not go into labour because of the movie. 'Don't do that to me,' she laughed.

The movie was scary but I knew it was only a movie. I felt my life was scarier, though I didn't know why. The implication of the female being pursed by the proverbial bogeyman resonated with me. I remember the part where Jamie Lee Curtis was hiding in the wardrobe in the bedroom. The wardrobe was fitted flush with the wall and had slatted doors. The room I was sleeping in at Aunt Helen's house had a freestanding wardrobe quite like it, with the same slatted doors. This picture from the movie stayed with me as I went to bed that night. In the dark, with the moonlight and streetlight filtering through the venetian blinds on my window, I looked at the wardrobe in my room.

Contemplating the movie, and no doubt also my own situation, I realised something had touched my head. As I looked up, my heart stopping, I saw a hand above me searching for something to grasp. I shrank down tight under the covers and held my breath. The hand disappeared. I flung back the duvet and lunged from my bed. I knew only Helen, Paul and baby Daniel were in the house, upstairs in bed. I ran upstairs, shouting for Helen in my panic. They came down still half asleep, and Paul, her husband, went outside while Helen and I waited, gripping on to each other, me trying to catch my breath.

The front door pushed open. 'Nothing there,' he said as he came in, shivering. 'Couldn't see anything.' He went into my room and switched the light on. Everything was as it had been; nothing was out of place. Then we saw that the curtain was billowing slightly. He went across to look at it and realised my window had been slid up, even though it was a chilly autumn night. It was slightly open. Paul and Helen looked at me.

'Well, I didn't do it,' I said.

Helen was standing in my bedroom doorway, clutching her dressing gown round her. 'What d'you think it was, Paul?' she asked him.

'Ghosts,' he said and grinned. He pulled the window tight shut and locked it, and they went back up to their room, but not before I checked the wardrobe and under the bed as well just in case.

It wasn't till the next day we discovered it was Ann, my cousin Helen's best friend. She'd been looking for me, not wanting to disturb the whole household, to ask me if Helen was still awake. She'd disappeared back next door when she got no result. Johnny, her boyfriend, lived there; he was the neighbour's son.

I knew by experience that my time here at my aunt's would be limited. One afternoon when my aunt Helen wasn't working, I was sitting on the couch downstairs listening to the radio and she came in dragging the Hoover.

'Here,' she said and tossed a yellow cloth duster over to me. 'While you're here, you might as well make yourself useful.'

I was happy to and dusting wasn't exactly heavy duty. So I dusted as she tidied up newspapers and the family's bits and pieces, then I made a cup of tea for us while she hoovered the living-room carpet. As she stored the Hoover, I brought the cups and biscuits through and put them down on the coffee table. The gas fire was on and the room felt warm and bright even though it was late October. No one else was in for some reason – it was always such a busy house – and with just her and me there it felt like the home I'd always wanted.

We chatted. I tucked my ankles up on the couch while we had tea and she laughed that I was still able.

There was a moment of silence. I reached over for a biscuit and she put her cup down. She asked me about Alex. Was he coming up to see me?

'I don't know,' I replied. We'd planned a visit but he was vague about dates and I'd begun to wonder if he was putting it off. Yet I still needed to feel he liked me.

I felt she was getting ready to say something to me. There was an edginess about her suddenly and I responded to that with my own anxiety, wondering what she was going to tell me. I dreaded being sent away.

I was eight months pregnant. A single girl that my father complained had brought disgrace upon his family.

'What?' I asked, unable to think of anything else to say but feeling I wanted the conversation to go on.

'Och,' she said. She fidgeted her hands, reached for a biscuit then changed her mind and put it back. She picked up her cup and sat back, nestling into her chair. Her hair was soft and curled but it was even softer today because she'd been doing her housework. She hadn't put any lipstick on yet and her face looked sad.

Whatever it was she wanted to say, she never did.

Rebecca Mower visited me at my aunt's and broached the subject of adoption. That, for me, was also out of the question. Times and attitudes had changed in much of society in the 16 years since I'd been born. Now it was deemed better for the child to stay with the mother, married or not. No matter how badly a child was treated, it was felt that it should still have family connections, as I had discovered in the relationship forced upon my father and me. As I understood, a child needed a mother and father. I also understood how badly that could go wrong, when, for instance, an adopted child didn't meet the expectations of the parents. While this could be true in many families, it was particularly true of many adopted families. As I knew so well. I couldn't consider adoption because of my experience and my instinctive fears of what could happen to my baby. I wanted to prevent that. It wasn't a simple decision for me, though.

My own fear that I couldn't cope with a child confused the issue for me. I just could see no way out other than accepting that the baby was my responsibility, despite the fact that I had no idea how to cope and that I had this dread of the world in general.

Halloween had passed and November had begun. Bonfire night passed, too. I had begun to spend much of my time organising and reorganising: from making and remaking my bed to perfection, to constant bathing, cleaning and making sure my clothes drawers were clean and all the contents folded and whereabouts known. All this in between resting. The pressure weighed down between my legs and my diaphragm area stretched uncomfortably. Anxious, I felt every odd sensation might be my labour starting. I began to will the process to start, as much as I was afraid of it. What I would do when it did, I had no idea, as I had no idea what to do once my child was born. I had told everyone I was having a boy. As I caressed him under my skin, I told him I had three names picked. I chose Craig, Anthony and Gregg, in that order. Several people told me I would be in for a shock, that there was a 50–50 chance I was carrying a girl, but I was so adamant my baby would be a boy.

My cleaning obsession grew in fever. On Saturday, 10 November 1979, I found myself cleaning worktops, otherwise known as bunkers, in my aunt's kitchen. My aunt was at work, as was my uncle Charles. I don't remember who else was in the house.

Despite having a mop and pail at my disposal, I decided to scrub the kitchen floor again, this time on my hands and knees. Every speck of dirt I could see, I rubbed away with a disinfected cloth; round and round the floor I went. I was still doing so when Lena arrived home from shopping with her friends and went upstairs. Eventually, about four o'clock, I conceded, my hand reaching round my belly. Something was happening. My muscles were tightening up and I was feeling a strange sensation of hardness that I couldn't ignore any longer. I rose from the floor and went upstairs.

By now my cousin Helen was home, too. I just looked at her and she looked back.

'Are you in labour?' she asked, quite still.

'I think so,' I said, nodding my head. I had held off and held off the inevitable as long as I could, afraid and also knowing that once I announced it there would be no going back. I had wanted to endure for as long as I could at home.

It was time to go. Soon, I found myself in an ambulance going to hospital. My aunt had been phoned and Lena had nearly fallen down the stairs in her rush to see me. Seeing how scared I was to go in the ambulance, the ambulance men gave me a cardboard sick bowl to use as an ashtray. Unimaginable and unheard of now. In my nervousness, I set it on fire in the ambulance. Off I went to hospital with the familiar feeling of life taking control while I was only in the passenger seat. I watched orange lights passing, the dark sky through the window. Another journey in which I was not driving.

30

Remembrance Day

Labour, like the surreal journey to the hospital, was happening to me and I was merely a passenger. However, this was different; this time I was physically involved.

When I arrived at the Bellshill Maternity, I was examined and then hurled in a wheelchair to a small room. Lying on a bed, I was told I had to be prepped. I had no idea what this meant, so I lay there waiting under a white linen sheet with my belly convulsing away. Over and over, the spasms kept coming. I felt like a lodger that was in arrears in rent in my own body, a lodger who couldn't leave till my debt was paid.

Soon, I discovered what 'prepped' meant. The brisk nurse arrived back at the bottom of my bed with a razor and some gel.

'Just to get you ready,' she said. 'If you can remove your underwear . . . ?' She spoke matter-of-factly.

Shame and embarrassment reared in me as I did as she asked. It felt to me as if she thought I was dirty and had to be cleaned up. Why did I have to have this done? What was its purpose? I felt like a piece of poultry waiting for the tin foil to arrive.

As the nurse shaved away, I had to remain perfectly still. I tried to focus on the ceiling, to disconnect myself from the embarrassment and the pain I was experiencing, afraid that one wrong move and the razor might be dangerous. I hoped it would not be long now. Since arriving in the ambulance, and that feeling of being a passenger, my muteness had appeared, my silence muffling a loud chaos in my head.

'Right, you can get up now and have a shower,' the nurse said.

Compliant, and without question, I got up from the bed and began to make my way over to the door of the shower room she had pointed out to me.

'Just a minute,' the nurse stated. 'I have to give you an enema.'

As I lay back down on the bed, uncomfortably on my side, I struggled to keep the tears away as she inserted the enema. Why? Why? Why? Why didn't she explain anything to me? I didn't know what was likely to happen to me. I hadn't been to antenatal classes – hadn't known about them, so didn't know they'd have helped me understand the process I'd be put through when the time came. I'd never been one of the in-the-loop troupe of well-informed mothers-to-be who traipsed excitedly through the hospital, months ahead of their first labour pains, to visit the scene where they'd give birth. I'd been prepped physically but hadn't been mentally prepared.

The nurse left with the words 'Have your shower,' and I was left alone.

I got myself into the shower and turned it on. I bent down to get the soap from my pre-packed toiletry bag from home. I leant against the wall of the shower, with one hand round my belly, the other holding the soap. I was so afraid. The pulse pains of the contractions became buddies with the spasms that began in my bowels. I had no control over either.

As I huddled against the wall, shaved, naked, waiting for respite from a contraction, my mind raced with panic. I felt humiliation. Was my baby going to be born, here, alone in the shower, or was I going to lose control of my bowels? A contraction passed. I managed to dash like a plucked turkey, naked and wet, to the adjoining toilet. As I sat there, the spasms that the enema created went into full flow and at the same time another contraction came. As the pain overwhelmed me, I gritted my teeth so as not make a noise. I felt I might lose my baby down the toilet.

Once that was over, I dressed in the white backless hospital gown and ung over the bed, head barely touching the mattress. In angry, scared ilence, I remember clenching my teeth.

The next thing I remember was being in a labour room. My aunt Helen was with me. A different nurse came in and told my aunt, 'She's oing well and not a sound from her.' She ruffled my hair as she left.

My aunt held my hand, the familiar smell of the rose hip oil she used n her face comforting me. I smiled at her and she was smiling at me. How she must have felt for me! Her eyes shone, on reflection probably ith empathetic sadness for me. I was a good girl not causing a fuss.

Soon I was given pethidene to ease the pain and time passed into he small hours. Midwives came and went, checking my progress. pparently the neck of my womb wasn't dilating as quickly as it should. didn't know whether to be worried about that or not. At least, with my unt beside me, I wasn't alone and that pacified me somewhat.

After a time, I was given a triple dose of pethidene to subdue the pain nd, as far as I remember, to slow the labour down. As I drifted in and ut of the pain and the room, my glazed eyes constantly searched out ny aunt's presence.

I heard a medical voice talking. 'She'll be a while; best go home.' In he grey fog, I felt a flicker of panic, then nothing. I was alone. Drugged nd tired, I went to sleep.

'Eileen. Eileen? It's time to take you down to the theatre.'

The voice sounded slightly anxious. It seemed to whisper from omewhere in the room. The flicker of panic lit again and I said, 'Phone ny aunt. Phone my aunt!' The voice agreed to do so.

I was transferred to a trolley and it trundled down corridors as I lently prayed my aunt would get there in time. Please don't let me do his alone, I was thinking, needing the only mothering influence I'd ver really had.

A large light above me is what I remember next. I knew I was in an perating theatre. With my legs placed up on stirrups, it was almost ine months since I had lain on a medical examination bed in a police tation. I remember panic. Was it mine? Was it present in the busy heatre? Most likely both.

'We are going to have to cut you,' a male voice said. Then an intense pain, to which my immediate response was to black out. No nauseou fainting feeling, just immediate blackout.

I came round. The theatre room was quieter. I was emptier. Betwee my legs there was pain.

'Hello,' the man said. 'We're just finishing stitching you up.'

I was taken from the operating table and into a recovery room in wheelchair.

'You've a baby boy,' the nurse who was with me told me.

I knew he'd be a boy. I just knew it would be. 'Where is he?' I aske her, trying to turn round in the chair so I could see any expression o her face.

Her face was calm and smiling. 'He's in special care,' she said, 'ju getting checked over. That was a long time he was struggling to be bor there!'

I lay in my bed exhausted but intensely hungry. Tea and toast wer brought to me. I felt wide awake, though I'd been in labour from yesterday afternoon and all through the night.

My aunt appeared, full of smiles. 'He's beautiful, Eileen.'

I gulped my tea and ate the rubbery toast, and it was delicious. I ha given birth to my Craig and how I wanted to see him. Eventually, I wa wheeled down to the special-care nursery. I stared through the glass a this little baby boy, lying there, so quiet, with slight bruising on hi forehead from the forceps and with a mass of blond curls. I was amazed It was amazing.

Craig weighed in at six pounds nine ounces. He was born on th eleventh of the eleventh, at four minutes to eleven. It was Remembranc Sunday. Poppy Day. The consultant who had looked after me durin my labour came up to visit me and told me Craig had been stuck in m birth canal. My body certainly wasn't wanting to let him go. And th intense pain I had felt was the 'slash and grab' episiotomy, followed b use of forceps. This experience was to terrify me and haunt me so badl over the years that I never wanted to give birth again.

I found myself on the postnatal ward, in a room of my own. M father's statement to my social worker that I was a disgrace, bringin shame on the family, preyed on my mind. With my low self-esteem an

lnerability, I thought I'd been shut away in a side room because I was
6 and unmarried. On reflection, it was probably because I wanted to
reastfeed Craig. I had seen that breast was best somewhere on a poster
nd I'd decided, idealistically, that I was going to try to do everything
ght for my baby from the very start, determined that his life would
e healthy.

Later on, I woke to tinny music playing from the back of my bed. I
cognised it immediately: 'Crazy Little Thing Called Love' by Queen
as on the hospital radio.

The memory that I had just given birth came back to me. I had
deed fallen in love. A nurse breezed into the room, smiling. How
ifferent it was from my entry to the hospital and shower room. She
amined me, feeling my stomach. 'My goodness,' she said, 'you have
flatter stomach than me and you've just given birth.' Having always
een skinny, there certainly was nothing much of me, even now.

I asked when Craig would be brought up to me. 'Today,' she replied.
nd he was. His little transparent incubator cot sat by the side of my
ed, under the glass window. He slept quietly as I watched and watched.
mazed that this little body had evolved from me. Still watching, as
y silent baby lay, I felt an uneasiness being conceived in my empty
omach. A fellow mother appeared from a room nearby. She seemed
iendly enough. 'What a beautiful baby,' she said.

I smiled and thanked her.

'We all think he's so quiet,' she added. Only I could hear the
mbling of my uneasiness at this comment. It was a feeling I did not
et understand.

I had been afraid I would not feel anything but relief after the birth,
ut I was consumed by one of the most powerful emotions I had ever
xperienced. His little fingers slowly stretched and wiggled as he slept.
wanted to touch them, to feel him. Afraid that I might disturb him,
had to wait. I struggled to contain my impulse to pick him up and
queeze him tightly. I desperately wanted to say hello to him.

31

Postnatal

As I returned to my aunt's home from the hospital with Craig and began to settle down to motherhood, my thoughts travelled the fragmented journey over my life that had brought me to this point. Here I was, back living with my aunt Helen, pondering my origins, genetic and social. When I held Craig in my arms, I was all too aware that, for the first time in my life, I was looking at another human being who was connected to me by blood. Throughout my life, since I was old enough to understand that I'd been adopted, I'd scanned people's faces, looking for resemblances and similarities. When I'd heard my aunt Helen or friends and neighbours look for likenesses in baby Daniel, it brought back my own perennial searching for someone that I looked like or who looked like me. The first blood relative I had ever laid eyes on was my son.

I began to think in earnest about what the blueprint for 'our' history was. What did it contain? What good things? What bad? Might it contain special skills and talents for him or hold special fears I should be aware of, like inherited disease? However, in thinking of tracing my genetic parentage, as much as I would have loved to and felt compelled to, I denied myself this. I was not a daughter to be proud of.

And just as I didn't want my genetic parents to know I was in care because it felt like my fault, so too I didn't want to bring them the shame I had brought my adopted father, of being a teenage mother of an illegitimate baby boy. History repeating itself. I decided I would wait till I had some reason to make them proud of me before I contacted them.

On the other hand, thoughts about my social blueprint drove round my head. I thought of Urquhart, the children's homes, the social workers who came and went, one day writing their impacting perceptions about me and my persona, only to disappear the next. It struck me as bizarre that, for children in care, so many people were allowed to come that close, closer than some couples and families, and they were allowed to impact on your life for short spaces of time, only to sometimes not even recognise you or, worse, ignore you as you rubbed shoulders with them later. What kind of blueprint was that in the creation of a child's personality?

I was many things, so I had been told by many of these people over the years, either verbally or by what they didn't say to me. Looks and actions, too, had given me the yardstick against which to measure myself. Many words and clichés had stuck over the years, projected sometimes, from people's own demons. I wasn't to understand this as a child. For me, it was about who I was, not who they were; people told me I was bad, so I believed them. I felt I had no right to judge anyone.

As I myself had been brought up in a bitter religious family, my reaction was to raise my son without it. I understood that people had their own rules according to what society they were born into. No because it was the 'right' or 'superior' religion, but rather that that was what they believed because that's what they had been told to believe. It was part of their upbringing. I considered this to be a worldwide experience. Why did people not question it? It seemed they stayed where they were comfortable, as far as views on life were concerned. I really didn't understand why they didn't question it. For me, it seemed unnatural not to. I thought about my adoptive father on the football terraces and swaggering in the Orange Order parades. To me, religion separated people. I decided that religion was an ideology that my son could decide about if and when he wanted to.

Having resolved one issue, I turned my mind to that other one from my past. At this time of my life the only label I had for Urquhart was that he was an 'interferer'. Having said that, I absorbed the blame swallowing whole what my mother had impressed on me during my upbringing when she'd called me a 'whore'. I couldn't comprehend it fully at this time. My terror of being killed held so strong, compounded by the way I held my secrets longer and longer.

I was already familiar with society's response to the female in general, labelling young women provocative or Lolitas, imposing dress codes, expecting a different standard of behaviour from men and women, boys and girls, just as Alex and Tim and the others were treated differently in Fernlea compared to me. Along with the ingrained verbal prejudice, I would have to face differences in class, the sub-classes or -cultures within them. My background was built from post-war dysfunction, immigration, blind religious observance, superstition and snobbery. It surely was a Frankenstein society. On top of this, alcoholism lent itself to the search for oblivion: the desperate suppression of the self.

All I knew was that I had a baby I was terrified I would lose or not be able to protect and there was no one I could confide in about my worries. As I held him, I wondered if the aspirins I'd taken would have any effect on him. I thought about the way I had neglected myself during the months of the pregnancy, staying out late or overnight, drinking. I thought about the tests at the hospital and the long labour that had caused him to become distressed. There was even the rash I'd had when Aunt Elspeth had sent me back to bed. I worried about them all.

Still at Aunt Helen's for now, but knowing that couldn't last for long, I wondered about my future. Our future. Yet he was such a settled baby. I lay in my bed at night, watching Craig sleeping, my mind quietly doing the rounds of noisy memories in my head. He literally gurgled with contentment. He was an 'easy' baby; within a week he was sleeping from seven at night to seven in the morning. A nurse had laughed and said if it wasn't for his skin colour she would have thought his father came from deepest Africa, such a mass of blond, tight curls he had, which had begun to loosen slightly as he was bathed morning and night. The gorgeous blue eyes, unlike mine, which are green, were like bright-blue moons that shone through his long, corn-coloured eyelashes. His little lips, perfect in their form and often wearing little bubbles of saliva that burst quietly with his breath, made him, as in any mother's eyes truly adorable.

Mother and baby were doing well. I had my son to take care of. I was free, escaped from the Urquharts, the children's homes, the case notes and the files. Now, free from other people's construction of my history, I thought I would begin to build my own.

Postscript

I first met Eileen in February 2007 when she arrived, flustered but grinning, half an hour late for an Open University day school I was teaching. The motorway into Glasgow had been blocked and she'd been obliged to find her own path. That more or less sums her up.

Her grin became more and more familiar to me as 2007 rolled on. In the spring, she approached me for advice concerning a major project she was undertaking: writing her autobiography. We met for coffee and she outlined the major milestones marking her life – those discussed in this book and many more, including serious health issues and personal loss. Throughout her life, she's retained her grin and her determination to find her own path no matter what the obstacle. Her story is often bleak but her attitude of laughing in the teeth of adversity made all of our writing sessions fun.

This volume of autobiography concerns the young Eileen from birth to the age of 16. We compiled it from extensive research through the detailed record of her social work case notes and other official sources. It's been a privilege to travel with her while she wrote it.

Carol McKay

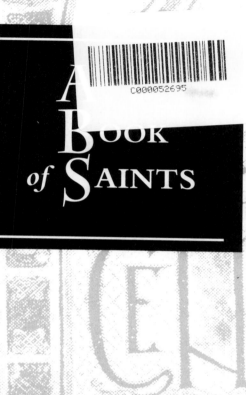

A
BOOK
of SAINTS

A
Book
of Saints

Stewart H Nicol

SAINT ANDREW PRESS
EDINBURGH

First published in 1997 by
SAINT ANDREW PRESS
121 George Street, Edinburgh

Copyright © Stewart H Nicol 1997

ISBN 0 7152 0693 1

British Library Cataloguing in Publication Data
A catalogue record for this book
is available from the British Library.

ISBN 0-7152-0693-1

Design concept by Mark Blackadder.
Printed and **bound** by
Athenaeum Press Ltd, Newcastle upon Tyne.

CONTENTS

CONTENTS

AUTHOR'S NOTE

MAJOR works consulted during the research for this book include many well known sources of information on the lives of saints. These include: Butler's *The Lives of the Fathers, Martyrs and other Principal Saints*; and the *Kalendar of Scottish Saints*, translated in 1872 by Alexander Penrose Forbes.

The modern edition of the *Oxford Dictionary of Saints* by David Hugh Farmer proved indispensable for quick reference. Also of great value was a much older book, *The Book of Saints*, by the Monks of the St Augustine Abbey near Ramsgate (published in 1931).

Other sources investigated are too numerous to mention, but include feature articles about saints, visits to churches and crypts, and interviews with priests and ministers on this topic.

Special thanks are due to my wife, Sarah, who has been something of a saint in helping out and encouraging me to stick to my deadlines, as well as keeping my writing up to scratch.

Stewart H Nicol BD

DEDICATION

This book is dedicated to my parents

HAROLD G NICOL   BELLA NICOL
(1912-1988)   (1915-1997)

A favourite song of my
father is particularly apt:

Shall we gather at the river ....
Yes we'll gather at the river,
the beautiful, the beautiful river,
gather with the saints at the river
that flows by the Throne of God.

ROBERT LOWRY 1826-1899
(words and music)

INTRODUCTION

STORIES that surround saints are often in the category of 'murder' or 'miracles'. The former may strike you as surprising when the subject is sainthood, but after reading many of the life stories contained within, you may find yourself convinced that the 'murder' part is not completely inappropriate for a book on holy people. For in this selection, several individuals destined for sainthood were put to death for their faith, for beliefs they were not willing to give up; and some met particularly violent ends for so-called 'judicial' reasons, often during political struggles. The tragic fate of Thomas More, for example, is an example of a conscience in conflict with the will of the State.

The 'miracle' aspect in the lives of saints is perhaps more recognisable to the reader. It is a word synonymous with sainthood and a miracle of one form or another is often the cause of an individual's eventual elevation to this status.

It continues to be the job of the Roman Catholic Church to confer sainthood on candidates who are put forward to them. The Vatican in Rome has a 'Devil's Advocate' who tests the cases before individuals are put forward for *beatification* (the first formal step towards sainthood), or are fully *canonised* (the official term for those individuals who show themselves to fit the criteria of sainthood).

The Vatican is the only body which formally turns ordinary men and women of faith into saints and, over the centuries, the Roman Catholic Church has carried out this task with great thoroughness. It is a difficult task, at times controversial, and later centuries have seen the reversal of some individuals who were originally accepted as saints.

The process over the years has become complex and lengthy, but changes made by John Paul II, the current Pope, have stream-lined the system, speeding it up considerably. Indeed, he has probably beatified more candidates than any other Pope in history – well over 200 in his time in the Holy See.

As mentioned above, the raw material for sainthood is ordinary people, like you and me. But what sets these people apart for sainthood is some *extra*-ordinary circumstance in their life or actions. These happenings, often seen as miraculous, must convince the Devil's Advocate that the case is without question and the individual should be put forward for the title of 'saint'.

The total number of saints to date is astounding. For this book I have chosen a selection from the shores of the United Kingdom and Ireland, in the hope that I may introduce you to some lesser known indivi-duals, as well as re-acquaint you with some of the more familiar personalities. All, I am sure, will interest and encourage you.

The criteria for inclusion in this book has

nothing to do with orthodoxy with regard to
the Roman Catholic system. Most of the
saints in this book will be recognised by
Rome, but there will be some who hark back
to earlier *Kalendars* of saints. (In Britain, Celtic
saints were all but thrown out in favour of
Roman ones as the influence of the Roman
Church grew. However, evidence of these
earlier saints has survived to this day in names
of places, wells, markets, local fairs and so on.)

We in this modern age often forget about
the saints, since their lives were so extraordinary and often difficult to identify with.
However, we can learn from their fortitude,
their strength in the face of adversity and
injustice. For, despite everything, amid all the
trials and tragedies, their faith in Christ shone
through. Few complained about their lot in
life; even fewer saw themselves as anything
above the ordinary. But later generations
recognised their worth and bestowed upon
them the honour of sainthood.

Indeed, that such men and women are
remembered in this way tells us much about
the enduring truth of our faith. The Church
exists today because of their special contri-
bution and their examples of stewardship and
education. And, as this special role continues,
I have included in this book two individuals
of more recent times who are candidates for
sainthood – John Duns Scotis and John Henry
Newman.

Finally, as this century comes to a close,
and a new millennium dawns, the process
continues and we may be witness to some
new saints canonised by the Roman Catholic

Church in the near future. On a recent Papal tour of the Pacific, a number of beatifications took place, including an Australian candidate – Mother Mary of the Cross (who was born Mary McKillop in 1842 to a Scottish father who came from Roybridge).

★　　★　　★

This book follows an alphabetical format and, in most cases, associated geographical locations have been pinpointed, so that the reader may visit a church or town or other religious/historical site, if practical. This may suggest to you a pilgrimage for picnics or a visit to a famous cathedral or place of religious interest. There may even be a welcome coffee shop in the crypt!

This book is designed to whet your appetite to learn more about saints. Dip into the text, enjoy it, and discover the stories about those who are not far below the angels.

The
SAINTS

Adamnan

*A*DAMNAN qualifies as a saint of our proposed territories – the United Kingdom and Ireland – for he has links with Ireland (where he lived most of his life), with Northumberland in north east England, and with Aberdeenshire (formerly part of Grampian Region, now involved in the reorganisation of local government returning it to its former title of Aberdeenshire – one of the unitary authorities in Scotland). Although he established a monastery in Dunkeld, Perthshire, his Scottish links are mainly in the areas surrounding the rivers Dee and Don, which finally reach the sea at Aberdeen.

I have some personal interest in Adamnan as he is linked with Aboyne in Royal Deeside where I went to school. I used to walk regularly down St Eunan's Road in Aboyne – 'Eunan' is a modified spelling of Adamnan which is found in certain references. 'Adamnon' is another variation.

Adamnan is reputed to have had an unusually long life span for his time. He died in his late seventies in 704 AD.

He was known for his skill as a writer and he completed a number of works of great importance – the best known, and possibly the most valuable, being his biography of the famous saint, Columba. Adamnan also wrote a history of Scotland and an account of the Holy Land. The latter was not written from experience, but dictated to him by a French bishop called Arculphus, who had travelled widely in that area.

According to legend, at one point in his life Arculphus found himself stranded in Britain after his ship was wrecked by a storm. There he met Adamnan and the result of this encounter was the latter's book on the Holy Land which he called *De Locis Sanctis.*

Legends exist which tell how it was the great Saint Columba himself who sent Adamnan to the tiny island of Lismore, off the west coast of Scotland. However, the chronology of Columba's death makes this impossible – he apparently died 20 or so years before Adamnan was born.

SCENE from the BATTLE of NECHTANSMERE carved on the ABERLEMNO STONE, PERTHSHIRE

Although Adamnan spent most of his life in Ireland, he also lived in the Northumbrian region of England, where it is known he negotiated on behalf of Irish hostages. This was most likely after the Battle of Nechtansmere (AD 685), where Adamnan may well have been like a

latter-day Terry Waite, negotiating for the
lives of hostages caught up in war.

Adamnan was also instrumental in
ensuring that women ceased to be placed
in the front line of battle – a common
practice at that time. You might say that
he was among the first to promote the
protection of women as a socially-acceptable
custom.

It is reported that Adamnan saw a
vision of the boy Christ prior to his own
death. This vision is mentioned in early
records – like the *Martyrology of Donegal,*
for example, which outlines the event in
some detail.

[The *Martyrology of Donegal* is currently
located in Belgium, although a copy exists
at Queen's University, Belfast. It contains
ancient liturgy and biographical accounts
of saints, their feast days and the proper
form of service for these occasions.]

Adamnan's life and work is celebrated
on September 23rd – his 'feast day'. Alternative sources suggest September 6th.

Aidan

AIDAN was a saint who was as much
at home in Scotland as the area of
Northumberland.

It was the Christian King of Northumbria – Oswald – who began Aidan's
missionary career when he sought someone from among the monks at Iona to
bring the Gospel to his people. When the

first missionary failed, Aidan was sent to do this task. He did it well and became an adviser to the King and his successors.

Eventually Aidan was consecrated a bishop and he chose the beautiful island of Lindisfarne, near Oswald's capital, Bamburgh, as his headquarters. There he established a small community, becoming Abbot of Lindisfarne around AD 634.

Aidan's symbol is a torch, which is linked to a tale of miraculous fire. It is said that an enemy king, Penda, set fire to Bamburgh. Aidan was on the nearby Island of Farne at the time, often retiring there to pray and to meditate. In the evening he saw the fire in the distance and prayed in desperation to God. At that moment the wind whipped up and turned the fire *against* those who had sought to destroy the city.

Aidan was probably a monk of the Celtic tradition. He is known to have had links with Hexham, Whitby, Coldingham and Melrose – daughter establishments of Lindisfarne. There is also evidence of his work in Iona and Glen Lyon.

A man who inspired others, he set up a school for young boys, including Chad and Wilfrid. The Venerable Bede (see page 19), in his famous *Ecclesiastical History*, wrote of him:

> *His course of life was so different from the slothfulness of our times, that all those who bore him company, whether they were shorn monks or laymen, were employed in*

meditation, that is, either reading the Scriptures, or learning psalms ...

He was wont to traverse both town and country on foot, never on horseback, unless compelled by some urgent necessity; and wherever in his way he saw any, either rich or poor, he invited them, if infidels, to embrace the mystery of the faith; or if they were believers, to strengthen them in the faith, and to stir them up by words and actions to alms and good works.

Aidan saw the importance of faith leading to an active life of simplicity and humility which resulted in good works.

His life is celebrated on the 31st of August.

Alkelda (Athilda)

WOMEN have a well established place among the saints and some of them have had more than their fair share of trials and troubles. Everyone knows, for example, about the French maid from Orleans, Joan of Arc, who was burned at the stake for her faith. (It is perhaps ironic that women can become saints in the Catholic Church, yet still be barred from the priesthood.)

In general, however, women saints are less well known. This is true of a Yorkshire girl by the name of Alkelda, sometimes recorded as 'Athilda'. She was a princess, possibly the daughter of a Cornish king, and yet it is an area of Yorkshire where she is remembered today.

Like many in the tenth century, Alkelda faced the constant threat from over the horizon, in the shape of Viking raiders from the north. (There is now archaeological evidence to suggest that the Vikings did indeed reach Yorkshire.) Where the raiders plundered, they had scant respect for religious men or women.

Alkelda's tale is thus a brutal one. She was a devout woman, probably a nun who served in the community. Sources record that she met her death at the hands of Danish pirates, rather than Vikings as one source notes. Other legends even suggest that she was strangled by 'women pirates'.

If you visit Yorkshire today there are still traces of Alkelda. A painting depicting her tragic demise is thought to exist in a church in Giggleswick. And places dedicated to Alkelda's honour and memory can be found. For example, a college was established in Middleham by Richard III in honour of Jesus Christ and Alkelda.

Many who became saints were murdered for their faith – or, to be more accurate, because they would not compromise their faith. Alkelda is one such example.

Her life is celebrated on March 27th.

Andrew

SOME saints become special not just to individuals or churches, but to entire countries. Scotland's saint is Andrew, the disciple of Jesus.

The cult of Andrew is linked to the story of Regulus or Rule (see page 87), who was shipwrecked off the coast of Fife in the eighth century (some sources say fourth) and who brought to the shores of Scotland the relics of Andrew, the fisherman from Galilee and disciple of Jesus. In response to a vision, the bones were subsequently buried at Kilrymont.

However, although exciting, it is much more likely that the seventh century clerics Wilfrid and Acca of Hexham, brought relics of Andrew back from Rome and the bones were presented, even *sold,* to the Pictish king, Angus MacFergus, who brought the bones to Fife, the heart of his kingdom. Kilrymont was the favoured destination, the place where St Andrews now stands.

What is known about Scotland's patron saint? A fisherman to trade, Andrew was one of the first disciples chosen by Jesus and was instrumental in bringing Simon Peter, his brother, to the Master. He certainly never came to Scotland during his life time, but the disciple would have had much in common with the fisherfolk of the Fife Kingdom.

Andrew, who was executed in AD 60, is thought to have been nailed to an 'X'-

SCOTLAND'S FLAG – 'The SALTIRE'

shaped cross. This particular cross, known in Scotland as the 'Saltire' from the Old French variation of the Latin *crux descussata*, inspired the famous Scottish flag – a white or silver cross out of a blue background. The Saltire is also present in the Union Jack flag, representing Scotland in the United Kingdom.

Andrew is also patron saint of the Amalfi region in Italy and his feast is still celebrated there to this day. Andrew is also thought to have been Greek in origin with links to Constantinople. However, few contemporary records exist.

Scotland's patron saint is celebrated on the 28th or 30th of November (religious calendars vary). In Scotland – and also within Scots' communities abroad – the day is still observed, even if many of the celebrations are not specifically religious in content.

One notable exception, however, is the St Andrewstide visit to London of the Moderator of the General Assembly of the Church of Scotland. There he preaches to the Scottish Members in the Houses of Parliament in St Steven's Crypt, as well as undertaking a scheduled visit to meet the Prime Minister.

Anselm

LET us now look at the saint known as Anselm (1033-1109). Anselm was a Benedictine monk and writer who rose to become a leader of the Church of his day. As Archbishop of Canterbury, he was a predecessor of the present holder of this position, the Right Revd George Carey.

This saint and theologian of some stature was born in Italy in the eleventh century of noble parentage and came to Britain via France. An early theologian and metaphysicist who was considered years ahead of his time, Anselm was also well travelled and worked tirelessly on Church councils.

In 1093 Anselm was enthroned as the Archbishop of Canterbury, but disagreements with the monarch led him to flee for his life from Britain to France. Politics and religion can be a volatile mix, then as now.

Only when the ruler at that time – King William Rufus – died, did Anselm return to serve as Archbishop under the new ruler. But he had to flee once more because of his unpopular views over who exactly was allowed to appoint bishops –

the Church or the King. Anselm favoured the former.

Anselm eventually returned to Britain for a third time – something of a miracle in itself given the basic transport available at that time – to continue his rule as Archbishop of Canterbury. This was at the request of the new king, Henry I of England.

It is true that being a bishop does not automatically set a man forth on the road to sainthood. Nevertheless Anselm went on to become a saint and, like that other famous scholar, Thomas Aquinas, did so undoubtedly by divine grace.

During his long and busy life Anselm wrote many distinguished works – his best known being *Cur Deus Homo.* As he became increasingly more famous for his writing, the city of Canterbury began to gain recognition as a centre of religious importance. The Cathedral city today is synonymous with the highest position in the Church of England and has a fine modern cathedral built from the ruins of the building destroyed during the Second World War. A visit will offer you an opportunity to learn more about Anselm and the other saints who are honoured there.

Anselm's feast day is on the 21st of April.

CANTERBURY
CATHEDRAL
in the
NINETEENTH
CENTURY

Baldred

BALDRED, known to be 'suffragan' – meaning a helper or assistant – to Saint Kentigern (better known to us as Mungo), was very pro-Scotland. This made him extremely popular north of the border – especially so when he prophesied that Scotland would extend from the River Tyne northwards!

This eighth century saint was venerated because miracles began to happen when people prayed to him. Miracles are often the first sign which inspires a petition to the Roman Catholic Church to investigate an individual's merit for sainthood.

Baldred himself was so popular in his day that, when he died, no less than three churches laid claim to his body. However, when they came to collect it, they were surprised to find there were no less than *three* identical bodies, each prepared in the customary manner befitting this most beloved individual.

This remarkable story of three bodies from one dead saint surely put him into a strong position for *beatification* – although multiplication of remains is not such a rare situation in saintly circles and appears in lore relating to a number of other saints.

Although associated with the monastic life at Melrose or Coldingham, Baldred spent his latter years as a hermit. Information on those hardy souls can be found in sources like the *Aberdeen Breviary*.

The Bass Rock

[Written in Latin, this *Breviarum Aberdonenis* is one of the few surviving books which provide an insight into the Church in Scotland prior to the Reformation. It lists a large number of saints' days, as well as the liturgy for the form of services used. The original *Breviary* belongs to the Strathmore family at Glamis Castle, but a copy is kept in the Aberdeen Reference Library and another – by the 'Bannatyne Club' – in the National Library of Scotland, Edinburgh.]

Rocky outcrops off the Scottish mainland were a favourite location for early hermits. Many who chose to live this way did so to meditate in peace, far from the distractions of life. Today most of the places they inhabited are completely empty of people, though evidence of the hermits' frugal and tough lifestyle is still obvious in places like the rocks north of the Butt of Lewis, south-western locations like Ailsa Craig (near the Isle of Arran), and, on the east coast, the Bass Rock, where Baldred has particular links.

Many saints were hermits for part, or even all, of their lives, but it was something of a trait for the Celtic saints.

During Baldred's long and extraordinary life, he is said to have been able, like Saint Peter, to walk on water. However, his best known miracle – the result is still visible today – was the moving of a rock in the Firth of Forth near North Berwick. The dangerous reef was located between the Bass Rock and the mainland and was a constant hazard to the boats which plied the Forth. By 'prayer alone', Baldred moved the rock from the path of shipping and placed it nearer the coastline.

If you visit North Berwick today, you will be able to see St Baldred's Rock from the shore. Baldred may not have moved a mountain in this context, but it certainly is an impressive enough structure!

In North Berwick you will find a notice beside the shore which gives details of Baldred's Rock. The location of this landmark – a dangerous reef – is between the famous Bass Rock and the mainland.

As you stand on the shore on a windy day it is easy to imagine just how hard life must have been for these hermits in such isolated and bleak locations, as they meditated on the Passion of Christ or some miracle of their Lord and Master.

Baldred's feast day is on the 6th of March. This is testified to in the *Aberdeen Breviary*. The same source also points to a tradition of ruins on the Bass Rock as the place inhabited for many years by Baldred.

Bartholomew

BARTHOLOMEW is a name linked to a number of different saints. When researching a book of this nature, it is interesting that, on a world-wide scale, there is often more than one saint who bears the same name. This makes research more difficult, as stories passed down by word of mouth or legend are often attributed to more than one saint, leading to some confusion. It is also why sometimes, even in scholarly circles, there are arguments over what is true and what is not about a given saint.

[For saints of earlier centuries, books like the *Aberdeen Breviary,* the *Stowe Missal* and *Martyrologies,* provide us with clues about these venerable men and women. The *Stowe Missal*, for example, is a great source of detail on the lives and work of saint, as well as providing an insight into the ritual of the early Celtic Church, illustrating the Roman *and* Gallic influences in its liturgy and in the form of the Mass.

Published for the first time in 1881, the original dates back as far as the sixth century (though some suggest the eighth). A more accurate interpretation of the *Missal,* according to some scholars, was published by a Dr MacCarthey in 1885.]

Bartholomew of Farne, who died in 1193, is the subject of this section. He was a hermit who lived on the island of Farne off the Northumberland coast.

The quaint coastal town of Whitby is

The RUGGED COAST off WHITBY

full of history and definitely worth a visit
if in the area. On the hill there, you can
see a church and monastery, which continue to provide hospitality as part of the
Youth Hostel Association. Although these
buildings are not directly linked to our
Bartholomew, it is possible that, since he
was a native of Whitby, he climbed the
hill and looked out across the same wild
seas.

Bartholomew of Farne was of Scandinavian parentage, but changed his name
to avoid trouble from local people who
were hostile toward those with Viking
associations. The ninth century Viking
raids had left deep wounds and people of
Scandinavian origin would not have been
particularly welcome.

Bartholomew's piety was clear even in
early life. He refused to marry ... *ever* –
even escaping to Norway on one occasion
when a marriage was planned for him.

In Norway he trained for the priesthood and worked for a while before

returning to his English homeland.

In later life, Bartholomew became a hermit on the island of Farne. Hermits, in those days, did not always live alone, but they did tend to live in very remote areas. Bartholomew, a rugged individual, took well to the hermit lifestyle, but shortly after he first moved onto Farne he disagreed with the other hermit in residence over, of all things, meal times and menus! A none-too-saintly way to behave ...

Bartholomew then decided to leave the island and go on to Durham. Some time later he rejoined the other hermit back on Farne and they lived together more amicably this time.

A strange story is attributed to Bartholomew. An old friend, a woman from Belgium, wished to see him. When she was refused permission to visit him on Farne, she was so angry that she ignored his refusal. When she arrived on Farne, the woman was thrown heavily onto her back as if hit by a sudden whirlwind. She only recovered thanks to the intervention of Bartholomew.

Northumbria is certainly an area of great religious significance. Many who lived and worked there in early centuries – like Aidan, Cuthbert and Bartholomew – were destined to become saints.

The feast day of Bartholomew of Farne is 24th of July.

Thomas à Becket

PERHAPS the most dastardly judicial murder of all was that of the Archbishop of Canterbury called Thomas à Becket (*circa* 1118–1170).

Becket was the Chancellor of England under King Henry II. He was an excellent negotiator and in 1162 the Church selected him as their leader.

The King was especially pleased. He expected his relationship with the Archbishop would be the same as it had always been. However, Thomas changed and took up a rather austere lifestyle as the leader of the Church of England. He then began to quibble with Henry and to criticise his way of life unreservedly. This aroused the wrath of the King and Becket had to flee in fear of his life.

Eventually this turbulent era in England's history ended. Becket returned, believing he could do so in safety – but his feeling of wellbeing was short-lived.

The ARCHBISHOP THOMAS à BECKET

The Archbishop of Canterbury continued to oppose Henry at every turn, especially over Church discipline, telling the monarch not to interfere in ecclesiastical matters. He also, in undiplomatic ways, opposed the king's oppressive tax regime. This constant niggling opposition led Henry, in a fit of rage, to speak indiscreetly to some courtiers about how he wanted this troublesome priest removed! They took him at his word.

Becket's death is well documented. He was brutally killed in his own church, in front of the altar. Hacked to death by the barons' swords, the Archbishop of Canterbury fell in a pool of blood, praying for the forgiveness of those who wronged him.

The King was shocked when he heard of the murder – the *whole* of Christendom was stunned – and in response to the outcry, Henry was forced to seek forgiveness and to do public penance for this terrible deed done in his name.

A visit to Canterbury Cathedral will provide ample evidence of this beloved saint, with stained glass windows depicting the tragic and senseless assassination.

The life of Thomas à Becket is honoured on the 29th of December.

The
ASSASINATION
of THOMAS
à BECKET

The Venerable Bede

THERE can be few historians who have travelled so short a distance as The Venerable Bede, but who have written so much of great value. Bede, who lived from AD 673 to approximately 735, wrote the famous *Ecclesiastical History of Britain*, a classic work of the history of his time. The following extract comments on the work of the first Archbishop of Canterbury, Augustine, sent by Rome to convert the pagan English by the Pope, Gregory the Great:

> **AD 597** *Augustine, thus strengthened by the confirmation of the blessed Father Gregory, returned to the work of the Word of God, with the servants of Christ, and arrived in Britain. The powerful Ethelbert was at that time King of Kent; he had extended his dominions as far as the great river Humber, by which Southern Saxons are divided from the Northern ...*

The *Ecclesiastical History* is a mine of information and it could be argued that without his written account, much of the early days of general British history would have gone without record.

Some of Bede's original work can still be seen at the Bodleian Library at Oxford University. The Library houses an original Greek and Latin copy of the *Acts of the Apostles* which, more than likely, is in Bede's own hand.

As mentioned before, the powerhouse of saints seems to have been at one time the north east of England. Bede also came from that part of the country; and if there is such a thing as a saint for home-lovers, Bede would fit the bill – he was born at Monkton on Tyne, County Durham and died in nearby Jarrow.

Bede was well known and much loved by his contemporaries, monks and bishops alike, who were influenced by his example. Dedicating his life to worship, he was known as a competent singer, as well as a talented writer. The present–day Church has a lot to thank him for.

Bede's worth was recognised centuries later. One Pope – Leo XIII – called him the 'Doctor of the Church'.

At the age of 62, like many saints, Bede became aware of his forthcoming death and prepared himself for that final adventure. After death, his bones were moved to Durham and in 1370 placed in a tomb in the Cathedral.

JARROW MONASTERY where BEDE lived and learned

The 25th of May is his feast day, although some sources list it as the 27th.

Boisil (Boswell)

IT is often difficult to track down authentic stories about the lives of saints. The Roman Calendar, once introduced, was a preferred source of names to the earlier Celtic or other 'martyrologies' (official listing of martyrs), thus Celtic saints were often replaced by Roman ones and details have become confused over time. Then, after the Reformation in the sixteenth century, saints were often forgotten or even ignored in the rush to move away from Roman Catholic practice.

With few historic facts remaining accessible or unaltered over the centuries, information on the lives and deeds of saints can be found only in literature, history books or the various calendar lists which have survived. Boisil is one such saint and it is to the martyrologies and other ancient writings that we need to look for clues to his story.

As a young man, Boisil was a very active preacher. It was later in his life that he became the Abbot of Melrose in the Scottish Borders. The well-known saint, Cuthbert, was numbered among his monks (see page35).

One thing you will notice about those destined for sainthood is that they often shared the company of others similarly fated. There seems to be something catching about such a vigorous and enthusiastic faith. Boisil and Cuthbert, for example, were the best of friends. Boisil, it is said, prophesied his own death, while indicating that Cuthbert would survive him. According to records, this was indeed the case and Cuthbert was with Boisil when he died, *circa* 661.

Boisil died young. Neither martyred nor murdered, he succumbed to pestilence. The plague tragically claimed the lives of many priests and monks in the early centuries, as they often worked closely with those afflicted with many contagious diseases. In their ignorance of medicine these carers did not take adequate precautions to safeguard themselves and truly risked their lives to help the sick.

Near Melrose today there is a place called St Boswell's. The town was named in honour of this saint. His relics, however, were removed to Durham in the eleventh century (although other sources say that they were actually moved to Jedburgh in the eighth century).

At Melrose, recently associated with the possible finding of Robert the Bruce's heart, you will experience the country-side around which Boisil must have wandered, preaching and praising God.

The feast days of saints can be some-what confusing. There are at least three dates linked to Boisil, depending on the source consulted – 23rd of February, 7th of July, or 8th of June.

Brigida

THE hallmark of a saint is something amazingly simple, yet far-reaching, in an individual's life. Perhaps they lived to teach, or to pray, or to help their fellow man or woman. In the sixth century there were several women whose exceptional lives were worthy of record. Among those who rose to sainthood was the Irish Brigida.

Brigida (also known as Bride or Bridget) was born in AD 455 and is held to be, in certain circles, on equal footing with such saints as Columba and Patrick, both her countrymen.

She was a learned nun who founded communities for women of similar devo-tion in various locations. Perhaps she could be compared to the present-day nun, Sister Agnes, who has brought the contemplative life back to Fetlar in the Shetland Islands.

Although Brigida has links with Ireland, the *Aberdeen Breviary* tells us:

> ... *Holy Brigida, whom God foreknew and predestinated into his own likeness, sprang from a good and prudent Scotic stock, having for father Dub Thacus and for mother Brocca* [and] *from her very youth profited in the study of good things.*

Brigida was determined to live a life of celibacy. When it was planned to marry her off, she prayed for some terrible deformity. According to legend, at that very moment her eyes burst and melted into her head.

Brigida's life is well documented and she has links throughout Scotland, as well as Ireland, which suggest that her cult was worshipped widely. However, she may not have actually visited or worked at any of the places where mention is made of her. Some churches may have taken her name centuries later merely because they appreciated her life story.

Brigida's cult goes back to the seventh century and many miracles were associated with her. She is particularly known as the patron saint of pity and mercy.

Her life is celebrated on the 11th of February.

Chad (Ceadda)

L INDISFARNE, known as Holy
Island, lies off the north east coast of
England. It has been a centre for spiritual
strength over many centuries. Many saints
in the first twelve centuries AD were from
that area and, by their lives and advice,
became very influential over successive
governments.

Chad (*d.* 672) was from the north east
of England. Sainthood ran in his family.
His brother Cedd, a Bishop of London,
was later canonised; and both brothers
were pupils of Aidan on Lindisfarne.

Chad was ordained Bishop of York in
AD 666 after the original nominee for the
rank, Wilfrid, failed to return from a visit
to France. But despite Chad making a
success of York, as Bede assures us in his
History, the then Archbishop of Canterbury, Theodorus, judged that the *See* of
York (a 'See' is an area overseen by a
bishop) should still belong to Wilfrid on
his return to Britain. Chad was therefore

HOLY
ISLAND

removed from the position. However, he was soon given another post – bishopric to the Mercians – and it was there that he began his own See of Lichfield.

At Lichfield a miraculous happening was witnessed. Bede's account tells us:

> *Among the eight monks whom* [Chad] *kept with him at Lichfield, was one Owini, who came with Queen Ethelred, commonly called Saint Audrey, from the province of the East Angles, and was her major-domo* [chief housekeeper], *and the first officer of her court till quitting the world ... clad in a mean garment and carrying an axe and a hatchet in his hand he went to the Monastery of Lestingay.*

Lestingay was founded by Chad in the Wolds of Yorkshire, known in his day as the mountains of the 'Deiri'.

Bede continues the account:

> [Owini] *declared that he one day heard a joyful melody of some persons sweetly singing, which descended from heaven into the Bishop's oratory, filled the same for about half an hour, then mounted to heaven again.*

The monks entered the oratory and received instructions from Chad, 'wherefore he earnestly recommended his passage to their prayers and pressed them to prepare for their own the hour of which is uncertain by watching prayer and good works'. Soon after this strange premonition of his death, Chad passed away and he was buried at Lichfield.

Chad, like many saints of that era, had a number of wells dedicated to him. The waters of the saints' wells were often said to have healing powers and so attracted pilgrims to them. In England many of these wells continue to be decorated on the individual saint's feast day. Chad's wells are mostly around the area of the Midlands. The best known can be seen today at Lichfield in Staffordshire.

Chad's feast day is celebrated on the 4th of October.

Columba (Colum Cille)

THIS best known and beloved of saints is long associated with bringing Christianity from the shores of Ireland to Scotland. However, recent scholarly rivalry, which has attempted to establish Ninian's credentials of note at Whithorn, have to some extent underlined the fact that Columba was not the only labourer in the first ripe fields of early Scotland. Nevertheless, Columba still by far out-weighs Ninian in the perception of the public at large.

Ironically, the year 1997 sees a double anniversary of Columba and Ninian. It is perhaps divine grace that puts these two names to the fore for combined celebration.

Ninian notwithstanding, today, all

around Scotland, Columba's name is found on churches he could never have reached during his life time. Even south of the Border, there are still obvious connections – for example, St Columba is the name of the Church of Scotland church in Pont Street, near the famous shop Harrods in London.

Adamnan's own record of Columba offers us a great insight into the life of this man. We do not often think of saints being excommunicated or being in any way rebellious. However, from Adamnan's history, we are told that Columba was in fact excommunicated from the Church in Ireland either for his part in civil war, or due to his frequent bouts of ill temper. In Adamnan's view, however, this was not a 'just' excommunication, but since Adamnan was of the same blood as Columba, perhaps his view was a little biased.

Whatever his experience in Ireland, Columba was encouraged to leave there and devote himself to missionary work. Scotland was to receive the benefit of his new direction in life.

Columba was a man with great zeal for the Gospel which had great effect around the whole of Scotland. When he originally left Ireland, he established his base on the island of Iona. From there he blazed his fiery trail of evangelism.

There are many stories and legends surrounding Columba, but it is the tale of his encounter with the monster of

The ABBEY on IONA

Loch Ness (another legend in its own right) which I have chosen to tell here.

On a visit north to what is now Inverness, Columba was being rowed across the Loch by some locals. All of a sudden a sea-monster rose up and attacked the boat, grabbing one unfortunate soul in its massive mouth. Columba was furious with the monster and reminded the beast that God gave Columba charge over it. Columba ordered the monster to leave the man alone and never, never to bother mankind on the Loch again.

The monster, according to lore, let the man gently down into the boat and slid back into the water, down into the icy depths and an acceptable diet of fish.

Little, if anything, of the writings of Columba himself remain, but a number of pieces are known about. One of these is the 'Altus of St Columba', a poem where each verse begins with a letter from the alphabet. The following excerpt was found in a nineteenth century publication:

The ALTUS
of ST COLUMBA

A NCIENT of days, enthroned on high!
The Father unbegotten He,
Whom space containeth not, nor time,
Who was and is and aye shall be:
And one-born Son, and Holy Ghost,
Who co-eternal glory share,
One only God, of Persons Three,
We praise, acknowledge, and declare.

B EINGS celestial first He made;
Angels and archangels of light,
In Principalities and Thrones,
And mystic rank of Power and Might:
That Love and Majesty Divine
Not aimlessly alone might dwell,
But vessels have, wherein to pour
Full wealth of gifts ineffable.

C AST from the highest heights of heaven,
Far from the Angels' shining state,
Fadeth from glory Lucifer
Falling in scorn infatuate.
Angels apostate share his fall,
Steeled with his hate, and fired with pride,
Banishèd from their fellows bright
Who in the heavenly seats abide.

D IREFUL and foul, the Dragon great,
Whose deadly rage was known of old,
The slippery serpent, wilier
Than living thing that earth doth hold:
From the bright realm of heaven he could
A third part of the stars entice,
In Hell's abyss to quench their light,
In headlong fall from Paradise.

E ARTH next and heaven, sea and sky,
Found shape within the Eternal mind,
And stood created. Next appeared
The fruitful herb, and tree in kind:

Sun, moon, and stars that climb the heavens,
    And birds and fishes, great and small,
And beasts and herds and living things,
    And man to be the king of all.

FROM every glad Angelic tongue
  Soon as the stars sprang into light,
Burst forth the wondering shout that praised
    The heavenly Creator's might.
And as His handiwork they viewed
    Arose from loving hearts and free,
The tribute due of wondrous song
    Swelling in sweetest harmony.

'GAINST Satan's wiles and Hell's assault
  Our primal parents could not stand:
And into new abysses fell
    The leader and his horrid band;
Fierce forms, with noise of beating wings,
    Too dread for sight of mortal eye,
Who fettered, far from human ken,
    Within their prison houses lie.

HIM, banished from his first estate,
  The Lord cast out for evermore;
And now his wild and rebel crew
    In upper air together soar;
Invisible, lest men should gaze
    On wickedness without a name,
And, breaking every barrier down,
    Defile themselves in open shame.

IN the three quarters of the sea
  Three mighty fountains hidden lie,
Whence rise through whirling waterspouts
    Rich-laden clouds that clothe the sky:
On winds from out his treasure-house
    They speed to swell bud, vine, and grain;
While the sea-shallows emptied wait
    Until the tides return again.

KINGS' earthly glory fleeteth fast,
  And for a moment is its stay:
God hath all might: and at a nod

The giants fall beneath His sway;
Neath waters deep, with mighty pangs,
    In fires and torments dread they rave,
Choked in the whirlpool's angry surge,
    Dashed on the rocks by every wave.

L IKE one that through a sparing sieve
    The precious grain doth slowly pour,
God sendeth down upon the earth
    The cloud-bound waters evermore:
And from the fruitful breasts of heaven,
    While changing seasons wax and wane,
The welcome streams that never fail
    Pour forth in rich supplies of rain.

M ARK how the power of God supreme
    Hath hung aloft earth's giant ball,
And fixed the great encircling deep,
    His mighty hand supporting all
Upon the pillars which He made,
    The solid rocks, and cliffs that soar,
And on the sure foundations rest,
    That stand unmoved for evermore.

N ONE doubteth that within the earth
    Glow the devouring flames of hell,
Wherein is prisoned darkest night
    Where noisome beasts and serpents dwell,
Gehenna's old and awful moan,
    And cries of men in anguish dire,
And falling tears, and gnashing teeth,
    And thirst, and hunger's burning fire.

O F realms we read beneath the world
    Where the departed spirits wait,
Who never cease to bend the knee,
    To Christ, the only potentate.
They could not ope the written Book,
    Whose seven seals none but He might break,
Fulfilling thus the Prophet's word,
    That He should come, and victory make.

PARADISE and its pleasant glades
  From the beginning God did make;
Out of whose fountain-head there flow
    Four rivers sweet, earth's thirst to slake.
And midmost stands the tree of life,
    With leaves that neither fade nor fall,
With healing to the nations fraught,
    Whose joys abundant never pull.

QUESTIONS the Singer, 'Who hath climbed
  Sinai the mountain of the Lord?
The echoing thunders who hath heard,
    And ringing trumpet-blast outpoured?
Who saw the lightning's dazzle whirl,
    And heaving rocks that crashed and fell,
Mid meteor's' glare and darts of flame,
    Save Moses, judge or Israel?'

RISETH the dawn; – the day is near,
  Day of the Lord, the King of kings;
A day of wrath and vengeance just,
    Of darkness, clouds, and thunderings;
A day of anguished cries and tears,
    When glow of woman's love shall pale;
When man shall cease to strive with man,
    And all the world's desire shall fail.

SOON shall all mortals trembling stand
  Before the Judge's awful throne,
And rendering the great account
    Shudder each hateful sin to own.
Horror of night! when none can work,
    Wailing of men, and flooding tears,
Opening the books by conscience writ,
    Riving of hearts with guilty fears.

THE trump of the archangel first
  Shall blare afar its summons dread;
And then shall burst earth's prison bars,
    And sepulchres give up their dead.
The ice of death shall melt away,
    Whilst dust grows flesh, and bone meets bone,
And every spirit finds again,
    The frame that was before her own.

UNLOOSED from the pole of heaven,
    Speedeth Orion's evil ray,
Far from the clustered Pleiades,
    Over the Ocean's trackless way.
Two years shall pass ere he return
    From East again with tortuous speed,
To shine instead of Hesperus, –
    Whoso hath wisdom let him read.

XRIST the Most High from heaven descends
    The Cross His sign and banner bright.
The sun in darkness shrouds his face,
    The moon no more pours forth her light.
The stars upon the earth shall fall
    As figs unripe drop from the tree,
When earth's broad space is bathed in fire,
    And men to dens and mountains flee.

YONDER in heaven the angel host
    Their ever-ringing anthems raise,
And flash in maze of holy dance,
    The Trinity Divine to praise.
The four-and-twenty elders cast
    Their crowns before the Lamb on high,
And the four Beasts all full of eyes
    Their ceaseless triple praises cry.

ZEAL of the Lord, consuming fire,
    Shall whelm the foes amazed and dumb,
Whose stony hearts will not receive
    That Christ hath from the Father come.
But we shall soar our Lord to meet,
    And so with Him shall ever be,
To reap the due rewards amidst
    The glories of Eternity.

★ ★ ★

There is another saint called Columba –
a woman this time. Little is known about
her except that she came from the
Cornwall area and reputedly gave her life

for the faith. Her demise was at the hands
of a heathen King of Cornwall at a time
when that part of England was a law unto
itself. Although her life time dates are
unknown, her feast date is on the 13th of
November.

Cuthbert

CUTHBERT (*circa* 634-687), whose
body lies at Durham Cathedral, was
among the pupils taught by Aidan on
Lindisfarne. If you visit Durham Cathedral
today you can find out more about this
beloved saint and actually see the location
of his burial behind the rood screen.

After Aidan's death, Cuthbert came to
Melrose in Scotland to study and work
with Boisil.

Cuthbert was a warm-hearted person
and very devout. The following miracle
is characteristic of his actions.

One day some monks, sailing on the
River Tyne, found themselves in danger
of drowning when their meagre raft was
pulled out to open sea by a strong wind.
Cuthbert, it is said, prayed earnestly, and
the wind subsided. The monks were able
to reach safety on the opposite shore.

Another story is told of the time when
he was travelling through the Teviot hills
in the company of a small boy. Cuthbert
asked the boy if he had any food, or if he
thought anyone would give them some.
The boy thought not, but Cuthbert said

simply, 'Cheer up! God will provide'.

Shortly after, the boy spotted an eagle with a fish. He ran towards it and the huge bird dropped the fish for him. He took it back to Cuthbert, who asked him if he had left some for their feathered friend.

'No,' said the boy truthfully.

So Cuthbert instructed him to return some of the fish. Despite giving half the fish back, the rest of the catch fed them quite adequately. There was even enough left to feed three other passing travellers in need of food.

This beautiful story illustrates Cuthbert's miraculous knack of producing food for the needy from virtually nothing.

When Cuthbert died, it is told how his body was wrapped in cloth and a consecrated wafer placed on his breast. Many centuries later his body was exhumed and found to be remarkably preserved – a sure sign in the eyes of many of someone destined to become a saint.

The life of Cuthbert is celebrated on his feast day, the 20th of March.

David of Scotland

DAVID was the son of another saint – Margaret (see page 67), who was the wife of King Malcolm Canmore of Scotland (also known as 'Bighead'). David, who lived from 1085 to 1153, was the youngest of six brothers.

Educated at the Anglo–Norman court, David was a devout man, with a practical interest in the welfare of the Church in his country.

He is thought to have been responsible for founding famous sites like Edinburgh and Berwick. He also founded various Scottish bishoprics – Aberdeen, Brechin and Dunblane being among them.

Two of his best known innovations in Scotland were a codified Law and the setting up of the feudal system over the former Celtic tribal system of land owner-ship. The codified Law was the first instance of a legal system set down on paper. It was devised and written down so that some type of consistent system existed to regulate land ownership.

In his life time, David I was considered a reformer, although at times his actions did appear somewhat violent. In death, however, he brought communications with the See of Rome much closer.

It is recorded that King David died in Carlisle, during prayer …

And, according to some sources, David was seen ascending towards heaven by the sixth century Mungo at the latter's own death. Given that the men lived centuries apart, Mungo's vision must have been prophetic.

Dunfermline Abbey, well-known for its connection with Robert the Bruce, is the resting place of both Scottish kings.

His feast day is on May the 24th.

David of Wales (Dewi, Dafydd)

THE number of saints who share the name David is surprising. Perhaps the best known are David, the patron saint of Wales (*circa* AD 520-601), and David I, King of Scotland.

David of Wales was a powerful preacher and a strong defender of the orthodox faith. He was in the forefront of the fight against the Pelagian heresy, which was pioneered by the Briton Pelagius (*circa* 383-409), a Christian moralist. The strange theology of Pelagius caused a lot of trouble in the early Church, as it was a view of humanity which appeared to overlook the problem of 'original sin' and the 'grace' of God. Pelagius felt that human nature had been created free from sin by God and therefore could do no wrong. Debated in the early councils of the Church, the Pelagian theory was declared a heresy.

However, in Britain the theory still held much influence in some areas and was fought against by individuals like David who laboured to ensure that a more accurate understanding of the grace of God was accepted.

David was a good Church leader who always ensured that his followers were aware of the dangers of sinful behaviour, and of the correct way to live. He is often portrayed as a man standing on a hill, a dove of peace resting on his shoulder.

The place we now call St David's in Wales, near Milford Haven, is where this saint spent his final years. There are a number of churches in that area dedicated either to him, or to Saint Nun (or 'Non'), who is reputed to have been his mother.

(The name 'Nun' is interesting, for it was not unusual for a widow in those days to join a convent.)

The spelling of David in Welsh – 'Dafydd' – is also interesting. The nick-name 'Taffy' for a Welshman comes from this root.

David's feast day is celebrated on the 1st of March.

Devenic
(Devinicus, Teauneck)

BANCHORY-Devenick is in the north east of Scotland and derives its name from Saint Devenic. It was the place the saint loved, despite all his travels, and he requested that he be buried there when the time came.

Devenic also travelled in the Caithness area in the final years of his life. This was around the time that Columba would have been preaching in Scotland.

St Devenick's Well on the other side of the River Ythan, near Aberdeen, is among the many places linked to this saint. He may also have been south of the border as far as Cornwall in his earlier preaching days. North east of Lizard

Point is a place linked to a saint called Dewednack – possibly a mis-spelling of Devenic. However, since there seem to be so many places which he visited and worked in around Aberdeen and the north east of Scotland, it would seem that he could not have had much time left to visit the south of Britain!

Devenic was considered a miracle-worker rather than a martyr, becoming a saint because miracles were effected in the wake of his death. People invoked him in prayers for the relief of their ills.

The story of his life is to be found in the *Breviary of Aberdeen*. This reference adds to the likelihood of north east Scotland as the principal locus of his works.

Devenic's feast day is on the 13th of November.

Drostan

LEGEND has it that Drostan, a saint who lived during the sixth century, was a nephew and disciple of Columba of Iona. This information can be found within the pages of one of Scotland's oldest sources, the *Book of Deer,* where we also learn something of Drostan's miraculous gifts of healing.

[The *Book of Deer* itself is a relic of the Celtic Church, providing a valuable insight into its ways. It has been difficult to track down the exact whereabouts of the original *Book of Deer.* However, in Scotland the 'Spalding Club' had an excellent copy and commentary which is now kept in the National Library of Scotland, Edinburgh.]

Reference to Drostan is also found in the pages of the *Breviary of Aberdeen:*

> *His parents handed him to his uncle,*
> *Saint Columba, then resident in Ireland,*
> *to be educated and he afterwards assumed*
> *the monastic habit at Dalquongale* [or Donegal as we know it better today].

Drostan founded the monastery of Deer and became its abbot. It served as a base for the evangelisation of the Moray Firth area. Aberdour, in the north east of Scotland, is particularly linked to Drostan, who came to the area on missionary journeys with his uncle, Columba.

In Aberdour today you will still find Drostan's Well, near the old church. It is thought that Drostan's relics were actually housed in that church.

There is evidence that a namesake travelled around the Galloway area in south west Scotland; and in places like Inverness, Insch and Markinch, you will find churches which suggest other links to Drostan. [In Inverness there is a church known as St Drostan's Urquhart; and there is a St Modrusta's (from 'Drostan') in Markinch.]

However it is the place known as Deer where Drostan was most closely associated, especially in medieval times, where he did much of the work in the art of healing that the *Book of Deer* bears witness to.

Drostan's feast day is on 11th of July.

Dunstan

SOME places which have a particular link with a saint have a special atmosphere. It may be one of tranquillity or excitement. Whatever it is, it leaves a lasting impression ...

Glastonbury, in the south west of England, is one such place. It has a myriad of links to famous saints like Dunstan who, as a monk in AD 943, worked to make the Glastonbury area of renewed importance to Christendom.

Even to this day, there is an annual pilgrimage organised to Glastonbury, and the surrounding countryside is certainly worth a visit.

Dunstan became Archbishop of Canterbury in the year AD 961 and died in 988 at 78 years old – something of a miracle considering that he nearly lost his life in the Cheddar Gorge while hunting years earlier.

He is known for his bid to restore and renew a sense of spiritual purpose to monastic life in England, under the original terms of the Benedictine Rule which was based on poverty, chastity and obedience. By the tenth century, various attempts had already been made to reform monastic life which had strayed from its original ideals.

It is said that Dunstan nearly married, but took vows instead, becoming a hermit. He was artistic and known to practice the arts of embroidery and painting and it is interesting to note that goldsmiths claim Dunstan as their very own patron saint. This is perhaps because of his artistic nature and skills.

There is a also manuscript of a Glastonbury book, housed in the Bodleian Library, which contains an illustration depicting Dunstan at the feet of Christ.

Like many priests Dunstan travelled the difficult way – on foot. It is known that he spent time in Flanders, where he 'filled Flanders with the odour of his sanctity'. According to some sources, the remains of his vestments are supposed to exist there even to this day.

During his life time Dunstan must have witnessed something of a golden age in the south of England. Indeed, he may well have been responsible for much of the change as Archbishop of Canterbury and he certainly remained influential with the kings of his time. Evidence that he was quickly moved to the level of sainthood is to be found in some pre-Norman Conquest documents.

Dunstan's feast day is on the 19th of May.

Ebba the Elder
(Aebba)

THE rugged St Abbs Head, down the Firth of Forth coastline from the city of Edinburgh, derives its name from the next saint on our list – Ebba.

'Celtic' in her outlook with regard to the development of monastic life, Ebba organised a 'mixed' monastery, which was disapproved of by the Roman Church. (It was destroyed by fire shortly after her death.) The Venerable Bede certainly frowned upon the idea of the mixed community and gave Ebba a 'bad press' when he came to write about her.

Ebba originally came to Iona and became a Christian. She worked around the Fife area and the piece of land named after her – St Abbs Head – is these days better known to ornithologists for its rich sea-bird life. She is also documented as having been the first Abbess of Cold-ingham in Berwickshire; and is known to have taught the nun Etheldreda (or Ethel-thryth) who founded Ely monastery.

Adamnan was another critic of the way Ebba ran her monastery, scolding her in his writings for her unusual attire. Ebba's nuns dressed in embroidered out-fits, described by some as bridal in style, rather than the more conventional habit.

Ebba is not widely documented, but it is known that this modern-minded abbess died around AD 683 and her feast day is on the 25th of August.

Edward the Confessor

THERE are a number of royal individuals who, as well as being 'crowned' in their temporal lives, received the crown status from the church of sainthood. Because of work done for the people of their kingdom, especially those without wealth or power, later generations were to recognise the goodness of these 'Royal rulers' and approach Rome to move them up the scale to sainthood.

Edward the 'Confessor' (*circa* 1003-66) is honoured among the saints, although historians remain undecided about him. Some see him as powerful and cunning; others as weak – the direct cause of the Norman Conquest in 1066. Edward had promised the English throne to William of Normandy, but, on his deathbed, bequeathed it to Harold instead. William invaded England to win back what he believed was promised to him.

Despite this, Edward is known to have maintained peace in his land for 20 years – an achievement in those days.

Without Edward we would not have the marvellous Westminster Abbey in London for, during his reign, he endowed almost a tenth of his considerable income to found this majestic building, 300 feet in length. It became, and remains today, an impressive setting for magnificent coronation and marriage ceremonies of the monarchy of the United Kingdom – a monument in stone to church and state.

The Shrine in Westminster Abbey
which contains the Ashes of Edward the Confessor

The status of Westminster Abbey is unique because it is a 'royal peculiar' and belongs to the Monarch rather than the Church of England. The Dean of the Abbey is answerable to Her Majesty alone.

Edward might be described as an early Anglo-Catholic as he strengthened links with the Papal authorities. He was also known to have healed people of the disease scrofula (ironically known as the 'king's evil') by his touch.

Many years after his death, Edward's body was exhumed and found to be incorrupt. He was canonised in 1161 and given the title 'Confessor' – a man loyal to his faith and resistant to worldly temptation.

Although his original feast day was in January, it is now officially recognised as the 13th of October.

Endellion

THE contacts between Scotland and
Cornwall in the extreme south west
corner of England are remarkable. A
Scots woman who had known links with
Cornwall is Endellion. She was a sixth
century virgin who dedicated her life to
the discipline of chastity. She is thought to
have particular links with Tregony where
a chapel was dedicated to her. She also
gave her name to the place St Endellion
in Cornwall.

According to legend, Endellion is said
to have brought a landowner in Tregony
back from the dead, after he had killed a
cow that had wandered onto his land. It
was the same animal that Endellion herself
depended upon for milk. Straying onto
the wrong pasture, the angry landowner
had simply slaughtered it.

When Endellion's godfather found
out about the incident, he was furious. As
he was a powerful man, he had the landowner killed!

Endellion, on discovering this extreme
act, went to the spot where the land–

owner lay and, according to legend, miraculously revived him.

Later, miracles happened when people prayed to Endellion; and these later miracles encouraged followers to begin the long process toward having Endellion declared a saint.

Endellion's feast day is on the 29th of April.

Fergus

OUR knowledge of the Scriptures, and of our own history, is due in great part to the individuals who people these pages. However, today we do not have to defend the Christian faith to the extremes these valiant souls did before us. Our view of the faith is from the shoulders of these giants, and one of these giants is the great saint known as Fergus.

Today a terminal bringing the North Sea's natural gas to the mainland is located at St Fergus near Fraserburgh, in the north east of Scotland. It is something of a miracle in itself that such modern technology exists in the first place, never mind the miracle of transferring a precious resource from the depths of the sea to its use as an energy source in our homes. This whole enterprise may well have appealed to Fergus, a man who never discounted the unusual or the impossible.

Fergus, who lived in the eighth century, was another of those Irish monks whose missionary zeal in and throughout Scotland continued unabated. He was thought to be a Pict and merits a mention in the *Breviary of Aberdeen* as a bishop in Ireland.

The place in north east Scotland which now takes the name of Fergus was known in his time as Lungley.

Fergus later went to Caithness and established Wick. His links there produce one of his more unusual stories. It is said that a stone effigy of Fergus was kept in the town and was greatly loved by the residents. After the Reformation in Scotland, in a bid to get rid of superstition, a local minister was so zealous in his 'mission' of destruction that he had the effigy of stone smashed up. Ironically he had signed his own death sentence! The people were so enraged, they threw the minister into the river where he drowned.

This is a legend, of course – its authenticity is fragile, as are many tales of miracles contained within these pages. However, it does illustrate an issue which the Reformers and the Protestant tradition of the Church have never quite resolved – that of the place of the saints. The fact that there is little or no calendar of saints' days in the Church of Scotland today, for example, is a result of the Reformed Church's reluctance to include the saints in its policy.

Returning to Fergus himself, like many saints he has a well dedicated to him. In this case it is in Glamis Castle in the Angus region of Scotland. His relics were for a time retained there, but they were later removed to Scone in the time of King James IV.

Fergus could well have travelled outside Scotland and Ireland – it is noted in some sources that he was present at one time in Rome, for a council in AD 721, but this is not certain.

He also appears in the pages of the *Book of Deer*, and it is thought that the relic of his arm may have been kept at some time in Aberdeen.

Fergus' feast day is celebrated on the 27th of November (15th of November in the Scottish Episcopal Church).

Fillan (Faelan)

SAINT Fillan – variously known as Faelan, Aengus or Colgan – is remembered in places which depict his name, or a derivative of it. These include Killin, Skelmorlie, Cunningham, Largs – as well as Kilphillane in Wigtownshire. The town of Pittenweem, where Fillan's east coast cave is reputed to be, is another location which can be visited these days. It is a popular tourist spot.

Fillan's dates are not recorded in detail, but it is thought that he lived around the early to mid eighth century.

It is certain, however, that his mother, Kentigerna, died around AD 735. She was also destined for sainthood.

Fillan's father, it is said, did not like his son and tried to have him cast into a lake. According to the legend, Fillan survived for a year in the water with the help of ministering angels.

Fillan is linked to the famous Battle of Bannockburn in 1314. According to the mediaeval historian Hector Boece, King Robert the Bruce prayed to Fillan before the battle in the mistaken belief that the relic of the arm of the saint had been carried into the battlefield with them.

The saint's arm was thought to have had special powers because one night a monk had observed Fillan writing in his cell – even though it was pitch dark! He wrote by the light which was shining from his other hand as he held it over the manuscript.

The priest, who had set up the altar before the battle, and who knew that there was no relic within, suddenly heard the silver case shake – the sudden appearance of the arm was indeed a miracle!

The priest was so amazed, he forgot the danger of telling the king that he had not carried out the original instructions to bring the relic. Instead he admitted he had been so concerned that the relic might be lost in the battle that he had removed it. By a miracle it had appeared again in its case!

Robert the Bruce thought the event was a sign of great importance, especially when the final result of the battle went in Bruce's favour.

Saint Fillan was not only credited with winning battles, but also with curing those who were mentally ill.

Strathfillan's Holy Pool was one location where they brought people who were considered insane to be cured by the waters – or, to be more accurate, *beside* the waters. The ritual was to tie the sick person to a bed. If, by morning, he or she were found untied, the cure was seen to be complete. They were then released, complete with sound mind and peaceful countenance.

Saint Fillan's feast day is generally held to be on the 9th of January, but some calendars suggest the 19th.

Finan (Finian)

THE pastoral and majestic landscape of Royal Deeside still makes it easy to imagine yourself back through the centuries, the saints trekking across the open countryside, through woods and fields, and down by the River Dee.

Among the many saints who went on missionary journeys was Finan. This saint was a follower of the better known saint, Mungo (or Kentigern, see page 71). He is known to have worked around the Aberdeen area and thought to have built several churches in the latter half of the sixth century.

We know that he certainly travelled inland, for you can visit a church building dedicated to him near the village of Lumphanan – although the church is no longer in use. It is located near the place where the real King Macbeth of Scotland took his last stand.

Interestingly, the village name – Lumphanan – is similar to LLanfinnan in Wales. Evidence suggests that it may well have been the same Finan who gave his name to both places.

Apart from liturgical calendars giving saints' feast days, a clue to the presence of a saint can be found in the name of a local fair.

[In the past many fairs were held throughout the country, but the advent of the supermarket or shopping centre has meant that many small outdoor markets have disappeared. Some local fairs and market days have survived, however – usually bearing names which echo a long lost saint or feast day. It was a special day for the whole community – a 'holy day'.

Fairs could last a day, sometimes more. There is an account of a fair in Newburgh lasting eight days! Market days, on the other hand, were held more often than fairs and were chiefly a time for buying and selling.

Other fair names in existence today which echo the custom of the past include St Barr's at Eddleston (from the saint known as Finbar); the Magnusmas Fair at Watten-Wester (from Magnus); Paldy's fair at Fordoun (from Palladius); and Hallowmas, Lammas, Kirk Dandy,

Middlemas, Candlemas and Whitsuntide (taken from the original feast days in the Calendar).]

In Finan's case, the 'Finzean Fair' used to take place in March or April at Migve, near Tarland, on Deeside. 'Finzean' is an unusual spelling which may well have been derived from Finan.

Finan's feast day is celebrated on the 18th of March.

George the Martyr

THE well-known tale of George and the Dragon is a legend linked to George the Martyr. Beyond this, little is known about the famous patron saint of England.

It is thought, however, that George died around the beginning of the fourth century. Since this is documented by Bede, this claim is likely to be accurate.

The reason George was elevated to sainthood is lost in the mists of antiquity and it is hard to distinguish legend from history. The following is what is thought to have happened to the famous fighter of dragons.

It is said that George was more than likely martyred *circa* 303. This may even be linked to the persecution of Christians by Diocletian. Diocletian was a Roman Emperor who lived from AD 284–305. He was a strict believer in the old Roman tradition which led him to undertake the ruthless persecution of Christians in 303.

The English link to George is difficult to trace, but the cult of George is closely connected to the golden legend of his fight with the dragon. His ability to slay the monster by first capturing it, and thus saving the King's daughter's life, resulted in the King agreeing to convert to Christianity and to looking after those who were professed followers of Christ. It is said that around 15,000 people were baptised as part of this agreement.

George's continued popularity as patron saint of England was probably due to the Crusades – a series of campaigns of war by Europeans into the Levant area of the Middle East between 1095 and 1291. In 1095 Pope Urban II proclaimed a War to reclaim the Holy Land – Jerusalem was to be restored as the Holy city by force – with the second crusade in 1147, the third *circa* 1187 and the fourth major one from 1228-29. There are some who suggest there were seven such crusades, but the four dates here depict the major battles.

The English king, Richard the Lionheart, led the way in 1187. He raised the money for the venture, fought across the miles, but failed to capture to Jerusalem.

The Crusades were embarked upon because the ground taken by the Moslems was increasing to the very door of Spain. The spread of Islam seemed as if it would overwhelm Europe if not stopped.

It is said that, during the siege of Antioch, a vision of Saint George was witnessed. Richard I immediately placed his army under George's protection and he won the battle, defeating the enemy Saracens.

Later in history, the feast day of Saint George was made a holiday – a significant measure of his growing importance.

The patron saint of England is very much the saint of the soldier, the protector of the Kingdom. He is synonymous with courageous, chivalrous knights resplendent in shining armour – and with soldiers as well as armourers. He is the kind of figure to aid the damsel in distress, to fight the dragon, to risk his life for what he believes in. He has confidence in his faith.

Although there is little evidence to prove that the dragon-slaying is true, it was clearly the influence of Saint George on the knights of the Crusades which really established his cult in England.

These days there are many churches dedicated to this saint and his feast day is celebrated on the 23rd of April.

Giles

THE High Kirk in Edinburgh's famous High Street is known as St Giles Cathedral. Tourists perhaps give little thought to who this particular saint was, as their interest is more likely to be in John Knox, founder of the Reformation in Scotland. (If the Kirk did have a roll of saints, Knox would probably head the list!)

There is very little known about Giles, but he is thought to have been a saint of Greek origin, although much of his life was spent as a hermit in Southern France. There are some indications, less clear, that he also spent time in Spain.

It is most unlikely that Giles came to Scotland, so how did he come to be associated with that country?

Perhaps, if Giles did study or work in France, he may have come into contact with Scots monks who frequented that country. Did his reputation spread from these early contacts?

The more likely answer to his fame, however, comes from the time of the Crusades. Many soldiers from Britain, on their way to and from the Holy Land, would have made a pilgrimage to the shrine of St Giles in the Rhone Valley area of France.

The SEAL of St GILES

There is an interesting legend told about Giles, maybe the only one broadly known. It happened when he was living as a hermit in the Rhone Valley. One day, while a king was out hunting, Giles was shot through the arm by an arrow from the king's bow. He had been doing his utmost to protect a deer which the royal hunter was out to kill.

The king was so ashamed for hitting this gentle priest he granted him land in the valley, which later became the location for a Benedictine monastery. The hind which Giles protected was later incorporated into the king's coat of arms.

The well-known St Giles Cathedral, the High Kirk in Edinburgh, is by no means the only church bearing this saint's name. There is also a St Giles, Cripplegate in London (near the Barbican), and a St Giles in Elgin.

The feast date of this saint is on the 1st of September.

Gwen (Blanche)

THE majority of saints lived in the early centuries of this millennium. However, many people who lived in the Middle Ages and after were also canonised by the Roman Catholic Church.

Since the process of becoming a saint was lengthy one, and often took centuries, it is useful to bear in mind that some stories have become confused over the years. This is true in the case of Gwen. The *Book of Saints* – a Benedictine work – mentions two women of this name.

'Gwen of Wales', according to sources, was a woman of character who suffered a violent death at the hands of the Saxons. The other 'Gwen', however, is associated with Cornwall.

It is thought that 'Gwen of Wales' lived in the fifth century. The name 'Gwen' means 'white'. Some sources suggest that she was the aunt of David of Wales.

Talgarth in Wales is the area where Gwen worked and lived, and where she was tragically murdered by the Saxons.

The feast day of Gwen of Wales is on the 18th of October.

Herbert

A COLLEAGUE of Cuthbert, Herbert was based originally at Melrose in the Scottish Borders. He is thought to have been Cuthbert's 'soul friend' and they met together on a regular basis to talk and pray. They were both Saxon in origin.

Herbert mainly worked in the Lake District and was a hermit in that area. The isle he lived on was later named St Herbert's Isle and in the fourteenth century the Bishop of Carlisle suggested that a mass should be said on the island's church, each year on the saint's feast day. He also said that any who attended this mass could expect some indulgence, a pardon for sins committed.

Herbert and Cuthbert met annually, usually on Lindisfarne. The final time they met was in Carlisle, however, and this may explain a later link to the saint. At this meeting Herbert predicted that the two men would die on the same day and prayed that they would be friends in death as in life. Herbert died in AD 687, March 20th ... the same day as Cuthbert.

Melrose was an important Christian

centre in the early days of the Church. Many of the priests who were taught there later became saints – like Herbert, Cuthbert and Boisil. Sadly many of the areas which were strong in Christian teaching in the past, are now no longer the centres of commerce or meeting-places for travellers they used to be.

Melrose, however, continues to have a distinctive spiritual atmosphere. The ruins of the Abbey and its environs are still worth a visit today.

The feast day of Herbert is on the 20th of March, although it was a less popular event in the earlier centuries than the feast day of his friend Cuthbert.

Hilda

HILDA, the first Abbess of Whitby, was someone who brought the best out of those she met and taught, inspiring some to great achievements. Hartlepool, on the north east coast of England, is not perhaps a place you would instantly link with religious fervour. However, it was there that Hilda began her organisation of a community for nuns.

According to the Venerable Bede, Hilda did not have a full-time religious life until she was over thirty years old. However she made up for this late start and, in a very short time, appeared to outshine her contemporaries with her achievements.

Hilda eventually left her community at Hartlepool and was called to Whitby. There she became the Abbess at a double monastery. This probably referred to one which housed monks and nuns together, in the same location, but not mixed as in the Celtic model.

The historic Synod of Whitby in AD 664 was, you might say, catered for by Hilda – no mean feat of organisation in those early days of communication.

Hilda was known to be an outstanding teacher. No less than five of the men she trained became bishops – including a Bishop of York.

Another famous name among her pupils was Caedmon, the first recognised English poet. Caedmon, who had been a simple cowherd when he came under her wing, was encouraged and tutored by Hilda. In time she inspired in him such confidence that he wrote his wonderful poetry.

Hilda died in AD 680 at the age of 66, having fought a fever for years. In the Yorkshire area no less than 35 churches are dedicated to her.

If you visit the town of Whitby today, take a walk along the clifftop and look out to sea. As the wind swirls around, you can begin to imagine the harsh life these dedicated people lived.

November the 17th is the feast day dedicated to Hilda.

Laurence

AMONG the first to bring Christianity to the south east of England was a man called Laurence. It is recorded that, in the sixth century, he travelled with Augustine to Britain to preach the Gospel and to convert the Angles and Saxons to the Christian faith.

Laurence was a trusted messenger between Augustine, the first Archbishop of Canterbury, and Pope Gregory in Rome. And Augustine was so impressed with Laurence that he named him as successor to the Primacy of all England.

However, the religious and political climate changed and some of Augustine's colleagues left Britain to escape growing danger. Laurence was about to do the same when he had a dream that Saint Peter beat him black and blue for being such a coward.

He knew then that he had to stay and, in the complicated and delicate relations with the Celtic Church which developed, Laurence seems to have coped rather well. Indeed, he was highly respected and was given honourable mention in the *Stowe Missal*, in the Canon of the Mass.

Laurence was among those seeking to solve the 'Easter Question', to decide *when* Christ's resurrection should be celebrated – a controversy which troubled the British Church at that time. Laurence, along with Justus and Mellitus, wrote to the Irish Bishops imploring them to conform to the Roman Easter. This difficulty took centuries to sort out, as the Celtic Church followed a different calculation from the Roman Church.

Laurence worked on this problem during his life, but it was much later in 619 before unity reigned in the celebration of Easter on a common date throughout Christendom.

Laurence's feast day is celebrated on the 2nd or 3rd of February.

Machar

*A*BERDEEN is the city linked to the saint known as Machar. The cathedral which bears his name stands proud near the banks of the River Don. The spot on the river which bends like a shepherd's crook was chosen by Machar himself.

Machar has known links with Iona and the saint, Columba. Of Scots-Irish stock, and a native of Ireland, Machar came to meet and work with Columba; and while in Scotland, he carried out his own work around Aberdeen. This was among the fierce warrior people who painted their faces and bodies – the Picts.

Machar (sometimes found in the form 'Mauritius', the name supposedly given to him by Pope Gregory) is said to have been instructed by the Church to go to Alba (*ie* Scotland). There he was told to build a church where the river resembled a shepherd's crook. He found this pheno-

St Machar's Cathedral, Aberdeen

menon near the mouth of the meandering River Don and where the river almost doubled back like a crook, he built his church.

Today the twin-spired cathedral bearing the saint's name is still working to spread the Gospel in that part of Scotland. At one time it took water for baptisms from a well also linked to the saint.

If you visit the cathedral today you will be able to see for yourself the meandering river resembling the pastoral staff Machar had been instructed to find!

Machar himself was known to be a man of great goodness and many miracles are attributed to him. It is said that one miracle was accomplished when he turned to stone a wild beast which had been bothering the neighbourhood for some time. There is evidence in the *Breviary of Aberdeen* to suggest that the beast was a wild boar. The *Breviary* alludes to the stone boar itself still being in existence at the time of the book's composition.

Machar also took on the false gods of that era and turned many of his contemporaries to the Christian faith in which he lived and preached and had his being.

He is known to have travelled widely and is thought to have moved eventually to Rome where, it is said, Pope Gregory named Machar as Bishop of Tours, and established yet another connection between France and the British Isles.

Machar's feast day is celebrated on the 12th of November.

Magnus

SAINT Magnus is synonymous with Orkney. The cathedral in Kirkwall which bears his name was founded in the twelfth century.

Jarl (Earl) Magnus Erlingsson was of Viking origin and considered a man of mild character. Ironically this gentle man met a violent and untimely death which was shrouded in political intrigue.

Magnus started off life as a Viking, but somewhere along the line he was converted to Christianity. At this time he was captured by another Magnus – Magnus Barefoot (known also as Bareknees) – who forced him to go on raids targeted at the east coast of Britain.

However, staying true to his new found faith, Magnus risked his life, remaining on board the longship reading his Psalter, instead of taking part in the pillage and plunder. Naturally this did not amuse his captors, especially Magnus Barefoot.

Magnus eventually managed to escape, seeking sanctuary on the mainland at the court of King Malcolm of Scotland.

When Barefoot died, Magnus returned to Orkney. This time he planned to work with his cousin, King Hakon. However, Hakon was power-hungry and decided to have the mild-mannered Magnus killed rather than let him interfere with his plans.

So Magnus was hacked to death by the swords of Hakon and his followers at Egilsay. Legend tells us that Magnus, like Christ, prayed for his murderers.

Magnus is much admired among the faithful in Orkney. However, his name is also known and loved further north on the Shetland Islands, and throughout other parts of Scotland as well.

The feast day for Magnus is the 16th of April.

Margaret

R OYAL saints certainly do exist. In Scotland, Margaret (*circa* 1045–1093) is one of the best known.

You will find a particularly beautiful stained glass window depicting Queen Margaret at Dunfermline Abbey. The Abbey was built at her instigation and was to be the Scottish equivalent of Westminster Abbey, and the place where she and her husband Malcolm were to be buried.

Margaret was born in Hungary to an English father, a member of West Saxon royalty who had been exiled from his homeland by King Canute. Having returned to England years later, with her sister Christina and brother Edgar, the intended successor to King Edward the Confessor, the events of the Norman Conquest in 1066 forced the family to flee to the north of England. Still at risk they escaped to Scotland. There she was noticed by recently-widowed King Malcolm III (Malcolm Canmore – 'bighead', as he was known) and she became the new Queen of Scotland.

Margaret arrived in a Scotland that was an inhospitable and violent place. Superstition and immorality were rife. It was in this less than civilised country, with its Church at a low ebb, that Margaret set out on her mission of improvement.

She was instrumental in carrying out a great deal of work among the poor, establishing hostels for the destitute. And, in common with the late Lord MacLeod of Fuinary, the island of Iona, off the west coast of Scotland, held a special place in Margaret's heart. There, she set about re-establishing Columba's Abbey.

She also had a great deal to do with re-establishing Sunday as a special day of rest and worship. Her own devout life, with its rigorous prayer routine, impressed those at the Scottish Court and the wider public of the time. This earned her the hard-won respect of her people.

Margaret appears in the *Breviary of Aberdeen*. It was Pope Innocent IV who canonised her in 1251 and authorised her feast day on the 16th of November. However, a later Pope, Innocent XII, moved the feast day to the 10th of June. This was done under the direction of King James VII who wanted this feast day to be on the same day as his son's birthday.

Margaret seems to have been a person of outstanding qualities. She not only achieved all the above, but bore no less than *eight* children. A number of them became kings in their own right, like David I of Scotland.

There is little evidence of miraculous stories attributed to Margaret, but there is at least one legend which suggests that she was able to recover a Bible from the bottom of a river without getting wet!

In the Bodleian Library, Oxford there is an exhibit on show which would have belonged to Margaret. It is a small, highly ornate Gospel, complete with gold initials.

Margaret died young, only 48 years of age. The 900th anniversary of her death was celebrated in 1993.

Recently, an elder at Dunfermline Abbey testified that the power and presence of Saint Margaret still works in that church. People come with their problems to pray in front of the stained glass window of St Margaret. Many leave saying that the special atmosphere in the church has helped them. And several bear witness to the fact that they feel refreshed and encouraged.

Margaret's life is celebrated on the 10th of June.

Thomas More

HERE is a tale of murder most foul. Thomas More is among the martyrs who was, you might say, judicially murdered. His only crime was to oppose the infamous King Henry VIII, the monarch who had six wives.

More was at first sympathetic to Henry, but his conscience would not allow him to agree to Henry's second marriage to Anne Boleyn since it would mean divorcing his first wife, the Spanish Catholic Catherine of Aragon.

Thomas More was a writer – and a persuasive one at that. It was his defence of King Henry VIII's work, *The Seven Sacraments,* to the Pope which earned

Henry the title, 'Defender of the Faith'. This support is ironic in the light of later events, when More could not in good conscience agree with Henry's marital plans.

When the Act of Succession of 1534 demanded recognition of Henry's offspring by his new wife Anne Boleyn, More's denial of the Act sealed his fate! Standing rigidly against this anomaly, he was accused of treason by a furious Henry and many of More's friends perished in the Tower of London in the wake of the king's anger. More himself was executed after 15 months of grim captivity.

THOMAS MORE

The fact that the Queen is the Head of the Church of England to this day stems from Henry's wish to divorce his first wife. In order to make this possible, the king gained control over the Church through an Act of Supremacy, making him Head of the English Church. Thus he was able to divorce at will *and* he had made himself Head of the Church, even above the Archbishop!

Thomas More was martyred for his courageous stance against the state. It was several centuries before he became venerated and finally raised to sainthood in the eyes of the Roman Catholic Church.

His feast day is celebrated on the 6th of July.

Mungo (Kentigern)

MUNGO, a saint from the sixth century, has links with the west of Scotland. The name 'Mungo' means 'dearest'. Although he is better known in the Deeside area as Kentigern, where he is much loved, Glasgow is the place which took Mungo as its patron saint.

Today's Glasgow is a large and busy industrial city well worth a visit. Its coat of arms tells us a great deal about Mungo, for the fish represents the salmon caught in the River Clyde by the saint. The story goes that the Queen of Cadzow had asked Mungo for help to find her wedding ring. Her husband was very angry with her, not believing that she had lost it accidentally in the river. So Mungo obligingly pulled a huge salmon from the Clyde and opened it up to reveal the ring which he returned to the Queen.

The life of Mungo is miraculous in itself, as he was an unlikely candidate for the priesthood – he was born illegitimate. In those days that normally meant automatic disqualification. Mungo was the exception and exceptional people have a habit of overcoming the impossible.

Thenew, his mother (see page 99), had been brutally attacked and raped. Yet, despite an attempt by her father to kill the unborn child by having Thenew stoned and thrown over a precipice, the baby survived.

In later years Mungo was educated at

Culross. He was tutored by another saint by the name of Serf (see page 93). An excellent pupil, Serf was sorry when Mungo left to work on his own.

Many stories are written about Mungo's miracles. There is the one about the fish and the royal ring, related earlier. Another favourite concerns Serf's pet robin. Serf is said to have had a favourite bird, a robin redbreast, which sadly died. Mungo, through fervent prayer and by making the sign of the cross, brought the little bird back to life. According to the *Aberdeen Breviary,* he also had powers of healing and is said to have revived a poor convent cook from the dead.

Mungo was a hard worker, much loved by his people. He was something of a Moses character as well, with at least one story telling how he parted the waters on one occasion – not the Red Sea in this instance, but the Firth of Forth!

GLASGOW CATHEDRAL

Mungo sent out many others in his way to preach the Gospel in Deeside, and he is remembered in places as far apart as Banchory near Aberdeen, parts of Wales, and Cumbria. There is also mention of him in Cologne, Germany, where in the cathedral there exists possibly the only centuries-old painting of this saint.

Sadly there are no relics of Mungo in Glasgow Cathedral – the Reformation ensured the destruction of much, if not all, of this type of worship throughout Scotland.

The feast day of this saint is on the 13th of January. Other sources claim the 14th.

Nathalan

NATHALAN is a popular saint in Royal Deeside, Aberdeenshire. He travelled widely, preached to many, and lived a simple but faithful life.

Like the rest of us, Nathalan had faults and failings. He often complained loudly about the miserable Scottish weather – Royal Deeside weather is notorious for producing four seasons in a single day – and when he wanted sun for the harvest preparation, it was cold and wet. Out in the field one day, in a fit of temper, he cursed the weather! The words had barely died on his lips when the clouds melted away. The sun came out and the resulting harvest was a bumper one.

This made Nathalan rather ashamed about his loss of temper. In penance he chained his ankle to his wrist, threw the key into the River Dee, and set out on a long pilgrimage to Rome to seek forgiveness for his sins. After many months of travel, which was painful and difficult in his shackled state, he arrived in Rome. There, confessing his sin, he was absolved.

On his way home, Nathalan bought a fish at a small market. Inside the fish, to his great surprise, he found the key to unlock his chains. This made his return journey very much easier and he felt forgiven, thanks to this miracle.

These days, if you journey up towards Ballater on Deeside, you will find Saint Nathalan's Well. In earlier centuries its waters were thought to cure various ills. Sadly the Well is no longer maintained to the same extent as some of the wells in England which are often beautifully decorated on feast days.

January the 8th or 19th are variously stated as Nathalan's feast dates.

John Henry Newman

RECENT years seem to have yielded fewer saints, but this man is on his way to becoming a 'saint' in the official sense. John Henry Newman (1801-1890) deserves sainthood simply for what he achieved in his life time in no less than two different denominations. For Newman was not only a leading figure in the Anglican Church of the Victorian era, *and* a prominent hymn-writer, but also a cardinal in the Roman Catholic Church of which he became a member in later life.

He is unusual for a 'saint-to-be' of recent times in that he has written so much. Intellectuals are few and far be-tween in the listings of saints, although there are certainly precedents – like the Venerable Bede of course; and Anselm, the man who stood intellectually head and shoulders above his contemporaries.

Newman, however, was one of the leading lights in what became known as the Oxford Movement in the Victorian Church of England. This was a group of like-minded clerics who did much for those in the worst positions of poverty. They had a special style of service and depended much on a liturgy which would not have been out of place in any Roman Catholic church of the time.

They sought to give their often poorly-educated congregations a very visual service. They used the brightest coloured vestments and glorious stained glass win-dows, as well as other sensual mediums, like incense. Indeed when Newman moved to the Roman Catholic Church, there were some who expressed surprise that he had taken so long to decide to do just that!

Newman reached the rank of cardinal at the end of his long service in the

Church. In recent years he has been one of those worthies put forward for the complex system of beatification.

However it may be a long time before Newman is officially put on the list of saints by the current Pope, John Paul II, who is in the process of streamlining the system of canonising those for the saint-hood.

Ninian

SAINT Ninian is rarely given the status in Scotland that he may well deserve, as Columba seems to be the saint popularly recognised as bringing Christianity to the Picts in the north. However, listed by the Venerable Bede, who refers to him as 'an honoured bishop', fifth century Ninian, thought to be the son of a British chieftain, settled in south west Scotland at Whithorn in Galloway, at the tail-end of the Roman occupation. The name of the church he established, *Candida Casa,* meant 'shining place' or 'white house'.

The recent archaeological survey of Whithorn continues to reveal more and more evidence about Ninian and his fellow workers in Christ. At the Whithorn Dig you will be able to see the outline of buildings which would have been in existence when the saint trod the earth.

Ninian took an interest in Christianity very early on in life and was baptised in boyhood. He eventually went to Rome where he studied hard and showed himself to be very devout. In doing so, he came to the attention of the Pope and was in time ordained, returning to his homeland to preach the Gospel.

At that time it was difficult to be an active Christian, since heresy and idolatry were rife. The Picts especially were a fierce nation and not inclined towards the new faith. Ninian, however, persuaded them of the error of their ways – a testament to his strong faith and character.

The
STAINED–GLASS
WINDOW
in ST NINIAN
PRIORY

Thus Ninian, who is thought to have lived during the fifth century, was in fact sowing the seeds of Christianity in Scotland long before Columba, who was born a century later.

Ninian's feast day is celebrated on the 16th of September.

Nothelm

MANY who held the position of Archbishop of Canterbury in the early centuries of the Church, later became saints. Their example of self-sacrifice for the people they served set them apart. Nothelm was one such saint.

Little detail exists about him, but it is thought that he lived around the eighth century and worked in the London area. He knew the saint Boniface and was a friend of the Venerable Bede whom he may well have assisted with his classic *Ecclesiastical History.* It is said that Nothelm provided Bede with some letters which passed between Pope Gregory and Augustine of Canterbury, but the authenticity of these letters has been questioned in some quarters and it is not known whether Nothelm was aware that they were possible forgeries.

Nothelm died in AD 740 and his body was moved to Canterbury around the eleventh century (later, according to some sources). His feast day is celebrated on the 17th of October.

John Ogilvie

JOHN Ogilvie was recently made a saint. He was a Scot whom the present Pope canonised just over twenty years ago. Indeed the man whose cancer cure was put down to prayer to John Ogilvie – a docker from Glasgow called John Fagan – was able to be present in Rome for the special canonisation ceremony which took place for Ogilvie in 1976.

There was much rejoicing in Scotland

at the time of his canonisation. He became the first Scottish saint since Queen Margaret, almost 750 years before.

John Ogilvie, born a Presbyterian, lived in Scotland at the end of the sixteenth and beginning of the seventeenth centuries. These were difficult times for the faith and he was brought up a Calvinist. He was educated in mainland Europe and in the process became a Roman Catholic, joining the Jesuits and working in Austria for nearly a decade.

John Ogilvie did re-visit the land of his birth, basing himself in Edinburgh for a time, fired up with zeal to return the Scots to the Roman Catholic fold. But by the time he had returned, the religious climate was stormy to say the least.

It was sadly an age of intolerance that greeted him, where the reaction against the Roman Catholic Church had reached terrible levels of violence and hatred. Many Catholics at this time were being forced 'underground' in the practise of their faith.

Ogilvie himself fell foul of the then Archbishop of Glasgow, who supported the Protestant James VI of Scotland in his new role as James I of England, ruler of the 'United Kingdom' since 1603. (The Archbishop had shown his loyalty to the King by speaking out vehemently against the Gunpowder Plot, the Guy Fawkes conspiracy to assassinate the monarch.) With such a powerful enemy, Ogilvie's days were numbered.

Ogilvie was tortured viciously in a fruitless effort to make him renounce his Catholicism. He was kept awake for days on end and it was said that he was thrown around so much his hair was torn out at the roots. But despite this horrific catalogue of torture, Ogilvie would not renounce his faith or name his co-religionists.

He was tried and ultimately convicted of treason. At his execution he requested the prayers of any Catholics hidden in the crowd.

Glasgow is the city that remembers John Ogilvie and was instrumental in his canonisation. In the Easterhouse area of that great city is the home of the John Fagan who was cured of terminal cancer through prayers to the brave Roman Catholic who died for his faith.

The feast day of John Ogilvie is on the 10th of March.

Osythe

IN the seventh century, one of the individuals assisting the then Bishop of London to establish Chertsey Monastery was a princess called Osythe. She had been brought up by a nun who in time was to become a saint herself and Osythe soon learned the ways of the Christian faith.

Osythe was determined to remain a virgin, but, coming under her parent's control again, she was ordered to be married off to a royal suitor – King Sighere. On the wedding day, during an early feast, a stag passed the castle. The king, being a keen hunter, left the feast for a while to hunt the animal. Osythe took her chance and fled to sanctuary with Bishop Acca at Dunwich.

Happily Sighere granted Osythe her freedom to become a nun, recognising the lady's devout wish to live the religious life. In addition he gifted her land at Chich on the River Colne. Today the saint's name is the more familiar version of 'Chich'.

Osythe's happiness was to be short-lived. Danish pirates raided the area and, according to legend, beheaded her. It is told that Osythe picked up her head and ran with it to the church door before dropping dead. There is supposed to be a spring marking the spot where she was killed which has, according to legend, miraculous powers.

Palladius

JULY is the month of this saint's feast. Although thought to have worked in Ireland, Palladius has been associated with the north east of Scotland. Legend has it that his relics were brought there in later times. His name is also linked with that of Serf.

It is thought that Palladius had been

originally sent to Scotland by Pope Celestine in the fifth century. Given this background, it is ironic that he is now credited with establishing almost a presbyterian system in the Scottish Church at that time, although with the emphasis on the use of bishops still very much in evidence.

Palladius appears in the *Aberdeen Breviary* as among the first to appoint solemn festivals and their observance. He was also one of the first to consecrate churches and to ordain clergy.

The formality of the early Scottish Church is all but lost. Only the later remnants of early Catholicism in Scotland, as recorded in such books as the *Aberdeen Breviary,* give any indication of the format of the service prior to the Reformation. The *Breviary*, for example, records the celebration of services and the hymns, psalms and prayers used in worship. As a record of liturgy which was in general use, the book is a valuable resource.

There is other evidence of Palladius in Scotland. It is known that 'Paldy's Fair' took place at Fordoun in Kincardineshire back in the nineteenth century. This is merely one example of a fair named in commemoration a saint of the 'Celtic' Church. The Roman Catholic Calendar of Saints replaced the Celtic connection for many other events and special days.

There are scholars who think that the links with Palladius in the north east of Scotland are tenuous at best. Some suggest instead that Palladius actually worked in Ireland, or even that he was none other than the more well-known saint, Patrick (see below) – although most scholars reject this outright.

Whatever the truth, Palladius is certainly believed to have been the person responsible for the ordination of Serf and Ternan, who have links to Culross and Banchory respectively.

Palladius is said to have instructed and baptised Ternan (see page 98), ordaining him a bishop to work among the Picts of the north east corner of Scotland. The town of Banchory, as it is best known these days, is also recorded as 'Banchory Ternan'.

The feast day of Palladius is on the 7th of July.

Patrick

THE patron saint of Ireland is Patrick. It is ironic that Patrick is best known in Ireland when, according to some sources, he may well have come from Scotland; and that Columba, one of the best loved of Scottish saints, originally came from Ireland to Iona.

It also appears that Patrick did not choose to go to Ireland, but was taken there as a slave against his will. And it is also known that he spent time in Gaul, possibly in study.

Whatever his background, this fifth

century man has provided history with a
long legacy of his legendary feats, which
may well be larger than life, and he is
often held responsible, single-handedly,
for spreading Christianity in the Emerald
Isle. In reality, however, Patrick's influence
was not that pervasive, although he
certainly did a great deal to advance the
cause of Christianity in Ireland.

Examples of rough or rustic Latin exist
which suggest Patrick was literate, though
not particularly learned. He is known to
have written his *Confessio* and *Epistola,*
and is associated, through the oral tradition, with the well-known eighth century
Celtic prayer *St Patrick's Breastplate*, from
which this extract, translated by N D
O'Donoghue, is taken:

> CHRIST beside me, Christ before me,
> Christ behind me, Christ within me,
> Christ beneath me, Christ above me,
> Christ to right of me, Christ to left of me;
> Christ in my lying, my sitting, my rising:
> Christ in heart of all who know me,
> Christ on tongue of all who meet me,
> Christ in eye of all who see me,
> Christ in ear of all who hear me.

Patrick was thought to have become a
bishop in the early Church in Ireland and,
as the centuries passed, his cult was to
become more and more popular. He also
has links to Palladius and may have taken
the latter's place as a missionary to Ireland.
Alternatively, the link may be due to the
confusion of the saints' life-stories over
the years.

There are also legends that tell us Patrick was good at getting rid of snakes. He is credited in some sources with the permanent removal of these beasts from Ireland.

These days we need not go to Ireland alone to find dedications to Patrick. The Cathedral in New York bears his name, for example, and there are thought to be relics of the saint at Glastonbury.

In the source which suggests the Glastonbury link, the saint's day is noted as the 24th of August instead of the 17th of March. This suggests today's feast date may be linked to a later calendar; or it may suggest the discovery of the bodies of more than one saint.

Today the life of this saint is celebrated on the 17th of March all over the world.

Probus

THE name 'Probus' means 'honest'. Various sources suggest that there was at least one individual of that name in the British Isles who may have been preaching during the sixth century or earlier. However, it was a popular name for priests and there is more information available about 'Probuses' from overseas.

We do know, however, about a Probus who served in the Cornwall area. He worked with his wife, Grace. According to traditional Cornish stories, they worked as a couple in their ministry. At least one church in Cornwall, at Tressillian, is dedicated in their honour.

There is also thought to have been a ninth century Probus who is said to have written a life of St Patrick.

The 5th of April is recorded as the feast day of this saint.

Ragener

RAGENER was a saint who met a violent end, martyred for his faith. Particularly linked with the Northampton area, he lived during the ninth century and met his death during this turbulent period of history in the British Isles with the country split into many small but volatile kingdoms, and over-lords fighting each other for power and territory.

One Easter eve, a tombside vigil was being taken by a severely crippled woman called Alfgiva. During the course of the evening she experienced a cure. In gratitude, she became a nun. After her experience, further miraculous cures were credited to the power within the tomb. It was opened and the body exhumed. A scroll was found with the bones, confirming that the body inside was Ragener and that he was the nephew of King Edmond.

In recognition of the miraculous cures attributed to him, including that of Alfgiva, the long process towards sainthood began.

Records suggest that Ragener was a

pacifist, but this is not entirely the case –
for he was also recorded as being a
soldier.

Ragener died around AD 870 and his
feast day is on the 21st of November.

Regulus (Rule)

THE next saint, it has been argued, was
responsible for two important events
in Scotland. First, legend has it that he
brought the relics of Saint Andrew to the
Fife area; and second, he established the
place which subsequently took the name
of the disciple of Christ – St Andrews.

In bringing the relics of Andrew to
Scotland in the eighth (Some say fourth)
century, Regulus (known also as Rule)
established the cult of Andrew as a special
saint whose status with the Scottish people
increased until he became accepted as
their patron saint. But is this more fiction
than fact (see page 7)?

The history of Regulus himself is
sketchy, but he was thought to have been
a talented individual who spent at least
some of his life on Patras in Greece.

However, the focus shifts to Constantinople where a pilgrim, Regulus, left
the city bearing the relics of Saint Andrew,
supposedly at the command of Emperor
Constantine, who had been instructed by
an angel in a dream to take the relic of
Saint Andrew to the most western part of
the Empire. This is alluded to in the

Breviary of Aberdeen: 'Regulus, after the relics had been removed to Constantinople, takes the portion he had concealed, and sails with them ....

The account notes that the journey took two years.

Then, off the Fife coast of Scotland, Regulus' ship was wrecked by a violent storm. By such a route it is told that he not only brought the precious relic of Saint Andrew to the Fife shores, but then went on to establish a church at Kilrymont.

As a result of Regulus' preaching, King Angus of the Picts had a vision. He saw a company of angels hovering over the precious relics Regulus carried. This vision impressed the Pictish king and he converted to Christianity on the spot. Angus then asked Regulus to baptise him and granted the saint a gift of land in the Fife area, which was to become an important religious foundation.

Today it is thought that St Andrews possibly benefited from the relics either by sale or by gift. Bishop Acca of Hex-ham, who is said to have procured the relics from Rome, is thought to have given them to the Pictish king. The romantic adventures of Regulus are the source of much confusion and were probably politically-influenced to give the new See of St Andrews increased plausability with the people of Scotland.

It is well worth a visit to the beautiful town of St Andrews. There you will find the ruins of St Andrew's Cathedral and the tower of St Regulus (or Rule).

There are other areas of Scotland which lay claim to Regulus, for he possibly travelled to places such as Monifieth or further north to Kennethmont.

In past historical records of old fairs, links can be found to the memory of saints. The Trewell (Rule) Fair, held in October, matches the feast date for this saint.

Rognvald (Ronald)

ROGNVALD, or Ronald as his name is sometimes recorded, was a twelfth century saint. He was the Jarl (or Earl) of Orkney and son of a Norwegian chieftain. He was also a nephew to Saint Magnus, to whom he dedicated the beautiful cathedral in Kirkwall.

In 1137 Rognvald began the building of the cathedral and it was there that the relics of Saint Magnus were enshrined.

An impressive edifice standing tall and proud in the island capital, the cathedral is an unusual building, for although it is served by a Church of Scotland minister and has a parish attached to it, it does not actually belong to the Church of Scotland. It belongs to the citizens of Kirkwall. Rognvald would have approved!

It is recorded that, during his life time, Rognvald made a pilgrimage to the Holy Land which took him away from Orkney for almost three years.

He was murdered in August one year, while travelling in Caithness. According to legend, the rock where his life was taken miraculously ran red with fresh blood ....

The Orkney Saga, which relates back to the thirteenth century, records:

> *... on the boulder where Earl Rognvald's blood had poured when he was killed, we can still see it, as lovely as if it had been newly split.*

Rognvald, known also as Ronald, has a following on the Scottish mainland. The church at Glenkindie, for example, is dedicated to this saint.

His feast day is on the 20th of August.

Rona (Ronan)

RONA (or Ronan) is thought to have worked in the Western Isles off the mainland of Scotland. Lewis, in particular, was the area favoured by him for his work.

There is an amusing tale told about Rona. According to legend, it seems he was very annoyed by the tongues of the Lewis women and their incessant nagging drove him from the island. He retreated out into the Atlantic Ocean to an islet which now bears his name – North Rona. Given such extreme action, their wagging tongues must have tested this patient man to his absolute limit!

Rona's life and work is celebrated on the 20th of August.

John Duns Scotus

JOHN Duns Scotus, a much forgotten Scottish philosopher, is now on his way to becoming a saint. He lived during the fourteenth century as a teacher and learned monk.

Little is really known about him, but he was probably born in Duns in 1265 and in 1290 went to Oxford. He was ordained a priest in 1291. Clearly academically bright, he was soon on his way to France to study at the University of Paris.

It was at Paris that he later became a

theology lecturer and skilled debater and philosopher. He pioneered a type of philosophical thought which went under his name – 'Scotism'. In addition, Scotus as theologian played his part in defending the complex Doctrine of the Immaculate Conception.

Scotus belonged to a Franciscan order of monks during his life time and he is remembered in Scotland now by a long overdue memorial – a statue in the public park in Duns, Berwickshire.

John Duns Scotus is buried in Germany in the city of Cologne. His gravestone states:

Scotia me genuit, Anglia me suscepit,
Gallia me docuit, Colonia me tenet …

meaning 'Scotland bore me. England accepted me. France taught me. Cologne holds me'.

This man is 'almost a saint', as far as official sainthood is concerned. As stated earlier, the process can take centuries, so we will have to wait a while before we can call him *'Saint* John Duns Scotus'! Although he has only recently been made venerable by the Catholic Church, as far back as the eighteenth century moves were made to have him canonised in Germany. It may have taken almost two centuries to move him up the list, but procedures are now well under way to elevate this scholar of note.

Serf (Servan, Servanus)

SERF, a Scottish saint, was, among other things, involved with the abolition of an unusual pagan cult.

He began his mission by evangelising the areas of Scotland on either side of the Ochil hills, as well as the western side of Fife, and he is credited in some circles with being the first to convert the pagan population in these areas. Some sources say that he was also an apostle to Orkney.

A key figure in the Christianising of the Scots, he may well be among the Celtic saints ordained by individuals like Palladius (see page 81) who travelled from Rome to Britain on a mission to ensure consistency in Christian thinking throughout Europe.

Later, Serf was based at Culross. It was here, according to other sources, that he is supposed to have taken on the education and ordination of that beloved saint we have already met – Mungo.

However, given the dates of the individuals concerned, to have been involved with Palladius and Mungo during a *normal* life span would have been a miracle in itself!

Serf lived a long and full life, but it was the manner of his life, which was accompanied by miracles and kindnesses, that eventually raised him to sainthood.

In one instance, it is recorded, he was credited with the removal of the strange pagan belief in the 'Green Man' in the area around the Firth of Forth. Today, at South Queensferry, under the impressive Forth Bridges for road and rail, an annual ceremony prevails which goes back to that era of the Green Man. In it a local man, whose identity is kept secret, dresses up as the 'Burryman', covered head to tail with burrs, bearing flowers, and walks the boundaries of the town.

Serf was certainly active in the central belt of Scotland. There is a well dedicated to him in Alva, although it is now no longer visible, modern housing developments paying scant regard to sacred memorials, wells or sites.

In the burgh of Auchtermuchty, the saint's motto is used – *Dum Sero Srero*, a pun on his name in Latin, 'Servanus'.

His links to the Ochil hills have in the past been confused by some scholars who credited the saint with going to Orkney instead. It is unlikely, though not impossible, that Serf worked in Orkney. It may be that confusion arose because of the similarity in the letters of 'Orkney' and 'Ochil' in some old manuscripts.

However, the majority of scholars suggest the Ochil area and central Scotland to be his place of *peregrination*. This is a pleasant word meaning 'to walk', used in past times of those who travelled, literally on foot, bringing the Gospel to people like the heathen Picts, Scots, Angles, Saxons and Gauls.

Serf's feast day is celebrated on the 1st of July.

Sexburga

NUNS in the early centuries were not necessarily virgins. It was, undoubtedly, a prized virtue, but then so was motherhood. (Saint Margaret is a good example.)

In the Kent area of England there lived a woman known as Sexburga. She was not only a nun – it was Archbishop Theodore who consecrated her to the veil – but she also acted as a ruler or regent on behalf of her son, Egbert.

If you visit the Isle of Sheppey, you will be going to the area where Sexburga established her monastery. Her eldest sister Etheldreda (another saint) was the Abbess of Ely. When Sexburga heard that the Abbess was at Ely Monastery, Sexburga went to join her there. When Etheldreda died, Sexburga took her place as the Abbess of Ely.

Sexburga experienced the rare privilege of learning that her sister was to become a saint in the course of time, because the body of the Abbess Etheldreda was found to be incorrupt when it was exhumed in readiness for a place of honour.

Etheldreda and Sexburga were of noble birth, two of the three daughters of the King Anna of East Anglia. The third daughter was called Withburga (see page 107). A holy family indeed.

Sexburga died in AD 699 after a long and full life. The feast day associated with her is on the 6th of July.

Swithin (Swithun)

IF you are interested in the weather –
and who isn't? – you will know all
about Saint Swithin. It is said that it will
rain incessantly for forty days and forty
nights if it rains on Saint Swithin's day,
the 15th of July.

The area around Winchester is worth
a visit if you are looking for evidence of
this saint. It is something of a miracle
(minor perhaps) that his shrine is still in
existence, for the Reformation resulted in
the destruction of many similar memorials.
Swithin's was among those torn down.
Happily, in 1962 it was restored and it
can be found in Warwickshire.

Saint Swithin (or 'Swithun') was
Bishop of Winchester in the ninth century.
He was a pious young man who started
out as a monk. But he excelled in his
learning and in time became a bishop.

Early in his life, Swithin was noticed
favourably by the king of the West Saxons,
Egbert, who entrusted the education of
the royal heir Ethelwolf to the monk.

Swithin's patient teaching of Ethelwolf
was finally repaid when the boy succeeded
to the throne. One of Ethelwolf's first
actions in AD 854 was to enact a law
giving a tenth of the land to the Church.

Swithin died on the 2nd of July which
became his feast day. However, over a
century after his death, plans were made
to remove his relics from his church to
the first Winchester Cathedral which was

in the process of being established. It is in connection with this event that the first Saint Swithin rains came down. When the removal of his relics was about to take place – *circa* AD 960 – under the direction of Ethelwold, Bishop of Winchester, torrents of rain hampered the removal. Similar delays at later dates (caused again by the rains) culminated in the famous meteorological prediction we know today.

If there is rain on Saint Swithin's day – beware! It may rain for a long time and it may be very heavy rain indeed!

Tancred, Tortha and Tova

THE Viking raids on the British Isles are well known in history. The Vikings were guilty of shedding a lot of saintly blood and they were also responsible for the removal of many relics that existed, especially those of any value.

In the Cambridgeshire area, Tancred, Torthred and Tova lived peaceful hermit existences. (Tova was in fact a woman.)

Hermits, living alone, were vulnerable targets for the marauding menaces and all three saints in this section met their deaths at the hands of the Vikings around the year AD 870.

Not murdered for gain, since they had few worldly goods, perhaps their quiet, self-sacrificing religious life was a source of irritation to the Vikings.

Ternan

THE school badge of Banchory Academy, in the north east of Scotland, depicts the saint of the town once known as Banchory Ternan. This saint is also thought to have been the founder of the Abbey of Culross in Fife.

Ternan was a Celtic saint who worked among the Deeside Picts. It is thought he may have held the highest position in the Pictish Church for, according to some sources, he was known as the High Bishop of the Picts.

Ternan, known to have been a contemporary of Saint Machar (see page 63), owned a favourite hand bell known as the 'Ronnecht', as well as a special Gospel of Saint Matthew which he used continuously. We have it on good authority from local historians that this precious book survived for centuries in Banchory (or 'Banquhory' as it was spelt in the past).

Spend a day or two in Banchory and the surrounding area and you will come across traces of this saint's existence around many corners. However, there are commemorative wells in other spots around the north east of Scotland which bear Ternan's name, and his fame is evident from other memorials in places like Slains, Banchory-Devenick, and Brechin. He also has links with Collieston near Aberdeen where the townsfolk in recent years celebrated his arrival by re-enacting the event. A simple cross in the graveyard indicates the respect still felt held for his life and work.

Ternan was supposed to have been consecrated as a bishop by Palladius, who recognised Ternan's hard work on behalf of the kingdom of God among the Pictish people.

His feast day is on the 12th of June.

Thenew (Enoch, Thenog)

THE mother of Mungo (or Kentigern) was known as Thenew (Enoch or Thenog). She is a seventh century figure shrouded in mystery and legend. Little historical detail about her survives. However she, like the son she bore, is well loved by the city of Glasgow.

Thenew was a woman of spiritual character who had wished to remain a virgin. Not looking to marry, she spent much of her time increasing her knowledge of the Christian faith. However, her father, King Loth (who gave his name to the Lothian area of Scotland), had other ideas and arranged her betrothal to the King of Cumbria's son for political gain.

Thenew, meanwhile, had other suitors. One of them would not accept 'no' as an answer. Continually hounded by this man, he eventually overpowered her and took her by force.

As a result of this violent crime, Thenew found she was carrying a child. When the news of this reached her father, he was furious. He did not blame the suitor, but directed his unreasonable anger at his daughter, giving out an order that she be stoned to death.

For good measure the execution team are reputed to have thrown Thenew down a mountain. Miraculously she survived, but when this was discovered by her father he sent his executioner to finish her off.

The executioner had at least some compassion for the tragic Thenew and could not bring himself to kill her. Instead he placed her in a boat and pushed the vessel into the Firth of Forth. It was not entirely an act of kindness, however – the executioner ensured that the boat had no oars and no rudder. Despite this, Thenew floated to safety in Culross.

There she gave birth to Mungo and it was the kindly Serf (see page 93) who looked after them at this time and who was to become Mungo's teacher.

In Glasgow today you will find place names which are derived from Thenew, particularly in the modified form of 'Enoch'. Although the modern shopping complex in the centre of Glasgow is called the St Enoch Centre, few people milling around the shops will realise that its name is derived from the mother of the patron saint of their city.

Thenew's feast day is celebrated on the 18th of July.

Thomas

THE saint known as Thomas, who became Bishop of Hereford, was well educated, well known and well thought of in his time. He travelled far beyond the British Isles, gaining a fit education in mainland Europe.

Although a devout and caring man, Thomas's career was not expected to be in the Church at first. It appears that he came to the attention of King Edward I because of his qualities in caring for so many parishes around the Herefordshire area and the king 'upgraded' Thomas' status. The attention was shortlived, however, for, like many others, Thomas fell foul of the monarch when he found himself caught up in the politics of the state.

Thomas was not martyred, but died from sheer overwork. After his death many people began to pray to him for acts of healing and well over four hundred miracles are attributed to him. It is not surprising that a cult grew up around Thomas, particularly in the late thirteenth, early fourteenth centuries. Later he was formally canonised.

There is a twist in the tale of this saint – he was excommunicated at one point in his life by the Archbishop of Canterbury. Despite this, he was canonised – possibly a unique situation in the history of the Church.

Thomas' feast day is celebrated on the 2nd of October.

Triduana

VISIT Edinburgh, a place itself full of history, and you will find a chapel dedicated to Saint Triduana. This chapel and a well are situated beside Restalrig Church.

Just who Triduana was is not absolutely clear, but various sources name her as the virgin from Colossae who accompanied Rule (or Regulus) to Scotland when he brought the relic of Saint Andrew over to the westernmost point of the Constantine Empire.

By all accounts, Triduana was a very beautiful woman and admired by many, including King Nectanevus, a dictator who was used to getting what he wanted. He sent messengers to bring Triduana to him – but she had other ideas.

She asked them what Nectanevus wanted with her.

They replied, 'He wants you for your beautiful eyes!'

She refused to go with them, but granted his request. Plucking out her eyes, she put them on stakes and handed them over, saying, as one account states, 'Take that which your prince loveth'.

This shocking gesture surprised the king, but he was not angry. Instead, he admired her devotion.

As a result of this story, many blind people prayed to Triduana as their saint. One particular case tells of an English woman who saw Triduana in a dream

telling her to go to 'Lestalryk' (the old
spelling of 'Restalrig'). There she would
recover her sight. And the woman did
indeed recover her ability to see near
Triduana's chapel.

The Reformation in 1560 caused this
holy place to be destroyed. There are
church records which state 'that the Kirk
of Restalrig, as a monument of idolatry,
be raysit and utterly cast down and
destroyed'. Today Triduana's Well and the
ruined chapel are well signposted beside
the kirk at Restalrig.

The life of Triduana is celebrated on
the 8th of October.

Verca

IN the seventh century there lived an
abbess called Verca. She is linked to a
particular water-into-wine legend which
provided ample drink for a whole group
of guests from only one glassful.

It happened one day that Verca was
entertaining the beloved Cuthbert at her
convent. Cuthbert requested a glass of
water which she duly gave him. He
blessed Verca's water and it turned to wine
– and wine in such abundance! There is
an illustration of this event in an ancient
manuscript about Saint Cuthbert, depicting this very scene, with the Abbess Verca
seated to his right.

The Tyne area of north east England,
near the mouth of the river itself, is the

region where Verca established her monastery and where this event happened.

Verca is also credited with providing a gift of cloth to Cuthbert. He stated that he would use the gift as his burial shroud in honour of this thoughtful woman.

Vigean (Fechin)

VIGEAN is still remembered in the Church of Scotland parish of Arbroath which takes the saint's name. This sixth (or seventh) century saint's name is best known in its latinised version – *Vigean* – although he would have been better known in his own day as Fechin. It is reputed that no less a person than Columba himself predicted Vigean's birth!

One well known story about this saint involves the taming of a wild beast. A wolf had been marauding among the pastures which Vigean was inhabiting. This wolf attacked livestock and eventually killed one of Vigean's calves. So he tackled the wolf and subdued it, tying the animal to a large stone.

But Vigean's talents did not just rest with converting wild animals into docile pets. He was also something of a healer in his time, according to some sources.

The Kirk of St Vigean in Arbroath bears testimony to the memory of this saint.

Vigean is celebrated on the 20th of January.

Wilfrid the Younger

HE historical city of York is well worth a visit. There you can see evidence of Saint Wilfrid. In some local churches, and in the magnificent York Minster itself, mention is made of this saint, a former Bishop of the city.

Wilfrid almost lost the See of York, for he spent a great deal of his time overseas. In his absence Chad was appointed Bishop of York (see page 25). However, Wilfrid was originally given this See by the then Archbishop of Canterbury who felt uneasy about the unorthodox installation of Chad. Thus, when Wilfrid came home, Chad was given his own See instead.

Wilfrid's life is characterised by hard work and an undeniable zeal for spreading the faith. He was eager to ensure that standards were upheld within the Church, especially in matters of doctrine.

On his travels, Wilfrid had visited Italy and spent time in Rome. There he was schooled in the major doctrines as outlined by the Roman Church. Wilfrid was recognised as a man of talent and met the Pope while in Rome. He learned well the Roman discipline and the Psalter according to the Roman version which differed from the more familiar Psalter of Saint Jerome that he used.

He also travelled around France and spent some years in Lyon with the monk known as Delphinus, whom he looked

YORK MINSTER

upon as his spiritual father. Wilfrid was almost martyred himself when he accompanied Delphinus to the latter's execution. Luckily Wilfrid escaped and returned to England.

Later his work took him to Friesland. Wilfrid is still credited with the bringing of faith to that part of the Netherlands.

His feast day is celebrated on the 12th of October.

William

WILLIAM is included in this book because he was a miracle worker who was associated with many acts of charity.

A twelfth century man, William was

the son of Herbert, an earl, and Emma, sister of King Stephen.

In 1144 William became a priest and was later ordained as Archbishop of York. But he had many powerful enemies, even though he did his best to improve life for his people and to look after their souls; and so, like many of his predecessors, he was eventually ousted.

William travelled to Rome to seek restoration, but it did not come immediately. On his *second* visit to Rome, and now newly restored to his position as Archbishop of York, William returned to find a huge crowd ready to welcome him back. But so large was the crowd of men, women and children, that the wooden bridge they stood upon crashed into the River Ouse under their collective weight.

William was so upset at witnessing this disaster, it is said he prayed to God with many tears. It is also recounted that he made the sign of the cross over the river. As a result, the crowd came to no harm ...

It was this typical gesture of care for people that set William on the path towards sainthood, and his life and work are now celebrated on the 8th of June.

Withburga

ANOTHER holy lady of note is the seventh century saint Withburga.

She was the daughter of a king and the sister of a saint we have already met – Sexburga. After the murder of her father, King Anna of East Anglia, by a rival king, she retreated to the Norfolk area where she established a nunnery.

The nuns under her leadership practised a life of poverty, but hardly had enough to survive on. On one occasion she prayed for guidance. Later, while out walking, she spotted two does. She was able to capture and tame them for their milk. The nunnery was at least better nourished with this unexpected supply.

Legend tells how a man tried to kill these precious does, but instead fell victim of his own hunt. Tripping over in hot pursuit of the animals, he broke his neck.

By the time that Withburga died, she was held in great esteem in the area of Dereham. When it was suggested that her body should be moved to Ely Cathedral, to rest alongside her sisters, Etheldreda and Sexburga, the move was resisted. But eventually Ely did become her final place of rest and a visit to the abbey there will reveal the burial sites of the three holy sisters.

Her feast day is on the 8th of July.

EPILOGUE

WE have met many saints within these pages. Each one has given us something to think about and, hopefully, brought us encouragement.

It is my sincere hope that you have enjoyed this 'peregrination' through the holy centuries and that this book will inspire you to delve deeper into the fascinating and often perplexing subject of sainthood, with its tales of miracles and murder waiting to be brought more fully to light.

ACKNOWLEDGEMENTS

THE following titles have proved very useful during the research and preparation of this book and are acknowledged with gratitude:

Miller, James P: *An Introduction to Celtic Christianity* (Edinburgh: T & T Clark Ltd), 1989, for the verse from *St Patrick's Breastplate* quoted on page 84.

Kalendar of Scottish Saints, The.
Book of Saints, The, compiled by the Benedictine Monks of St Augustine's Abbey, Ramsgate (London: A & C Black), 1931.
Parbury, Kathleen: *Women of Grace* (Oriel Press).
Sprott Towill, Edwin: *Saints of Scotland* (Edinburgh: Saint Andrew Press), 1994.
Butler, Revd Alban: *The Lives of the Fathers, Martyrs and Other Principal Saints*, in four volumes.

PICTURE CREDITS

ILLUSTRATIONS used *in this book have been taken and/or adapted from the following sources:*

Cassell's *Illustrated History of England* (London), volume I, n.d.

Grant, J: *Old and New Edinburgh* (London: Cassell), 1887.

Green, Samuel: *Scottish Pictures* (London: Religious Tract Society), 1891.

Macfarlane/Thomson: *The Comprehensive History of England* (Blackie & Sons), 1861 (in 12 volumes).

Story, Robert H: *The Church of Scotland: Past and Present* (Wm Mackenzie), 1890 (in 5 volumes).

(page 2) – detail from the Aberlemno Stone in Perthshire; photograph © Paul Turner.